Beyond
Early Writing

Beyond Early Writing

Teaching Writing in Primary Schools

Edited by David Waugh,
Adam Bushnell & Sally Neaum

**CRITICAL
TEACHING**

First published in 2015 by Critical Publishing Ltd

British Library Cataloguing in Publication Data
A CIP record for this book is available from the British Library

ISBN: 978-1-909682-93-1

This book is also available in the following ebook formats:

MOBI ISBN: 978-1-909682-94-8
EPUB ISBN: 978-1-909682-95-5
Adobe ebook ISBN: 978-1-909682-96-2

The rights of Kate Allott, Kirsty Anderson, John Bennett, Petula Bhojwani, Adam Bushnell, Adrian Copping, Eve English, Alan Gleaves, Steve Higgins, Catherine Hunt, Geeta Ludhra, Sally Neaum, Rob Smith, Caroline Walker and David Waugh to be identified as the authors of this work have been asserted by them in accordance with the Copyright, Design and Patents Act 1988.

Cover and text design by Greensplash Limited
Project Management by Out of House Publishing
Printed and bound in Great Britain by Bell & Bain, Glasgow

Critical Publishing
152 Chester Road
Northwich
CW8 4AL
www.criticalpublishing.com

Contents

Meet the editors

David Waugh is subject leader for primary English at Durham University. He has published extensively in primary English. David is a former deputy headteacher, was head of the education department at the University of Hull, and was Regional Adviser for initial teacher training (ITT) for the National Strategies from 2008 to 2010. In addition to educational writing, David also writes children's stories.

Adam Bushnell is a full time author who delivers creative writing workshops in the UK and internationally in both state and private education to all ages of children. His books have been selected by the School Library Association for the *Boys into Books* recommended reading list. Previously a teacher, Adam now delivers continuing professional development (CPD) to teachers and others working in education on how to inspire writing in the classroom.

Sally Neaum is a senior lecturer in early childhood, and teaches primary English in ITT working at Teesside and Durham universities. She has worked as a nursery and primary school teacher and as an adviser in early years and inclusion. Her doctoral research focused on the pedagogy of early literacy. Sally has published extensively in early years and primary education.

Meet the authors

Kate Allott is a lecturer in primary English at York St John University. She has also worked as a literacy consultant for North Yorkshire County Council and as a regional adviser for the National Strategies Communication, Language and Literacy Development programme.

Kirsty Anderson is a former deputy headteacher and literacy consultant for the National Strategies. She recently became a teaching fellow at Durham University.

John Bennett is a lecturer in education at the University of Hull. His main roles are in primary initial teacher education, particularly providing primary English teaching courses for post-graduate and undergraduate trainees. He previously spent 25 years working in schools, as a teacher and an advisory teacher, culminating in 12 years as a primary headteacher.

Petula Bhojwani specialises in raising boys' attainment. She has worked across the East and West Midlands as a primary school literacy co-ordinator, regional adviser and consultant for the Primary National Strategies. Petula was senior lecturer in primary education at Birmingham City University and is an associate lecturer at the University of Nottingham. She is currently based in Nottinghamshire where she works as an independent literacy consultant supporting schools to close the gap for vulnerable groups. Her research interests are in multimodal literacies with particular attention to boys and looked-after children.

Adrian Copping is primary PGCE programme leader and senior lecturer in English and literacy at the University of Cumbria. He has worked as a primary school teacher, and regularly takes the opportunity to return to schools using teacher-in-role strategies and developing writing projects. Adrian has published on many aspects of teaching and teacher education including practitioner research, reflective practice, creativity and school partnerships.

Eve English, a former headteacher, is a lecturer in English on the PGCE (Primary) and BA (QTS) courses at Durham University. She has published extensively on primary English.

Alan Gleaves is a lecturer in computing and learning technology at Durham University. He has also worked as a technology consultant for the Department for Education, and as a regional adviser in schools for various programmes, including the National Grid for Learning, Building Future Schools and the new primary computing curriculum. He has published widely in the area of mobile technology use in informal learning.

Steve Higgins is Professor of Education at Durham University. A former primary school teacher, he has a particular interest in how children's thinking and reasoning develops, and in the use of research evidence to inform professional practice. He is the lead author of the Sutton Trust-EEF *Teaching and Learning Toolkit*.

Catherine Hunt is a learning support teacher at a pre-prep school in Oxfordshire. She has worked in a number of primary schools both in the UK and internationally. Currently, her main role involves teaching children with specific learning difficulties, in particular those with dyslexic tendencies, using a structured, multisensory approach. She also supports and advises classteachers.

Geeta Ludhra is subject leader for primary English at Brunel University, and has led the primary PGCE for several years. She has taught in challenging primary school settings in the West London area, where she became very interested in the language and cultural identities of bilingual pupils, and ways in which their needs are planned for to support effective progress and inclusion. She has worked in various school leadership roles and is a former deputy headteacher.

Rob Smith is the creator of *The Literacy Shed*, a bank of visual literacy resources which are now being used around the world to inspire writing. Rob is currently teaching part time in a large primary school in Manchester, while travelling the country delivering CPD and writing workshops based on embedding high quality visual literacy into the classroom.

Caroline Walker is senior lecturer in special education and inclusion at Durham University. She has worked as a secondary teacher in schools and secure settings in the UK and overseas, and as an adviser in special educational needs, educational attainment of looked-after children, and parental involvement in their children's education.

Acknowledgements

The editors are very grateful to everyone who has contributed to this book as authors of chapters. In addition, we would like to thank the many teachers and trainee teachers who allowed us to use examples of their teaching as case studies.

Introduction

DAVID WAUGH, SALLY NEAUM AND ADAM BUSHNELL

This book focuses on children's development from early to more sophisticated writing. It offers both ideas and a rationale for developing children's writing once they have mastered the early stages. In considering strategies for developing writing, it is important to understand how we learn to write in the first place.

Becoming a writer begins long before children start school. To become writers, children need opportunities for sensory integration, symbolic play, mark-making and engagement with the functions and forms of print. This is achieved through play, which allows children to gain control over their bodies, engages their curiosity, stimulates their imagination and enables them to make meaning in their world.

Physical movement and play are essential for sensory integration. Children need to develop a strong sense of balance, when moving and when still, and need to develop their *proprioceptive abilities*, a sense of their body in space. This enables them to control their fine and gross motor movements, to sit still, to judge spatial differences and to respond effectively to visual and auditory information. Also, specifically linked to writing, children need to have integrated their *vertical midline*, which forms *bilateral integration paths* between the left and right sides of the brain (Johnson, 2014). All this is achieved through activities such as climbing, running, jumping, hopping, skipping, cycling, scooting, circle games, ball games and activities, clapping and tapping games, dressing and undressing, using puppets, and cutting and chopping.

In addition, through play children learn to symbolise, that is, to use one thing to represent another – a doll becomes a baby, beads become money, a box becomes a house. This ability to symbolise acts as a natural precursor to writing, a trajectory from using playthings symbolically, to the understanding of writing as the setting down (symbolic representation) of speech.

Mark-making begins with children making marks in sand, in paint, on walls, floors and paper, developing from large circular and lateral marks to more intentional marks that eventually become representational. These early child-initiated play-based experiences for mark-making are vital, both as developmental moves towards representation and as ways in which children make, and express, meaning in their world. Evidence suggests that these early marks are purposeful: they have meaning and intention for the child (Lancaster, 2013).

In their engagement with print in their environment, children come to know about the functions and forms of print. They learn that there are different domains of print (drawing, writing, number, musical notation, maps etc), what they are, and how they are used (Neaum, 2012). As children begin to recognise print in the environment (shop signs, food packets, words and logos on clothes and toys, and in the media), they develop an understanding that writing carries meaning. This is evident in its earliest stages as children begin to ascribe meaning to what they see and the marks that they make, for example, recognising the name of a supermarket, identifying a computer game from the logo, or telling you what their own marks represent. This then develops through their play as marks are increasingly used meaningfully in context, for example, *typing* on a phone or tablet to send a message to someone, mark-making in a notebook when playing at being police officers, making marks to put their name on a painting, *signing* a list to say that they have had a turn on the computer program. In these ways children come to know why writing is important, and the ways in which it is used.

With support, and when a child is developmentally ready, children need to begin to understand the forms of print that enable us to access meaning: recognition of letters and letter sounds, and moving from left to right and top to bottom of script (in English). They will begin by recognising letters that are important to them, the initial letter of their name, and letters and words that they regularly see in the media or in their environment. Engagement with books and observing people write will enable children to recognise the difference between different domains, allow them to create a visual map of what writing looks like, and will model their reading and writing behaviours, for example starting on the left and tracking print from left to right and (predominantly) top to bottom. This knowledge becomes evident in children's emergent writing as their marks start to take on the appearance of writing, small curved shapes in a line, some early formations of letters, and marks that track left to right and top to bottom.

These early play-based experiences enable more formal aspects of learning to write to be built on firm foundations. So what can we learn from the way we first learn to write that will help us when we develop at subsequent stages?

This book explores the development of children's writing as they move from early attempts towards increasingly sophisticated writing. It examines, in Chapter 1, the research on writing and asks if some approaches are more effective than others and, if so, how this information can be used effectively in the classroom.

In Chapter 2 Adam Bushnell draws upon his experience as a teacher of a wide range of children and adults to show how children can be inspired to write. He looks, too, at the importance of oral storytelling as a prelude to writing.

Adrian Copping explores, in Chapter 3, the place of drama and scaffolding in encouraging children to write, basing his discussion around the example of a murder mystery.

In Chapter 4, Eve English takes up the theme of drama as a stimulus for writing, providing examples of this in practice. Interestingly, Eve focuses upon both fiction and non-fiction writing as outcomes from dramatic activities.

Chapter 5 explores poetry writing, examining ways in which we can engage children's interest in poetry, as well as the importance of teachers possessing a wide knowledge of poems. The chapter suggests experiences which children need to have before they can write poetry and explores different types of poems children might write.

Kate Allott asks what the potential rewards and difficulties of non-fiction writing might be, and which text types should be taught, in Chapter 6. Her chapter looks closely at what children need if they are to become successful writers of non-fiction texts.

In Chapter 7, Rob Smith, whose Literacy Shed website is a rich resource for teachers, looks at the potential of film and visual image as a stimulus for writing and for engaging children's interest. He poses and answers the question: How does visual literacy scaffold the writing process?

Chapter 8 by David Waugh examines how we can develop children's grammatical understanding through writing, a key issue as the 2013 national curriculum and forthcoming national tests have made grammar a preoccupation for teachers.

In Chapter 9, Caroline Walker and Alan Gleaves ask. Do children need to be able to write longhand in the twenty-first century? Acknowledging that they do indeed need these skills, and not just because the national curriculum demands them, the authors look at practical ways in which teachers can develop pupils' good longhand writing habits.

Chapters 10, 11 and 12 examine strategies for children who face particular challenges in writing English, with Chapter 10 focusing on the specific writing needs of boys, who are consistently outperformed by girls in national and international tests. Petula Bhojwani explores ways to encourage boys to see the point of writing and asks what role technology can play in the classroom to support boys in engaging with and producing multimodal texts.

In Chapter 11 Catherine Hunt looks at the indicators of dyslexia and offers strategies for supporting dyslexic children with their writing. She also offers suggestions for creating a dyslexic-friendly classroom.

Kirsty Anderson and Geeta Ludhra, in Chapter 12, look at what we can learn from pupils with English as an additional language (EAL) and at how effective strategies for pupils with EAL can be for all pupils. They go on to explore ways in which we can draw on visual and multimedia literacies to support the progress of bilingual pupils.

Finally, in Chapter 13, John Bennett examines how we can ensure the national curriculum goes beyond pen and paper, and looks at what and how children write digitally. John examines the skills needed to write digital texts and ways in which developing digital writing can enhance the development of writing skills.

Each chapter provides critical questions, points and reflections to encourage you to consider your own practice in light of what you have read. There are also case studies to demonstrate how teachers and trainee teachers have used developed writing in the classroom. The chapters also include recommended further reading to enable you to develop stronger insights into how teachers can help children move beyond early writing.

References

Johnson, S (2014) A Developmental Approach Looking at the Relationship of Children's Foundational Neurological Pathways to Their Higher Capacities for Learning. [online] Available at: http://www.youandyourchildshealth.org/youandyourchildshealth/articles/teaching%20our%20children.html (accessed 11 November 2014).

Lancaster, L (2013) Moving into Literacy. How It All Begins, in Larson, J and Marsh, J (eds) *The Sage Handbook of Early Childhood Literacy*. London: Sage.

Neaum, S (2012) *Language and Literacy for the Early Years*. London: Sage.

1 Research-based approaches to teaching writing

STEVE HIGGINS

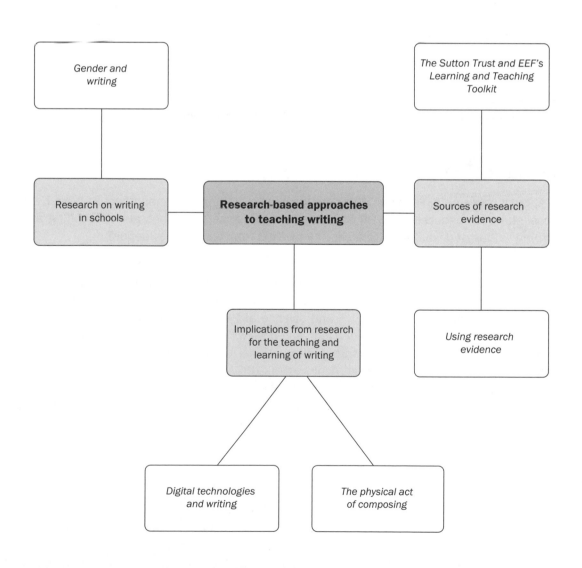

Teachers' Standards

2 Promote good progress and outcomes by pupils

- demonstrate knowledge and understanding of how pupils learn and how this impacts on teaching

3 Demonstrate good subject and curriculum knowledge

- have a secure knowledge of the relevant subject(s) and curriculum areas, foster and maintain pupils' interest in the subject, and address misunderstandings

- demonstrate a critical understanding of developments in the subject and curriculum areas and promote the value of scholarship

- *if teaching early reading, demonstrate a clear understanding of systematic synthetic phonics*

Critical questions

» *What can we learn from research about the teaching of writing?*

» *What does research about children's progress tell us?*

» *Are there approaches which are more effective than others?*

» *How can this information be used effectively in the classroom?*

Introduction

What does research have to say about the teaching of writing? What approaches have been successfully (or unsuccessfully) tried? What are the general lessons about teaching and learning writing and what specific advice can we get from research evidence?

In this chapter, an overview of what research has to say about the teaching of writing is presented. The evidence on pupil progress in England indicates that teaching children to write is a significant challenge. Writing is the subject in England with the worst overall performance compared with reading, mathematics and science at Key Stages 1 and 2. There are also persistent gender differences between girls and boys which tend to increase as pupils move from primary to secondary. Comparative international evidence from studies such as the Programme for International Student Achievement (PISA) and the Progress in International Reading and Literacy Study (PIRLS) is not available as they use measures from reading to assess literacy and do not include writing in their assessments. There is, however, research evidence which can help and which indicates that there are teaching techniques and strategies for pupils to use that can improve their writing.

Activity 1: What do you remember about learning to write at school?

» *Do you remember learning to write? Were you taught handwriting? What about keyboarding skills? Were you taught how to compose different kinds of texts? What strategies for writing were you taught? How successful did you feel as a writer?*

Research on writing in schools

There is less evidence about teaching writing in schools than other areas of literacy, particularly compared with learning to read, but there is still a substantial quantity of information available about how children learn to write at different ages and approaches to improve their writing. It is not possible to be familiar with all of these articles and studies. It is also important to bear in mind that a single research study is never going to be conclusive in education. Even when you find evidence that something has been effective, you have to consider whether there are any differences between the contexts in which the research was conducted and the setting where you might want to make improvements based on research. Just because something has been shown to be effective at improving writing quality in, say, 20 schools in the United States with 9-year-old children, this approach may not help you teach your class of Year 6 or Year 2 children to write better, but it might contain ideas or techniques that would get you off to a good start.

FOCUS ON RESEARCH

Pupils' progress in writing in England

In 2012 the Department for Education produced an analysis of the evidence about pupils' performance in writing in England (DfE, 2012).

Writing is the subject with the worst performance compared with reading, mathematics and science at Key Stages 1 and 2.

There is a consistent gender gap in pupils' performance in writing with girls outperforming boys throughout all key stages.

At the Foundation Stage, 71 per cent of children were working securely within the early learning goals of the communication, language and literacy learning area.

At Key Stage 1, 83 per cent of children achieved the expected level of national teacher assessments in writing; at Key Stage 2, 81 per cent of pupils achieved the expected level.

At GCSE, only 69 per cent of pupils achieved grades A*–C in English.

Gender and writing

Although girls consistently outperform boys in writing tests, it is important to keep this in perspective (Jones, 2012). At primary school level the extent of this difference is small (usually only a couple of percentage points). The majority of boys and girls perform at the same level, but there is an overall trend which worsens after Key Stage 2 (DfE, 2012). The reasons for this difference are less well understood. The overall quality of teaching is vital, as more effective teachers tend to have smaller gaps in attainment between boys and girls. This includes aspects such as the use of writing strategies, maintaining the engagement of all pupils, effective behaviour management, and the use of digital technologies (Graham and Perrin, 2007a). Ineffective approaches are thought to include the overuse of techniques such as writing frames and a lack of connection between oral and written work. However, approaches which work to improve writing for boys tend to work as well (or better) for girls. It is therefore important to focus on having high expectations for all pupils and to set motivating tasks with a high level of challenge and support to ensure progress (DfE, 2012; Graham et al, 2012) (see also Chapter 10 of this book).

Sources of research evidence

There are two broad approaches here: first is the evidence about general teaching and learning strategies and second is the specific evidence relating to improving writing. A good place to start is with summaries, reviews and overviews of research for teachers. There are several trustworthy internet sites available (see links below and the references).

- The US Government funds the What Works Clearinghouse (WWC). This focuses on identifying thematic areas which represent challenging areas of interest in US education, such as *beginning reading* or *character education*. Within each selected topic area, the WWC collects studies of interventions that have rigorous research evidence. These include *programs, products, practices, and policies* which are potentially relevant to an area of teaching and learning, and they undertake comprehensive and systematic literature searches. The studies collected are then subjected to a three-stage review process. Some areas do not get past the first stage where there is insufficient evidence; others are reported as meeting evidence standards: www.whatworks.ed.gov.

- In the UK, the Sutton Trust and the Education Endowment Foundation (EEF) have produced a *Teaching and Learning Toolkit*. This has been endorsed by the Department for Education and the government as a *What Works* centre for education evidence in the UK. It aims to provide an accessible summary of educational research as guidance for teachers and schools on how to use their resources to improve the attainment of disadvantaged pupils in particular. It is different from other summaries of research, in that it includes an estimate of the potential benefit in terms of months of progress, an estimate of costs, as well as an indication of the strength of the evidence. It is also unusual in that it reviews areas which the evidence indicates have *not* been effective, as well as those which show more promise: http://educationendowmentfoundation.org.uk/toolkit.

- The EPPI-Centre, based at the University of London, has been undertaking and developing methods for systematic reviews since 1993. There are summaries of research into the teaching of writing, as well as other aspects of teaching, learning and assessment: http://eppi.ioe.ac.uk/cms/.

- The Best Evidence Encyclopaedia UK (BEE UK) presents reliable, unbiased reviews of research-proven educational programmes for primary and secondary education to identify what works best in education, with an emphasis on those offered in the UK today: www.bestevidence.org.uk.

Activity 2: Review two of these sources of research evidence

» *What did you think? How easy were the sites to navigate to find evidence which interested you?*

» *Were there any surprises? Did the evidence match what you expected?*

» *How could you use these sources to inform your teaching?*

The Sutton Trust and EEF's Learning and Teaching Toolkit

This section looks at one of these evidence resources in more detail. The *Teaching and Learning Toolkit* sets out a range of different approaches to improving learning in schools. It assesses the quality of the evidence and identifies how well each approach has worked from over 150 detailed summaries of the impact of education research. These are meta-analyses which synthesise or pull together the quantitative findings from a large number of research studies.

The potential gain in attainment is presented in terms of the additional months' progress you might expect pupils to make as a result of the successful use of a research-based approach. For example, if an effective feedback intervention has an impact of nine-months' progress, it means that, for two classes of pupils which were the same before the intervention, afterwards the class which adopted the effective feedback intervention would be better than the control class by a large margin. The average pupil in a class of 25 pupils in the feedback class would now be equivalent to the sixth best pupil in the control class, having made 21-months' progress over the year, compared with an average of 12-months' normal progress in the other class. The Toolkit comparisons are based on these systematic reviews of research, and the detailed quantitative summaries are published in over 150 meta-analyses.

Cost estimates are based on a rough calculation of how much an approach for a class of 25 pupils would cost. Where an approach does not require any additional resource, estimates are based on the cost of training or professional development which may be needed. An estimate of the quality or security of the evidence, indicated by padlocks in the table, is also made based on the methodological quality of the evidence and the reliability or consistency of this impact.

Overall there are some clear general messages about teaching and learning from this Toolkit. For example, it is very effective to provide feedback to learners which helps them to improve. Also important is the teaching of strategies which encourage learners to plan, monitor and review their own learning (*metacognition*) and take responsibility for managing their own improvement (*self-regulation*). A specific example of an EEF-funded writing project which focuses on metacognition and self-regulation is described in Table 1.1. Other general messages are about the value of peer interaction and collaborative learning. It is also clear that intensive tuition for pupils who are falling behind can enable them to catch up, either in small groups or with one-to-one teaching.

There are also some surprises in the findings. For example, the deployment of teaching assistants (TAs) makes less of an impact than many schools expect, especially considering that this has been one of the most popular ways that primary schools have spent additional funding from the *pupil premium*. This is additional funding which is given to schools for pupils who receive free school meals (FSMs). Research, summarised in the Toolkit, indicates that classes with TAs assigned to them make, on average, only the same progress as classes without TAs. This does not mean that TAs do not have any effect on learning. But it does suggest that about half the TAs are deployed in a way that has a positive effect, and about half in ways which are ineffective or even detrimental to learning. A recent UK study (Blatchford et al, 2012) showed that the more support pupils with special educational needs (SENs) received from TAs, the *less* well they did in terms of attainment, when compared with similar SEN pupils in classes without a TA. This means that it is vitally important to work out how support staff can best support pupils' learning, as this is does not happen just by them being present in the classroom or in the typical ways that schools choose to use them. Recent research by the Education Endowment Foundation (EEF) suggests that one approach to deploying TAs effectively is to provide training so they can help small groups or individual pupils with targeted support in reading, writing or mathematics, with specific and monitored targets for improvement which are reviewed regularly.

Another surprise concerns the popular approach of ability grouping, a common practice in literacy teaching in the UK. On average, the benefits are seen only for high attaining students. The impact over time on the learning of low attaining pupils as a result of ability grouping tends to be negative, particularly on pupils' beliefs about themselves as learners and their aspirations for future learning (Marks, 2013). If your school decides to use these kinds of grouping, you should think about how you can limit or overcome the probable detrimental impact on your lower attaining pupils. This might be by looking at other approaches in the Toolkit which are more effective, such as significantly reducing the size of lower attaining classes (to about 15) or by increasing the amount or the quality of feedback that learners get about their work or by providing more intensive teaching in small groups or pairs. Overall, the research shows that providing effective feedback is one of the most successful things that a teacher can do.

Using research evidence

Of course, there are no guarantees when drawing lessons from the research evidence. The Toolkit summarises approaches which have been effective in the past, in other contexts. It is not really a summary of *what works*, but what *has worked*, for other teachers, with other pupils, in other schools. The quality of the evidence, even with the strict inclusion criteria adopted for the Toolkit, is still variable. This means that the potential gain identified will not

Table 1.1 The findings of the Learning and Teaching Toolkit

Approach	Cost estimate	Evidence estimate	Average impact
Arts participation	£ £	3/5 padlocks	+ 2 Months
Aspiration interventions	£ £ £	1/5 padlocks	0 Months
Behaviour interventions	£ £ £	4/5 padlocks	+ 4 Months
Collaborative learning	£	4/5 padlocks	+ 5 Months
Digital technology	£ £ £ £	4/5 padlocks	+ 4 Months
Early years intervention	£ £ £ £ £	4/5 padlocks	+ 6 Months
Extended school time	£ £ £	2/5 padlocks	+ 2 Months
Feedback	£ £	3/5 padlocks	+ 8 Months
Homework (primary)	£	3/5 padlocks	+ 1 Month
Homework (secondary)	£	3/5 padlocks	+ 5 Months
Individualised instruction	£	3/5 padlocks	+ 2 Months
Learning styles	£	3/5 padlocks	+ 2 Months
Mentoring	£ £ £	3/5 padlocks	+ 1 Month
Metacognition and self- regulation	£ £	4/5 padlocks	+ 8 Months
One-to-one tuition	£ £ £ £	4/5 padlocks	+ 5 Months
Parental involvement	£ £ £	3/5 padlocks	+ 3 Months
Peer tutoring	£ £	4/5 padlocks	+ 6 Months
Phonics	£	4/5 padlocks	+ 4 Months
Physical environment	£ £	1/5 padlocks	0 Months
Reading comprehension strategies	£ £ £	4/5 padlocks	+ 5 Months
Reducing class size	£ £ £ £ £	3/5 padlocks	+ 3 Months
Setting or streaming	£	3/5 padlocks	− 1 Month

Approach	Cost estimate	Evidence estimate	Average impact
Small group tuition	£ £ £	🔒🔒🔓🔓🔓	+ 4 Months
Social and emotional aspects of learning	£	🔒🔒🔒🔒🔓	+ 4 Months
Sports participation	£ £ £	🔒🔒🔒🔓🔓	+ 2 Months
Summer schools	£ £ £	🔒🔒🔓🔓🔓	+ 3 Months
Teaching assistants	£ £ £ £	🔒🔒🔓🔓🔓	+1 Month

automatically be achieved in a new context. Each school and each teacher will still need to work out what is likely to be the most effective approach for their particular school and their pupils, and then monitor the impact to ensure that any new approach or any spending of additional funding is effective in actually improving the learning of the disadvantaged students it seeks to help. What the Toolkit aims to do is to provide information about how different approaches have (and have not) been successful in other contexts, as a guide to where there is likely to be potential benefit as a *good bet* or more of a risky choice. The evidence suggests that this is not always straightforward, as many of the approaches we intuitively believe will be beneficial for attainment, such as smaller classes or additional adult support, are not always the *best bets* to improve learning that we think they are.

FOCUS ON RESEARCH

A meta-analysis of writing instruction for adolescent students (Graham and Perin, 2007a)

The authors were motivated by the widespread concern that the majority of young people do not develop the competence in writing, which they need to be successful in school, the workplace or their personal lives. So, in order to identify effective teaching practices for young people (from age 9 to 18) who are learning to write effectively, the authors undertook a meta-analysis of the writing intervention literature, focusing their analysis on experimental and quasi-experimental studies. They located 123 studies with 154 effect sizes for quality of writing. The authors calculated an average weighted effect size (in parentheses below) for the following interventions: strategy instruction (0.82), summarisation (0.82), peer assistance (0.75), setting product goals (0.70), word processing (0.55), sentence combining (0.50), inquiry (0.32), pre-writing activities (0.32), process writing approach (0.32), study of models (0.25) and grammar instruction (– 0.32).

(Note: an effect size of 0.82 represents an additional ten-months' progress in writing; 0.32 is about four-months' additional progress.)

Implications from research for the teaching and learning of writing

Writing is a complex skill and takes years to develop and improve. This section summarises the evidence from quantitative studies about what improves children's writing. One aspect of this is the importance of explicit teaching of the *process* of writing. This should include the use of tools (such as writing frames) and strategies which emphasise the different stages, such as planning, drafting and sharing ideas. It is also important to emphasise self-evaluation and developing pupils' capability to assess their own work through revising and editing. Other effective strategies include summarising texts in writing (such as through précis) and combining sentences. Overall, what is effective is a teaching approach which models specific skills, provides tools or strategies to support pupils, but where the support is deliberately faded out so that there is a gradual shift in responsibility from the teacher to the pupil so that they become independent writers. Engaging pre-writing activities which help them to develop a range of strategies are also important. This could be by helping them to work out what they already know, research an unfamiliar topic or arrange their ideas visually or thematically.

Evidence (Graham et al, 2012) indicates it is also important to expose pupils to a *variety of forms of writing* and to practise these so that they learn to write for a variety of purposes and master different genres of writing (eg, description, narration, persuasion or argumentation, information and explanatory texts). Seeing examples of good writing in these different forms and being given positive feedback when they develop key features is essential here. Teaching explicit strategies is valuable here too. For example, in descriptive writing one approach which has been shown to be effective is to link written descriptions with the senses: *What did you see? How did it look? What sounds did you hear? What did you touch? How did it feel? What could you smell? What did you taste?*

Writing is a complex skill which makes it difficult for pupils to know what to focus on to improve. It is therefore important to set specific goals for pupils which they understand. These goals can be set by the teacher or by the pupils (then reviewed by the teacher). They could include adding more ideas to a text or including specific features of a particular writing genre. It is also important to encourage self-motivation such as through personal target setting, so self-referenced or ipsative assessment is helpful as learners are judged by how well they improve on their previous performance. A writing task which requires inquiry skills can be structured by agreeing a clear goal for writing, identifying specific sources to summarise and being clear about the purpose or audience for the writing. Overall, it is important that teachers know and then use a range of strategies to develop children's writing (Hebert et al, 2013). There is no magic shortcut to developing these skills. It takes time and effort to develop physical and compositional fluency. Regular (daily) time to write is important and should be a priority (Graham and Perrin, 2007b).

Writing should also be purposeful. You should model writing in front of your pupils, and share real examples with them such as a letter or an email. Providing pupils with opportunities to choose the topics they write about will help to maintain engagement. Collaborative writing with peers can also maintain engagement, as well as increasing time spent writing and providing opportunities for informal feedback and discussion. In terms of more formal feedback, you should provide opportunities for pupils to give and receive constructive comments throughout each of the stages of the writing process. Writing for a purpose and an identified audience can help focus learners' attention.

FOCUS ON RESEARCH

A meta-analysis of writing instruction for students in the elementary grades (Graham et al, 2012)

To identify effective practices for teaching writing to elementary grade (primary school) pupils in the United States, the authors conducted a meta-analysis of the writing intervention literature, focusing on robust designs such as true and quasi-experiments. There were 115 reports that included the data for computing an effect size (ES). They calculated an average weighted ES for these writing interventions. To be included in the analysis, a writing intervention had to be tested in several studies. Six of the writing interventions involved explicitly teaching writing processes, skills or knowledge. All but one of these interventions (grammar instruction) produced a statistically significant effect. These strategies were strategy instruction (ES = 1.02), adding self-regulation to strategy instruction (ES = 0.50), text structure instruction (ES = 0.59), creativity/imagery instruction (ES = 0.70) and teaching transcription and writing skills (ES = 0.55). Four writing interventions involved procedures for scaffolding or supporting students' writing. Each of these interventions produced statistically significant effects. These were pre-writing activities (ES = 0.54), peer assistance when writing (ES = 0.89), clear product goals (ES = 0.76) and assessment of writing (0.42). They also found that word processing (ES = 0.47), extra writing (ES = 0.30) and comprehensive writing programmes (ES = 0.42) resulted in a statistically significant improvement in the quality of students' writing. Moderator analyses revealed that the self-regulated strategy development model (ES = 1.17) and process approach to writing instruction (ES = 0.40) improved how well students wrote.

(Note: an effect size of 1.02 represents an additional 12-months' progress in writing; 0.30 is about four-months' additional progress.)

CASE STUDY

Self-regulated strategy development

A recent successful writing project in Calderdale, funded by the EEF, exemplifies many of these principles (Torgerson et al, 2014). The project aimed to use memorable experiences and an approach called *Self-Regulated Strategy Development* to help struggling writers in Years 6 and 7. The strategies provided a clear structure to help pupils plan, monitor and evaluate their writing. The strategies aimed to encourage pupils to take ownership of their work and could be used to teach most genres of writing, including narrative writing. Memorable experiences, such as trips to local landmarks or visits from World War II veterans, were used as a focus for writing lessons.

When teaching a specific genre, all teachers were asked to include the following elements:

- discussion about the genre;

- pre-assessment – carried out by classteachers before starting work on any genre;

- the use of mnemonics to help remember strategies (eg IPEELL: **I**ntroductory paragraph; **P**oints; **E**xamples/elaboration; **E**nd; **L**inks (connectives, openers); **L**anguage (wow words, genre specific vocabulary, punctuation);

- the use of graphic organisers – all schools were asked to use the same writing planner (graphic organiser);

- self-scoring and graphing (pupils used a self-scoring system and graphed the results);

- *positive talk* and *motivational messages*;

- the use of peer scoring;

- a final assessment.

Overall, the project, based on a robust randomised evaluation design, had a dramatic impact on pupils' writing, with the average improvement being about an additional nine-months' progress compared with similar pupils who did not participate in the intervention: http://educationendowmentfoundation.org.uk/projects/using-self-regulation-to-improve-writing/.

Activity 3: Applying self-regulated strategies with your class

» *Could you adapt these strategies for your class?*

» *Are you familiar with graphic organisers? Try searching Google or Bing Images with the phrase* graphic organisers for writing. *Which might be helpful and why?*

» *Do you use mnemonics with your class? Could you develop your own? How else could you help children to remember writing strategies?*

Digital technologies and writing

The nature of writing has changed over the past 30 years. Most people no longer write much with pen and paper (see Chapters 9 and 13). We text, email and draft writing on computers, laptops or tablets where we can edit, amend and revise what we write with much greater ease. Using digital media increases the opportunities for communicating with people (eg, we can email experts or children in another class learning about the same things, whether a few miles away or on the other side of the globe). There are also opportunities for digital publishing online through blogs and wikis which have the potential for an audience outside of the classroom and to get feedback from others about that writing. This is not without its challenges, however. Managing access to technology and developing the digital skills needed to develop composition skills takes time, and, of course, following school guidelines for internet safety are essential, but research indicates that the use of digital technologies can help develop children's writing skills (Goldberg et al, 2003). Each of these digital formats and outputs offers increased educational possibilities, but they also increase the challenge of digital literacy with the breadth of online opportunities for writing in today's technological culture.

FOCUS ON RESEARCH

The effect of computers on student writing: a meta-analysis of studies from 1992 to 2002 (Goldberg et al, 2003)

A meta-analysis was undertaken on 26 studies published between 1992 and 2002, which focused on writing with computers compared with paper and pencil for 6–18-year-olds. There was a significant advantage for computers for *quantity* of writing (an ES of 0.50, representing about six-months' additional progress) and the *quality* of writing (an ES of 0.40). Overall, the articles reviewed indicate that the writing process is more collaborative, iterative and social in computer classrooms as compared with paper-and-pencil environments. The authors maintain that, for educational leaders and teachers who question whether computers should be used to help students develop writing skills, the results of the meta-analysis suggest that, on average, students who use computers when learning to write are not only more engaged and motivated in their writing but also produce written work that is of greater length and higher quality.

The physical act of composing

Schools face a particular challenge in our contemporary culture in teaching the physical process of writing. How much emphasis should be placed on handwriting and how much on digital writing and keyboard skills or other text-input devices (see Chapter 9)?

Young children need to learn how to hold a pencil or pen so that they can become fluent with their handwriting and correctly form letters efficiently. Handwriting requires extensive practice. There is evidence that self-instruction can be an effective way to teach pupils to improve their handwriting, as can structured handwriting programmes (DfE, 2012). Keyboarding or other text entry skills can certainly also be improved with practice or through the use of tutoring software and keyboarding games.

The challenge is that the process of writing composition differs between handwritten text and digital text composition. When writing by hand, you need to have the sentence thought out in advance, and understand the place of that sentence in the text overall. With digital composition, you can write words, notes, ideas and edit them, with the text developing along with your thinking. With handwritten text, aspects of this composing and editing process need to be completed earlier, either on paper or in your head.

Most tests in schools are undertaken with pencil or pen and paper. It is therefore important not to disadvantage pupils who will not succeed unless they are able to write fluently and quickly by hand. It is also important that children develop digital writing skills, as this is likely to be the main way that they will write outside of school. This creates a tension which will not be solved until pupils are assessed through writing in digital form.

Conclusion

Using research about what is effective to improve teaching and learning and being able to interpret and apply research evidence is one of the hallmarks of a professional teacher. You should not accept the argument that experience is sufficient to improve practice. Experience alone will lead to blind spots in both our individual teaching and the kinds of practice we accept as *effective* in the UK. Writing is a complex skill and requires sustained teaching and practice to develop learners' skills and confidence. Overall, the evidence indicates that a range of approaches can be useful. In particular, strategy instruction, especially when this includes self-regulation by the learner, teaching about text and genre structures, and pre-writing activities, such as fostering creativity or the use of imagery, can all help improve writing outcomes. In terms of the process of writing, peer assistance and collaboration, clear end goals and the use of peer- and self-assessment have all been shown to improve children's writing skills and performance. There is also evidence that digital technologies can be beneficial, especially where these encourage pupils to undertake longer writing tasks or write purposefully for an audience

Critical points

» *Writing is a complex skill that requires sustained practice and explicit teaching to develop fluency to compose texts in a variety of genres.*

» *Rigorous research can inform classroom practice, giving us good bets for developing and improving our teaching and learning activities.*

» *A key issue in developing writing is engaging the learner. The evidence indicates that the most effective approaches involve the pupils themselves in planning, monitoring and evaluating their own learning and therefore taking responsibility for using writing strategies which can improve what they do.*

Critical reflections

» *Do you feel you have the skills to find relevant research to help you with the teaching of writing? Which sources of information do you think you would use in the future? As a professional teacher, knowing the research evidence helps you to make more informed decisions about your practice and to be confident about the effectiveness of your teaching. How will you help your pupils to engage with and take responsibility for their writing?*

Taking it further

Hattie, J (2011) *Visible Learning for Teachers: Maximizing Impact on Learning.* London: Routledge Pages.

Hattie provides a summary of several hundred meta-analyses of educational research, with implications for teaching.

Marzano, R J, Pickering, D J, and Pollock, J E (2001) *Classroom Instruction That Works: Research-Based Strategies for Increasing Student Achievement*. Alexandria, VA: ASCD.

This book focuses on evidence-based strategies for teaching, such as summarising, note taking and the use of graphic organisers.

Taber, K (2013) *Classroom-Based Research and Evidence-Based Practice: An Introduction*. Sage Publications Limited.

Taber focuses on the nature and logic of the research process and supports practitioners in critically evaluating the strengths and limitations of published studies.

References

Blatchford, P, Russell, A and Webster, R (2012) *Reassessing the Impact of Teaching Assistants: How Research Challenges Practice and Policy*. Abingdon, Oxon, UK: Routledge.

Department for Education (2012) *What Is the Research Evidence on Writing?* Research report DFE-RR238. London: Department for Education. [online] Available at: https://www.education.gov.uk/publications/eOrderingDownload/DFE-RR238.pdf (accessed 11 February 2015).

Goldberg, A, Russell, M and Cook, A (2003) The Effect of Computers on Student Writing: A Meta-analysis of Studies from 1992 to 2002. *The Journal of Technology, Learning and Assessment*, 2(1): pp 1–52. [online] Available at: https://ejournals.bc.edu/ojs/index.php/jtla/article/view/1661 (accessed 11 February 2015).

Graham, S, McKeown, D, Kiuhara, S and Harris, K R (2012) A Meta-analysis of Writing Instruction for Students in the Elementary Grades. *Journal of Educational Psychology*, 104(4): 879.

Graham, S and Perrin, D (2007a) A Meta-analysis of Writing Instruction for Adolescent Students. *Journal of Educational Psychology*, 99(3): 445.

Graham, S and Perrin, D (2007b) *Writing Next: Effective Strategies to Improve Writing of Adolescents in Middle and High School*. Washington, D.C.: Alliance for Excellence in Education.

Hebert, M, Simpson, A and Graham, S (2013) Comparing Effects of Different Writing Activities on Reading Comprehension: A Meta-analysis. *Reading and Writing*, 26(1): 111–38.

Jones, S (2012) Mapping the Landscape: Gender and the Writing Classroom. *Journal of Writing Research*, 33: 161–79.

Marks, R (2013) 'The Blue Table Means You Don't Have a Clue': The Persistence of Fixed-Ability Thinking and Practices in Primary Mathematics in English Schools. *FORUM*, 55(1): 31–44.

Torgerson, D, Torgerson, C, Ainsworth, H, Buckley, H M, Heaps, C, Hewitt, C and Mitchell, N (2014) *Improving Writing Quality: Evaluation Report and Executive Summary May 2014*. London: EEF.

Websites

Best Evidence Encyclopaedia UK (BEE UK): www.bestevidence.org.uk.

EPPI-Centre: http://eppi.ioe.ac.uk/cms/.

Sutton Trust/EEF Teaching and Learning Toolkit: http://educationendowmentfoundation.org.uk/toolkit.

'What Works' Clearninghouse (WWC): www.whatworks.ed.gov.

2 Finding a written voice

ADAM BUSHNELL

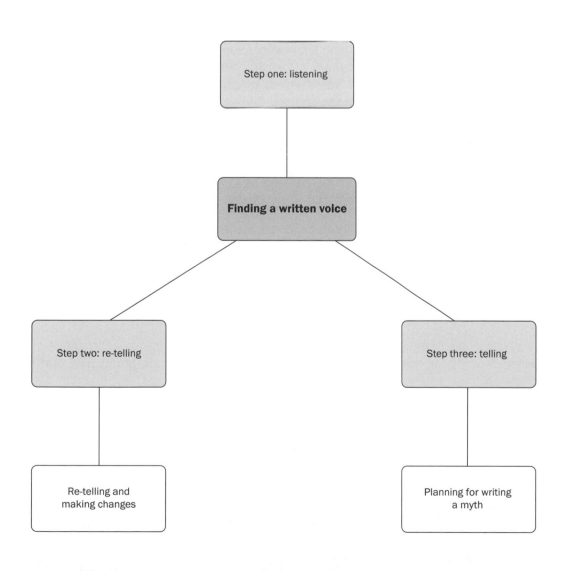

Teachers' Standards

3 Demonstrate good subject and curriculum knowledge

- demonstrate an understanding of and take responsibility for promoting high standards of literacy, articulacy and the correct use of standard English, whatever the teacher's specialist subject

Critical questions

» *How do we inspire children to want to write?*

» *What steps lead to effective creative writing?*

» *How can we extend oral re-telling of stories and experiences into independent writing?*

Introduction

How many times do children say, '*I don't know what to do*'? It is a statement that has echoed through classrooms more times than any of us can count. It is a statement that is as frustrating as it is frequent. You have delivered a clear introduction to your lesson referring to the learning outcomes. You have modelled examples. The children have then discussed with *talk partners* what they are going to do. You have reinforced, several times, what the task will be. Yet, despite all of this '*I don't know what to do*' can still be heard. Why? It is because children need to develop the ability to listen.

It is listening that empowers children. It empowers us all. By listening we *do* know what to do. We may not be able to do it but at least we know what is expected of us.

This chapter explores the skills children need to know exactly what to do and *how* to do it. This is a triadic approach: listening, re-telling and telling. The chapter looks at techniques to enhance listening skills and then uses these to fuel re-telling, leading to talking, then writing as an individual. The first step is listening because it is through this that we are able to re-tell past experiences, such as a visit to the zoo or the plot of a movie we have watched or a joke we have heard. Re-telling these experiences requires us to have listened.

Once children become confident *re-tellers* you can show them how to apply these skills to become confident *tellers*: that is, they can independently create brand new oral and written work.

Step one: listening

As a teacher or someone working in education, you need to listen. You need to listen to children, you need to listen to parents and you need to listen to your colleagues.

You are an amazing listener. You are such an amazing listener that you are able to sit in a pub or a restaurant with a friend, realise that the conversation you are having is not that interesting but the conversation on the next table really *is* very interesting. You are able to *zone out* your friend, *zone in* to the more interesting conversation and yet still nod and say '*yeah*' in all the right places. You are amazing. Yet it is not a skill that you were born with. You have developed your talent.

Children need to be taught the ability to listen. In the early years children enter the classroom to a sea of noise. Their homes may be filled with voices of siblings and other family members but these voices are familiar. Their homes may be filled with noise from speakers, televisions, laptops, iPods etc, but the classroom noise can be a new experience. Filtering this noise when an adult is giving instructions can be almost impossible for children to do, so lots of early years environments have a sound that indicates a time to listen, for example, buzzers and bells, whistles and wands, shakers and shouters.

The best listeners are those children who are used to having a designated speaking and listening area in their classroom – what can best be described as a *story space*. This is an area in the classroom with a place for the teacher or communicator to sit with the children. The communicator could be seated on an unusual looking chair decorated with materials or images. It could be a carved *storytelling chair*; it could just be a plastic chair with a few stickers on it. But this chair should stand out from the other furniture in the room. The listeners could be sitting on the carpet, on beanbags or just in their places on chairs. What is important is that when the communicator sits on this chair it should be clear that it is a special time for listening.

There are also fantastic examples of these spaces in many outdoor classrooms. But these work to their best effect inside because they can be accessed at any given moment in any lesson.

John Hattie (2003) discovered with over 500,000 studies that classroom environment was one of the top three factors that influence children's learning.

This *story space* is an excellent way of creating a specific speaking and listening space in any classroom from the early years to Year 6.

CASE STUDY

Reception class discussing their topic People Who Help Us

A reception classteacher was introducing a new topic, *People Who Help Us*. The teacher sat on her *story chair* and the children on a carpeted area in their *story space*. Images of the local area were displayed on the interactive whiteboard behind the teacher.

The teacher started by telling the children that she had met the Big Bad Wolf that morning on her way to school. She explained that he had seemed very pleased with himself, and when she had asked him why, he told her that he had something amazing that he had stolen from Old Mother Hen.

The teacher asked the class if they would like to see this amazing object.

There was great enthusiasm and a cacophony of noise which was instantly silenced when the teacher held up something wrapped in a brightly coloured cloth. She then revealed a stone. This was discussed. Why would the Big Bad Wolf have a stone?

The traditional tale of *Stone Soup* by Tony Ross was then read to the children.

The teacher revealed that she had told the Big Bad Wolf that Old Mother Hen had tricked him. She asked the children if they agreed and discussed how the wolf had been tricked.

The teacher asked the children what they would do if the Big Bad Wolf came to school. The children took turns discussing how they would barricade doors, block windows, where they would hide and finally they were asked who they would call to help them. Each suggestion was then discussed in *talk partners*.

Finally, the children decided upon who would be best to call for help in this situation, and a top three list was made on the board. The images of the local area on the interactive whiteboard were then referred to, and the children indicated where people who could help them might be found near to the school.

The case study contained lots of speaking and listening, and the children were clearly used to working in this way. To introduce the *story space* to enhance listening skills in the classroom takes very little time.

- As a quick five-minute activity before beginning a lesson: This can set the tone for any lesson; the children are used to joining in with class discussion in a fun and informal way before you even begin. It is like a warm up activity for classroom contribution.
- Other quick activities include asking riddles, telling jokes, playing charades, making up *tag team* stories etc.

The communicator on the story chair can be a teacher or teaching assistant or pupil or visitor etc.

Once the children are used to this process, longer activities can be introduced such as sharing work for discussion.

Activity 1: Using the story space

Read through the case study above in which a teacher introduces a topic using the story chair. Remember that the aim of this session is to encourage children to listen as a starting point to developing their ideas.

» *Think of a different topic that you could introduce in this way.*

» *What interesting objects or images could you use to introduce it?*

» *What stories could you tell to draw the children in and get them listening and engaged?*

» *List some books that you could use to develop the ideas?*

» *What other resources would get the children listening and engaged? How could you integrate the use of technology into this session?*

» *What might you ask them to discuss? How would you manage this?*

FOCUS ON RESEARCH

The Ladder of Participation

The Ladder of Participation (shown below) is based on a model from Weitzman and Greenberg (2008), who found that children's levels of participation can be understood with the help of this diagram.

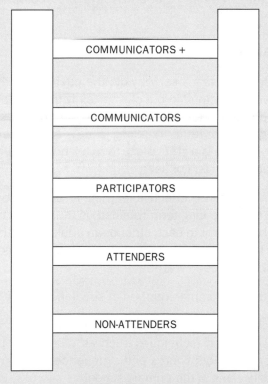

COMMUNICATORS +

COMMUNICATORS

PARTICIPATORS

ATTENDERS

NON-ATTENDERS

• The children who are on the *Non-attenders* rung are not those absent from school but rather those children who are present but in body only. They are distracted either by something good that is happening to them in the near future, such as a trip to Disney Land, or perhaps distracted by something bad.

• The children on the *Attenders* rung are those who are listening but do not wish to participate in the lesson. They do not put up their hands to answer questions or join in with discussions.

- The *Participators* will put up their hands and join in with discussions.

- The *Communicators* not only participate but give extra relevant information too. For example, they will not only tell you that a police officer is someone who helps them, but they will also tell you that they work in a police station.

- The *Communicators* + are those children who can fill an entire lesson with their answers, be they relevant or not.

A story space can help to make the *Non-attenders* attend, the *Attenders* participate, the *Participators* communicate and hopefully *reign in* the *Communicators* +.

Children can also be helped to listen and communicate effectively by using the strategies in this chapter throughout the day as they model effective and appropriate speaking and listening skills.

Step two: re-telling

A four-year-old in a nursery told this joke: Why did the pasty cross the road? It was meat-n-potato. She may not have understood it, but she certainly understood the delivery of a joke. She understood that there needs to be a question followed by a response, then she needs to give an answer. Telling jokes, or rather *re-telling* jokes is an excellent way to introduce children to re-telling.The story space is a great place to re-tell not only jokes but also experiences and stories that have been told, read or seen.

Re-telling has been shown to be an effective learning strategy. The National Literacy Trust (2012) found that children in the long term retained as much as 90 per cent of information by explaining what they have learnt to each other or an adult. This requires children to understand a concept before they explain it to others, but it clearly shows the benefit of re-telling in order to fully retain what has been learnt.

Re-telling is probably the most common method of speaking activity used in schools.

In the early years, re-telling stories happen frequently, but it is important to continue this throughout the school. Re-telling techniques such as stories through puppets, character studies in costume, events through figures and experiences through pictures would, therefore, be of benefit for every class in the primary school.

Nurseries often have boxes of themed toys: African animals, farms, dinosaurs, Arctic animals, rainforest etc. These same boxes of toys can sometimes be seen in Year 6 classrooms and they are just as effective. They work well as a wet play resource rather than sitting watching a screen, but they also work well as part of a lesson.

For example, a Year 6 class retold the story of the Last Supper in Lego. A Year 5 class retold the encounter between Henry VIII and Francis I of France on the Field of the Cloth of Gold. A Year 11 GCSE farming class explained the qualities of a healthy animal using a box of farm toys.

Re-telling is an essential tool for children to master in order for them to become independent and creative writers of their own stories.

CASE STUDY

Year 2 class re-telling a story

Little Rabbit Foo Foo is a traditional song and story. It contains a sufficient level of violence to keep even the most hardened Year 2 entertained. It involves a rather psychotic rabbit hopping through a forest and *bopping* animals on the head. Along comes a Good Fairy who gives the *furry nutter* three chances to change or she will turn him into a *goonie*.

Yasmin, a Year 2 teacher, read her class a version of the story by Michael Rosen. She was seated on her *story chair* and the children were on the carpet in the *story space*. Even the children who had not heard the story before were soon joining in, encouraged by the book's repetitive language and structure.

Yasmin then asked the class to work as *talk partners* in mixed ability duo groups. The children were asked to use a *tag team* technique to re-tell the story that they had heard.

Six images of the six characters were displayed on the interactive whiteboard. These six were Little Rabbit Foo Foo, The Good Fairy and the four animals that had been assaulted – wriggly worms, field mice, tigers and goblins. The children were familiar with *tag team storytelling*, so, if one child forgot what happened next in the story then they would *tag* their partner. If they both forgot then they missed out that section of the story and moved on to the next. Soon the whole class had re-told the story.

Building on this, a few volunteers swapped places with the teacher, one at a time, and sat on the *story chair* to model their re-telling.

The children recorded the story using a six-part storyboard. This was differentiated in three ways.

1.   The less able recorded their story through six images.

2.   The middle ability groups used both pictures and sentences.

3.   The more able wrote in sentences to re-tell the story.

Re-telling and making changes

The lesson in the case study above is a basic one and a variant can be seen in many schools. It is using *re-telling* as a vehicle towards *telling* and it works to great effect.

Remember that the aim of this session is to encourage children to become confident re-tellers.

You could start with a traditional tale such as *Little Rabbit Foo Foo*. Remember to choose a tale that follows a basic storyline with a triadic structure, that is, a story with three major events or following some kind of repetition in threes. Once all of the changes have been made the children can now tell a brand new story.

Activity 2: Using books with a repetitive structure

Read through the case study above in which a teacher uses a traditional tale as a basic structure that the children can have access to, before adding their own detail to create a new story. Remember that the aim of this session is to encourage children to move towards independent story writing.

» *Think of a different story you can use.*

» *Make a list of suitable books for this activity.*

» *What can the main character be changed into? What about the other characters?*

» *Does the change of characters mean that the setting needs changing too?*

» *Can the children perform their stories in talk partners or groups or as a class?*

» *What digital media can be used to record the stories and how can you share them with other classes?*

FOCUS ON RESEARCH

Long-term retention

The National Literacy Trust (NLT) (2012) states:

> *1 person in 6 in the UK has poor literacy skills which will impact on every area of their life. Without good reading, writing and communication skills a child won't be able to succeed at school and as a young adult they will be locked out of the job market. They will be unable to reach their full potential or make a valuable contribution to the economic and cultural life of our nation. Their poor literacy skills will also affect them as parents as they will struggle to support their child's learning and generations of families will be locked in poverty and social exclusion.*

The NLT decided to combat this by testing pupils' long-term memory retention after a variety of teaching styles were employed. They not only tested children's long-term memory retention through explaining concepts to others, but they also tested lessons taught predominantly with audio visual techniques and others dominated by listening, practice by doing, reading, demonstration and discussion. After this testing, they found that children retained the following percentages of information:

Method of teaching	Information retained (%)
Explaining to others	90
Practise by doing	75
Discussion	50
Demonstration	30
Audio visual	20
Reading	10
Listening	5

This may not come as a great surprise, but it does illustrate the importance of talking in the classroom. Talk fuels retention of concepts. Talk is the key in the classroom to help children re-tell with accuracy and to create new ideas with confidence.

Step three: telling

Telling tales is something that children find very easy. They do it all of the time – and not just '*My dog ate my homework*' either. A Year 6 pupil told his teacher that he had previously trained to be a Ninja in Japan. He said that his training had taken three years to complete. She asked him when he had done this. He replied that it was in the six-weeks' holiday. It was at this moment that she began to doubt the authenticity of his tale.

A Year 3 pupil told her teacher that she had over 100 pets at her house, ranging from llamas to giant pythons. Actually, that one turned out to be true, as her parents owned a rescue centre for animals.

When a Year 5 class sat in their *story space* after lunch, the teacher asked them if they knew how the stick insects had escaped over the half hour she had been out of the classroom. One boy had a think and then said, '*I think that the big stick insects ganged up on the little stick insect then used him as a battering ram to get out of the cage!*' He then smiled, triumphant at his storytelling techniques.

Good teachers are always happy to hear children being creative and telling their own made up stories. Most of the time anyway!

Before any piece of creative writing, it is effective for children to talk their ideas through with others. This solidifies what they are going to do before they do it.

We often get frustrated when children simply re-tell a video game or a movie when they are meant to be producing an original piece of writing. Quite often children do this as a safety net. They are afraid that their own ideas are not going to be good enough. By following the triadic structure of this chapter, children can build on their language and re-telling strategies in three steps.

It is important that children know that there is nothing wrong with *borrowing* ideas for your own writing. All authors *borrow* to some extent. When J K Rowling wrote the Harry Potter series she *borrowed* characters from many myths and legends from all over the world: the Basilisk from France, Cerberus from Greece, Cave Trolls from Norway etc. The spells, the beasts, the magical items are all familiar to us and yet have been woven together expertly and uniquely. It is a fantastic model to learn from.

If children want to add characters from other stories into their own, it is good to get them to adapt them, so for example, instead of having Hermione they have a good witch. By making the characters generic, the children can put their own unique mark upon them. Scooby Doo is now a talking dog character in their story, but perhaps a poodle rather then a Great Dane. Steve from Minecraft is now an explorer, perhaps a mapmaker rather then a miner. Percy Jackson is a boy with powers, not the power of water but the power of fire.

In this way, children can use the strategies they have developed in re-telling with changes, and apply them to new writing of their own.

CASE STUDY

Year 5 class writing about their own mythical creature

A Year 5 class had been studying myths and legends, and had had lots of examples read to them. Joe, the teacher, had the class on chairs in the *story space* and he was sitting on his *story chair* in front of the interactive whiteboard. He showed the class www.switchzoo.com and created a new mythical creature by making online selections and mixing animals together.

The children worked on iPads where the Switch Zoo Free app had been installed.

They created their own creatures and sketched them inside a box on a worksheet.

Names were invented using verbs and nouns, such as Flying Death, Slithering Doom, Sneaking Shadow etc.

After some discussion and sharing of these creations, the children then labelled them on the worksheet with four different writing techniques. They independently added adjectives, and after some input from the teacher, added adverbial phrases.

Then, following more input, they added some phrases with alliteration. Finally, similes were added.

To finish, there was a plenary where some children sat on the *story chair* and shared their ideas with the class before everyone worked in *talk partners* to share their ideas with one another.

Planning for writing a myth

Lessons like the one described are perfect for planning a myth. The children not only have a mythical character ready, but they also have a word bank of descriptive language to insert into their story.

The aim of the session is to become an independent teller of stories, but they still need the support of the structured approach. There are many websites to support the topic of myths and legends. *Switch Zoo* is ideal as it is so easy to use. Nursery children are able to step up to the board and make the selections with their fingers. The noise of the animal selected booms out across the carpet often to a squeal of delight from the children as a new creature is made, morphing before their eyes.

Also, www.buildyourwildself.com allows you to create more human looking mythical creatures. www.myths.e2bn.org is fantastic for looking at a range of both written and animated stories in this genre.

Once examples have been explored and monsters have been made, it is time to make your own myths. The creation of myths is something that most children enjoy as they can really let their imagination run wild.

One teacher described a class who wanted SpongeBob to be in everything they wrote about. In anticipation of this, when they were writing a myth about sea monsters the teacher used *Story World* cards by John and Caitlin Matthews and selected the *stories of the sea* pack. The children had to use characters from the cards in their story. The characters they choose in Story World are generic characters, so you do not have Captain Jack Sparrow, you have a pirate; you do not have Ariel, you have a mermaid.

Lots of myths and legends follow a basic structure. For example, in Goldilocks, she first goes to the house of the bears. The last thing that happens is that the bears come home. The three major events in the middle are the porridge, the chairs and the beds.

Longer stories follow this same structure too. In *Percy Jackson and the Lightning Thief*, Percy finds out he is a demi god and goes to camp Half Blood. At the end of the novel he travels to the Underworld to confront Hades and learns the truth. The three major events in the middle are meeting Medusa to collect a pearl, meeting the Hydra for the second pearl and collecting the third pearl in the lair of the Lotus Eaters.

Of course, other smaller events happen along the way but this is a basic structure that we can imitate in our own myth.

The Story World cards can be used to help children with ideas here as they can be grouped into characters, settings and objects and displayed around the classroom.

Adding individual detail makes the children's stories uniquely theirs.

An example of this planned story could be:

•   A girl goes off to save a prince from a monster.

- She meets a bad crow on a farm and collects a flaming sword.

- She meets a good witch on a hill and collects a helmet that makes her fly.

- She meets a bad giant in a village and collects a ring that can shoot out smoke.

Once this basic plan has been made, then the children can work with talk partners to add detail, such as the setting at the beginning for their main character and the setting at the end for their monster.

Talk partner questions could include, '*Why does the girl go to save the prince? Who sends her? How did the monster kidnap the prince and why?*' etc. More detail is added to the story map as these questions are answered.

By the time this planning is complete, the paper will be a mass of words, sentences and phrases but they will all be in chronological order. The children will understand their own writing and pictures even if it looks like a right mess to us! After some time sharing their stories orally with each other, the children should be not only ready but also *excited* to write!

Activity 3: Independent creation of stories

Read through the case study above in which a teacher encourages writing about a newly created character. The next step is writing a myth. Remember that the aim of the session is to encourage children to produce independent writing.

»   *What character will be the hero or heroine? What might others say about him or her? Can you add speech bubbles to do this? What catch phrases does the hero or heroine use? What are the past actions or events that they have lived through?*

»   *What resources can you use to inspire ideas about why the main character goes on a quest? What images could be used?*

»   *Which other characters appear frequently in myths? What objects are often associated with this genre of story? What settings are usually included?*

»   *How can the writing be edited and improved? How can the story be developed? How can talk partners help to build on the writing?*

FOCUS ON RESEARCH

Scaffolding

This method of planning with lots of discussion and taking it step by step is very appealing for reluctant writers. It gives them the scaffolding necessary to create independent stories and pieces of writing. It boosts confidence, ability and enthusiasm for writing, but, perhaps not so for more able students who are not used to working in this style. They often just want to get on with writing a story. This method of planning in a structured way can be frustrating to the more able forcing them to challenge their own writing techniques.

Carol Dweck (2000) maintains:

You might think that students who were highly skilled would be the ones who relish a challenge and persevere in the face of setbacks. Instead, many of these students are the most worried about failure, and the most likely to question their ability and to wilt when they hit obstacles.

Conclusion

It is important that you take *all* children out of their comfort zone frequently in order to establish an all round work ethic. If children find a method in their writing that works for them then this is not the only method that they should employ. Trying and failing is a part of life. It should be a part of school life. It is essential for children to know that failure is all right and how to learn from it. It is essential they know how to make it a positive experience. Employing writing strategies of a varied nature is the best strategy for any writer to take, whether they are early writers or experienced authors.

The methods described in this chapter will help children to find their own written voice. The chapter is set out in three parts but this is **not** so that Step One will be employed in the early years, Step Two in Key Stage 1 and Step Three in Key Stage 2 – definitely not. Indeed, the intention of the chapter is that you can select where your own group of children are on this continuum. You may have a class of Key Stage 1 children who are ready to tell and write their own stories. You may have a group of Key Stage 2 children who have not yet learnt how to listen. Use whichever strategies you feel are best for your children. However, it is important to realise that the first step of listening is the foundation to all written work. We learn to listen then we learn to speak. When we learn to speak we imitate and mimic. Finally, we find our own voice and express ourselves in our own way.

Critical points

»   *It is important that children develop their listening skills in order to develop their writing skills, which in turn leads to a desire to write.*

»   *It is important that children are given a structured approach to writing to promote effective creative writing.*

»   *Giving an independent written voice to children can be developed and encouraged in a structured way by extending oral re-telling of stories, using past experiences and the other techniques outlined in this chapter.*

Critical reflections

»   *This is not a chapter to suggest what you should do but rather what could be done. These are all real strategies that work in the classroom. How could you use these strategies in your classroom to enable children to find a written voice?*

Taking it further

For practical ideas and a rationale for talk and writing see

DCSF (2008) *Talk for Writing*. Nottingham: DCSF. [online] Available at: http://webarchive.nationalarchives. gov.uk/20110809101133/nsonline.org.uk/node/163592 (accessed 12 February 2015).

Corbett, P and Strong, J (2011) *Talk for Writing Across the Curriculum*. Maidenhead: Open University Press.

Clipstone- Boyles, S (2012) *Teaching Primary English through Drama*, 2nd Edn. Abingdon: Routledge.

References

Dweck, C (2000) *Self-theories: Their Role in Motivation, Personality, and Development (Essays in Social Psychology)*. London: Psychology Press.

Hattie, J (2003) *Teachers Make a Difference: What Is the Research Evidence?* Auckland University, Auckland, Australia.

Matthews, J and Matthews C (2009) *The StoryWorld Cards: Stories of the Sea*. Dorking: Templar Publishing.

National Literacy Trust (2012) *Words for Life: Impact Report*. [online] Available at: www.literacytrust. org.uk/assets/0001/4600/Impact_report_2011-12.pdf (accessed 12 February 2015).

Ross, T (1995) *Stone Soup*. London: Picture Lions.

Rowling JK (2001) *Harry Potter and the Philosopher's Stone*. London: Bloomsbury Publishing plc.

Riordon, R (2013) *Percy Jackson and the Lightning Thief*. London: Puffin.

Weitzman, E and Greenberg, J (2008) *Learning Language & Loving it: A Guide to Promoting Children's Social, Language, & Literacy Development in Early Childhood Settings*. The Hanen Centre, Ontario, Canada.

3 A murder mystery

ADRIAN COPPING

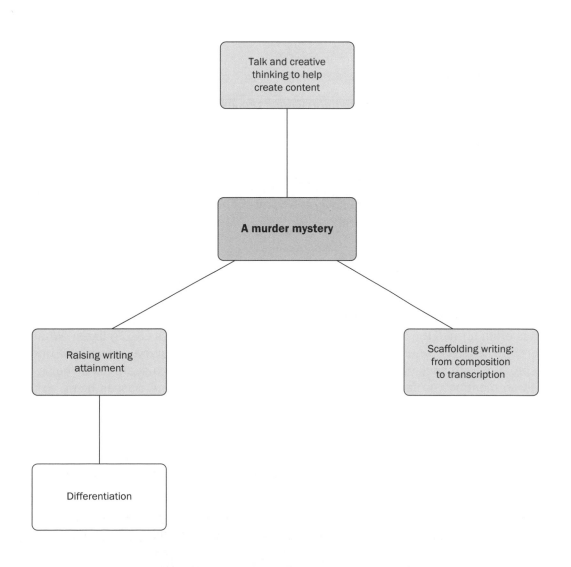

Teachers' Standards

2 Promote good progress and outcomes by pupils

- demonstrate knowledge and understanding of how pupils learn and how this impacts on teaching

3 Demonstrate good subject and curriculum knowledge

- have a secure knowledge of the relevant subject(s) and curriculum areas, foster and maintain pupils' interest in the subject, and address misunderstandings

- *demonstrate an understanding of and take responsibility for promoting high standards of literacy, articulacy and the correct use of standard English, whatever the teacher's specialist subject*

4 Plan and teach well-structured lessons

- contribute to the design and provision of an engaging curriculum within the relevant subject area(s)

Critical questions

» *How can you engage children in the writing process?*

» *How can you help children to think creatively and explore possibilities?*

» *How can you embed dramatic techniques to develop children's learning?*

» *How can you involve children in assessment of their writing?*

» *How can you help children get over the hurdle of not knowing what to write and then scaffold the process with them?*

Introduction

Children find writing difficult. In fact adults find writing difficult too. As I sit here and write this chapter I am thinking about all sorts of things: sentence structure, spelling, punctuation and whether what I am writing actually makes sense. Like me, children do get preoccupied with what is often termed the secretarial aspects of writing. David Wray's (1993) paper 'What do children think about writing?' emphasised this. The children he surveyed often saw writing as a product, with spelling, neatness and underlining the title with a sharp pencil being the top three mentions. In fact I remember a child in one of my Year 4 classes being so pre-occupied with neatness and spelling that he was not able to demonstrate his understanding of the concepts being taught. Interestingly, the National Literacy Trust's 2012 annual survey 'Children's and young people's writing in 2012' found that where most young people enjoy writing, it is with technology: text, email, social networking where of course many of these secretarial aspects are removed through context or spelling and grammar checkers, and neatness determined only by choice of font.

In this chapter, a case study of a Victorian murder mystery is used to provide a context for writing, engage children in writing and give them a purpose for it. The process of developing writing, the thinking, discussion and knowledge creation that goes on around it is the focus. This chapter also contends that motivated, engaged children who want to write have high expectations set for them and the process is scaffolded, so that they reach higher levels of attainment. Brownhill (2013) states that:

> it is strongly believed that it is our job as teachers to put fire in the 'writing bellies' of the children that we have the good fortune of teaching.

(2013, p 2)

Activity 1: What is your writing journey?

» *What do you remember about writing at school?*

» *Did you enjoy writing?*

» *What do you remember being told was good about your writing?*

» *Did this change in secondary school?*

THE CASE STUDY

Setting the context

John was doing a two-day writing project with his Year 5 class. He wanted to remove the complaint '*I don't know what to write*' from their lips. He decided to do this by helping them create some interesting content that they could later work on. His topic for the half-term was local history with a focus on *Victorian Britain*. John therefore decided to create a murder mystery, as he felt this would engage everyone particularly his boys and so *Death at Denscombe Park* was born. John's murder mystery revolved around Prime Minister William Gladstone being found dead on an upstairs toilet at Denscombe Park manor house. He had created evidence in the form of witness statements, recorded conversations, letters, diary extracts and pen portraits of the characters involved. The outcomes for these two days were not only around thinking, discussion and enquiry but also to create a *case file* which included several types of writing that might appear in such a document:

- an entry in the parliamentary record *Hansard*;
- prosecution and defence counsel speeches;
- a newspaper report;
- a diary entry;
- an epitaph;
- a coded letter addressed to the victim.

John had created a working wall to act as a police-style evidence board and had decided to present the murder mystery himself in role as *Stokes*, butler to Lord Denscombe.

As the children entered on the first morning, they were immediately asking questions; they noticed the board, the pictures and an old newsreel playing. They noticed their teacher speaking differently and dressed in *olden days* clothes, as one child put it. There was an immediate buzz of excitement and enquiry about the classroom.

FOCUS ON RESEARCH

Fostering play, engagement and teacher in role

In '*Teaching English Creatively*' (2009), Teresa Cremin draws on the influential work of Fisher and Williams (2004) who state that:

> *if the spirit of play and imagination is encouraged, then teachers and learners are more open to new and different opportunities, to try new routes and paths less well-travelled.*
>
> (2009, p 7)

Cremin goes on to discuss the importance of the process of learning stating that:

> *Creative English learning is a motivating and highly interactive experience involving a degree of playfulness and the potential for engagement in multiple contexts. In such contexts, creativity will not simply be an event or a product, although it may involve neither or both, but a process involving the serious play of ideas and possibilities.*
>
> (2009, p 7)

She considers the technique of teacher in role, which is distinctive in that it is about the teacher imagining themselves to be someone else. Cremin suggests that the teacher must take on the role with commitment and belief, so the teacher takes part with the children in creating a collaborative context. The teacher in their role acts as navigator, guiding the children through the experience, extending and challenging thinking from inside it rather than from being a distant figure outside. As a result, they can guide and shape the intended learning, consider any incidental learning and influence the enquiry taking place.

Talk and creative thinking to help create content

Corbett and Strong open their influential text *Talk for Writing Across the Curriculum* with these words:

> *It is impossible to write any text without being familiar with the language rhythms and patterns that it involves. Indeed, it is impossible to write a sentence pattern without being able to say it – and you cannot say it, if you haven't heard it.*
>
> (2011, p 1)

Children need an experience to get their minds engaged and their creative juices flowing. They need to be inspired and motivated and also see a reason for what they are doing. In the context of this case study, they were helping Stokes the butler solve a tragic crime in the public interest, and then create a file of evidence so the authorities could bring the perpetrator to justice. This was motivating, slightly alternative and certainly purposeful within the context of the topic they were studying. But the children needed to hear the language of solving crimes, the language of Victorian England and the language of the upper classes in order to talk about it so that they could then write about it.

THE CASE STUDY

Getting into character

It was important as a teacher in role that John modelled the language required. He began by inviting the children to stand, with their hands on their hearts, and read an adapted historical pledge that officers for the crown had to recite during Victorian times. The children swore to 'well and truly serve our Sovereign Lady Queen Victoria' and to 'do right to all manner of people after the laws and usages of this realm without fear of favour, affection or ill will'. Already they were into the language of the time.

A murder mystery is a perfect context for debate, discussion and exploration, which in turn provide content for whatever writing will be taking place. However, this debate needed to be structured so that the children remained on task.

John provided character information cards and distributed them to each small group that he had set up. Each group had to explore their character, discuss what they would say about the incident and what their opinion about the victim was. One of the group would then be in the *hot seat* to answer questions from the rest of the class. Any information gained from this would be added to the working wall to again support ideas and provide content.

However, the new national curriculum (DfE, 2013) for English, Key Stages 1 and 2 states that pupils should be taught to:

> *Use spoken language to develop understanding through speculating, hypothesising, imagining and exploring ideas.*
> *Consider and evaluate different viewpoints, attending to and building on the contributions of others.*
>
> (p 7)

More therefore needed to be done to refine, shape and construct new ideas, rather than just stay with initial thoughts.

A key aspect of creative thinking is allowing the exploration of different possibilities. Within the context of a murder mystery, it is hard not to purely focus on who did it. John had devised his mystery so that all of the key characters in the story could have been involved. In order to help his groups refine their ideas and address some of the speaking and listening skills above, John used a technique called *Six hats thinking*.

FOCUS ON RESEARCH

Edward de Bono's Six Hats Thinking

Edward de Bono's work is mainly within the world of business. His book *Six Hats Thinking* was first published in 1985 and has the strapline '*run better meetings, make faster decisions*'. However, the approach can be used in many different contexts, especially when trying to deal with a murder mystery! Six hats thinking is used to look at decisions from a number of perspectives rather than the one you may normally employ. The technique forces you to move outside the thinking style that you primarily use and consider an event, a decision or a situation from a variety of perspectives.

De Bono's thinking hats are:

1.   Black hat thinking is about judgement. It may lead you to ask: What is wrong with this? Will it work? What could some of the challenges be with this?

2.   Green hat thinking is about creativity. With this hat on you may ask: What new ideas are possible, what is my suggestion? Can I create something new?

3.   Red hat thinking is about feelings. On wearing this hat you may ask how you feel about the issue and what your likes and dislikes about the issue are.

4.   The white thinking hat draws attention to information: What are the facts? What information do I have and what do I need?

5.   The blue hat is thinking about thinking: What process will we go through? How will we decide?

6.   Finally, yellow hat thinkers ask about the benefits: What are the good points? Why is this good and why can it be done?

Applying all of these types of thinking to a situation or decision forces a much rounder response.

THE CASE STUDY

Using the six hats technique

After introducing the children to de Bono's six hats technique, John gave each group of six a hat and their responses in the discussion had to involve some of the questions stated in the research focus above. As a result, lots of perspectives shifted; children were analysing their ideas, adapting their thinking, building on the ideas of others and were able to add a lot more detail to their initial ideas. They were developing their skills of negotiating and questioning as well as beginning to frame some new hypotheses as to who could have been responsible for the prime minister's death. The discussion also resulted in new questions to ask the characters to gain more information and establish motive.

John had also created information packs on William Gladstone, including different perspectives on his life, political cartoons from the period, census documents and other useful information to help the class build more of a picture of this Victorian prime minister.

Scaffolding writing: from composition to transcription

In addition to engaging his children with writing, John's aim was to raise their attainment levels. Through the use of formative assessment over the year, John had recognised that many of his children were capable of a higher level of attainment in writing, and while many had good ideas, the organisation, grammar, punctuation and in some cases spelling was letting them down. John's challenge was therefore how to turn the sophisticated hypotheses and orally articulated ideas into the file of evidence. How would he be able to support his children to write the documents and so fulfil his outcomes?

John knew he needed to give children some examples of the texts he wanted the children to write. Chamberlain in Cox (2011) states that:

> Children need to be exposed to quality texts, both fiction and non-fiction. So that they interact with and read, good models of a range of texts, both print and electronic which will support their own writing.
>
> (2011, p 48)

Chamberlain is discussing writing in general, but this principle can be applied to specific genres. These models provide keys to unlock the door of style, language use, sentence structure and type, and also audience. They provide a way in for the children to begin to answer the question of 'How do I write this piece?' and 'What should it look like?'

This idea is referred to by Barrs and Cork (2001) as 'the reader in the writer'. They posit the notion that reading provides a scaffold for writing and is an essential part of the writing process.

Activity 2

Supporting children to create content for writing, usually referred to as composition, is fundamental to writing success. This cannot just be left to chance: children who are scaffolded through an experience so as to ignite the ideation process then navigated through the development of their ideas tend to write more successfully. The major stumbling block of what to write is removed. If those ideas are developed through exploration and discussion, the likelihood is that they will become more concrete and therefore easier to articulate.

» *How have you seen this composition process scaffolded for children? Give details.*

» *Was it successful?*

» *Plan a lesson where you will use this technique. Outline the stages you will go through showing how you will scaffold the child's writing at each stage.*

THE CASE STUDY

Modelling writing

John was able to find relevant period writings including, where possible, reproductions to use as models. The children were given these models in groups and provided with some prompts to enable them to explore the language, purpose, audience and structure. Below is an example grid that John used.

What is the text?	
Why was this text written? What is it for?	
Who will read it?	
Is it formal or informal?	
Find some examples of language that stand out as being important for this text. Give reasons.	

Raising writing attainment

While guidance from the Department for Education (DfE) is that assessment levels have been removed and will not be replaced (DfE, 2014), they do recognise that many schools have strong tracking systems which, as long as they work within the new national curriculum, can still be used. John's school uses attainment level descriptors; therefore John was assessing his pupils' progress through writing assessment tracking grids which indicated the level, the different assessment focuses for writing and criteria to meet that level. There are a number of example grids available online. You may wish to look at: www.tes.co.uk/teaching-resource/APP-Writing-Assessment-Grids-in-Word-format-6059072/; or a more child-friendly language grid, using *I can* statements available from: www.millhill.derbyshire.sch.uk/eng_res/writing/writing_levels.doc.

John recognised that he had raised the bar quite significantly with some of his texts. Examples from the parliamentary record *Hansard* from the time of William Gladstone's time as prime minister and examples of nineteenth-century defence and prosecution counsel speeches were significantly challenging for the children to interact with. The language, structure and formality were challenging for the children, as was the fact that these were text types few had come across before. Interestingly, some of the children went out for break using their newly acquired language in mock role play.

As well as these models, so that the children have ideas of what to write and how to write it, they need to know what is expected and what the teacher is looking for. Many teachers call these success criteria; often on a lesson plan format there is a section to put in your *success criteria*.

It would have been easy for John to have provided a sheet of criteria for what he was expecting. In this case, John was aiming for level 5 writing. To put this in context, primary schools across England have attainment percentage targets to meet for children at the end of Year 6. These are measured against results of Standard Assessment Tests (SATs) completed by Year 6 during May. The expected attainment level for Year 6 is level 4, with additional targets being given for level 5 and now in some cases level 6. So John had aimed high. John had created the grid using level 5 expectations in child-friendly language for each of the writing assessment focuses (see Table 3.1).

Table 3.1 *Level 5 expectations for writing in children-friendly language*

Assessment focus (AF)	Level 5 descriptors
AF1: To write imaginative, interesting and thoughtful texts	I can write using relevant ideas and I develop my material with some imaginative detail. I develop my ideas appropriately and establish a clear viewpoint and add detail where possible.
AF2: To produce texts which are appropriate to task, reader and purpose	I can write so that the main purpose of my writing is clear and consistently maintained. I can write using the correct form and features of specific types of writing and this appropriate style keeps my reader interested.
AF3: To organise and present whole texts effectively ...	My writing is structured clearly and I can organise my sentences into appropriate paragraphs. I can manage the development of my writing, for example closings refer back to openings. I write using clear links between paragraphs.
AF4: To construct paragraphs and cohesion within and between paragraphs	My paragraphs clearly structure my main ideas across the text to support my purpose, for example clear chronological or logical links between paragraphs. Within my paragraphs/sections, I can use a range of devices which support cohesion, for example secure use of pronouns, connectives, references back to text. I make good links between paragraphs throughout my writing.
AF5: To vary sentences for clarity, purpose and effect	I can use simple and complex sentences in my writing to make my ideas clear. I regularly use connectives in my work to show the relationship between my ideas, for example although, on the other hand, meanwhile etc. I can also add in extra detail and change the word order of my sentences for effect.

Table 3.1 (*cont.*)

Assessment focus (AF)	Level 5 descriptors
AF6: To write with technical accuracy of syntax and punctuation ...	I use a full range of punctuation accurately to demarcate sentences, including speech punctuation. The word order and punctuation within my sentences are generally accurate including commas to mark clauses although I sometimes make errors where ambitious structures are attempted.
AF7: To select appropriate and effective vocabulary	I choose my vocabulary to have an effect on my reader. I use a reasonably wide vocabulary although I do not always choose the best word.
AF8: To use correct spelling	I use correct spelling of most common words which have a function within a sentence. I can spell most suffixes and prefixes. I sometimes make mistakes with words that are not spelt how they sound.

Grid adapted from: www.millhill.derbyshire.sch.uk/eng_res/writing/writing_levels.doc.

John wanted to give children ownership of the assessment process and interact with the criteria. While each one was written in child-friendly language, which he was sure his children would understand, he still wanted them to take control of the assessment process. Briggs et al (2008) states that:

> For the children to become successful writers, it is essential that they feel part of this whole process and do not simply become involved at the point where they receive targets set by someone else for no apparent reason.

(2008, p 70)

FOCUS ON RESEARCH

Assessment

Shirley Clarke has written and researched extensively on involving children in the assessment process, mainly through sharing learning outcomes and success criteria as well as the purpose for doing the work. In her interim report (2001), alongside Lopez-Charles and McCallum, Clarke discusses her work with Gillingham Partnership schools. Her findings included these key points: When children were more aware of the learning outcomes, intentions, success criteria and purpose of their work, it sharpened their focus and made them more able to talk about their work and ask for clarification. It also helped guide their thoughts before they started. Clarke maintains that specific target setting makes assessment easier and makes it a more collaborative process. It also helps children take more ownership of their learning by being able to ask themselves if they have been successful rather than it be left to chance. An interesting question to ask children at the end of a lesson is '*Do you think you've been successful in this lesson?*' Then follow it up by asking them for a reason. You might be surprised at the results.

John therefore gave each group a copy of the grid and asked them to look at the examples, use their knowledge gained from interacting with the text and then plot which level 5 criteria they thought they could achieve and why.

For many of the children this proved very enlightening as it helped them determine their own success criteria.

Differentiation

John knew that not all his class would be able to write at level 5; therefore some of the writing outcomes for the file of evidence such as the coded letter, epitaph and diary were more suited to those in his class he knew may achieve level 4 and some only level 3. He used a similar grid to the one above and asked the children in those groups to complete the same activity. John worked with the coded letter group for this activity and used the activity as a guided reading session. Using the concept from Barr and Cork (2001) of a reader in the writer, John wanted to make sure that his lower attaining children would still be able to take part in the murder mystery as their idea creation, development and thinking was of a higher level than their writing attainment.

Activity 3

Think about any guided reading practice you have seen.

» *Was it separate from an English lesson?*

» *Was it organised where everyone reads and the teacher works with a group, or have you seen it used as a tool to scaffold the writing process?*

» *Was it an effective learning experience for the children?*

» *Did they know what the purpose was?*

» *Did the teacher know what the purpose was?*

Using their sample text as a model, John asked each group to create a writing frame for their own text. Writing frames can act as a very helpful scaffold as they help the writers structure their writing in a genre-appropriate way. Medwell et al (2012) state that not only does it help structure but

> *The skeleton framework consists of different key words and phrases, according to the particular generic form. The template of starters, connectives, sentence modifiers which constitute a writing frame gives children a structure within which they can concentrate on communicating what they want to say rather than getting lost in the form.*

> (2012, p 118)

Asking children to work together to create the frame continues their interaction with and understanding of the text. It also helps them to cement their understanding of the form, purpose and audience and supports their interaction with the language used.

Using their writing frames, the children began to draft their work in small groups. Chamberlain in Cox (2011) affirms this process approach to writing. She says that writing should be allowed time to develop, be reworked and refined. According to Chamberlain, English books should be messy to reflect the process of editing rather than focus on all writing as a product.

John decided to facilitate the children's oral rehearsal of their drafts before compiling their files of evidence to *hand over to the Judge*.

THE CASE STUDY

Teacher in role and drama as a scaffold for writing

During the lunch break, John transformed the classroom into a court room. He created a dock for the accused to stand in. He created defence and prosecution counsel benches, a jury area, court reporters' seats and of course the judge's chair. The idea was that, with John in role as the judge, the children (primarily those with counsel speeches, but also space for the other groups) would have chance to read their work out at the drafting stage in a simulation of the context that matched its purpose. This would support any redrafting and editing needed. John proceeded to hold court, complete with gown and wig, using the language of the courtroom.

The trial of the accused from the *Death at Denscombe* murder mystery began to take place. Members of each group shared their evidence and John came out of role to support points for editing. Further opportunities for questions were given and children had an opportunity to add any additional information to their drafts.

Here was drama being used as part of the process of scaffolding writing, not as a presentation at the end but as a specifically planned teaching tool to support the drafting process. Gardner (2010) supports this, by likening the process of *doing drama* to the process of writing. He states that:

> The process of doing drama, of making considered selections as a group in order to shape a narrative is akin to the writing undergoing the same process in isolation. As such then, drama is not only important for English as a subset of speaking and listening, it can be used as a device for rehearsing writing.
>
> (2010, p 56)

With a cry of *court dismissed*, John's class returned to their groups to amend their drafts, continue with the editing and checking that their sentence structure, spelling, language and punctuation was fit for purpose. Having already read their work out loud, they were able to identify whether it made sense by hearing it themselves. With the drafting complete, the children were ready to put together their class files of evidence. Using Chamberlain in Cox's (2011) language, the messy stuff was now ready to be presented.

Conclusion

Scaffolding the writing process for children is absolutely fundamental for facilitating effective writing. Within English teaching there can be a tendency to produce a *wow factor* opener to really engage children, get them talking and motivated. However, at the end of the lesson or unit of work, a teacher can then be bemused because the writing was still not very good. That *wow factor* opening to a unit of work has to then be built on. Children do not learn to write by osmosis, they have to be taught, they have to see the reason for it and they have to want to do it. This requires a lot of good subject knowledge about genres, about what makes those genres in terms of text structure, language features, purposes and what the writer needs to know. It also requires pedagogical knowledge in terms of how children learn to write, and how to use scaffolding tools such as shared and guided work, drama, and writing frames to develop them as writers.

Critical points

» *Children can be engaged in writing through the use of an enquiry-based simulation that forces them to ask questions and get involved.*

» *Children need to know what to write. They do not automatically know. You can help them with that by using talk techniques, giving them an experience and a purpose. Children tend not to have anything to write unless they have something to say.*

» *How do children know that their writing is what the teacher is looking for? How do they know they have been successful? You can involve them in the assessment process by using child-friendly targets and sharing your intentions with them.*

» *Writing does not just happen. Children need to be scaffolded through the process in order to be successful; otherwise they will not develop. Scaffolding tools may involve writing frames, drama techniques, working wall, tools that support children's interaction with text.*

» *Speaking, listening and reading scaffold the writing process.*

Critical reflections

» *How secure do you feel about teaching writing? How secure is your understanding of the writing process and what children need in order to develop as expert writers? There are many helpful and readable texts that support key aspects of teaching writing in a very engaging and practical way. It is worth exploring some of those mentioned below.*

Taking it further

For lots of practical ideas on how to get children writing but also underpinned by theory:

Brownhill, S (2013) *Getting Children Writing*. London: Sage.

To develop your understanding from a theoretical perspective of the role that talk plays in learning, read Chapter 5 from:

Lambirth, A (2005) *Reflective Reader; Primary English*. Exeter: Learning Matters.

and for a more practical read regarding *talk for writing*:

Corbett, P and Strong, J (2011) *Talk for Writing Across the Curriculum*. Maidenhead: Open University Press.

To focus a bit more on writing and the writing process:

Chamberlain, L (2011) *Writing*, in Cox (ed) *Primary English Teaching*. London: Sage.

Glazzard, J and Palmer J (2015) *Enriching Primary English*. Northwich: Critical Publishing.

References

Barrs, M and Cork, V (2001) *The Reader in the Writer*. London: CLPE.

Briggs, M, Woodfield, A, Martin, C and Swatton, P (2008) *Assessment for Learning and Teaching in Primary Schools,* 2nd Edn. Exeter: Learning Matters.

Brownhill, S (2013) *Getting Children Writing*. London: Sage.

Chamberlain, L (2011) *Writing*, in Cox (ed) *Primary English Teaching*. London: Sage.

Clark, C (2013) *Children's Reading Today: Findings from the National Literacy Trust's Annual Survey*. London: National Literacy Trust.

Clarke, S, Lopez-Charles, G and McCallum, B (2001) *Interim Report on the First Term of the Project. Communication Learning Intentions, Developing Success Criteria and Pupils Self-evaluation.* Gillingham 1 Partnership Formative Assessment Project. London: Institute of Education, University of London.

Corbett, P and Strong, J (2011) *Talk for Writing Across the Curriculum*. Maidenhead: Open University Press.

Cremin, T (2009) *Teaching English Creatively*. London: Routledge.

De Bono, E (2000) *Six Hats Thinking*. London: Penguin.

DfE (2013) *English Programmes of Study: Key Stages 1 and 2. National Curriculum in England*. DfE: London.

DfE (2014) National Curriculum and Assessment from September 2014: Information for Schools. [online] Available at: www.gov.uk/government/uploads/system/uploads/attachment_data/file/358070/NC_assessment_quals_factsheet_Sept_update.pdf (accessed 12 February 2015).

Fisher, R and Williams, M (2004) *Unlocking Creativity: Teaching Across the Curriculum*. London: David Fulton.

Gardner, P (2010) *Creative English, Creative Curriculum*. London: David Fulton.

Medwell, J, Wray, D, Minns, H, Coates, E and Griffiths, V (2012) *Primary English: Teaching Theory and Practice,* 6th Edn. Exeter: Learning Matters.

Wray, D (1993) What Do Children Think about Writing? *Educational Review*, 45(1): 67–77.

4 Writing and drama

EVE ENGLISH

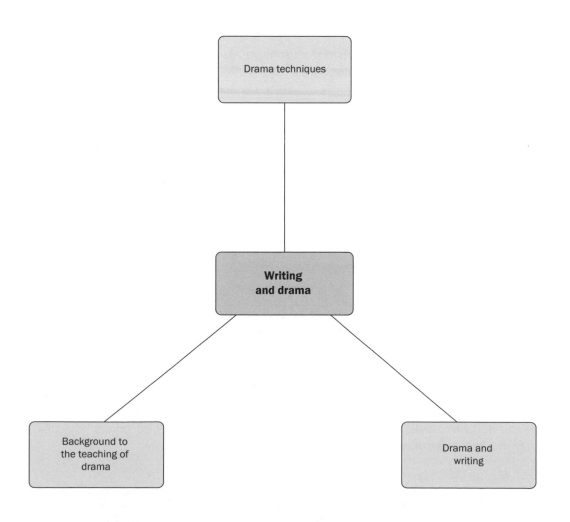

Teachers' Standards

3 Demonstrate good subject and curriculum knowledge

- have a secure knowledge of the relevant subject(s) and curriculum areas, foster and maintain pupils' interest in the subject

- demonstrate an understanding of and take responsibility for promoting high standards of literacy and articulacy

Critical questions

» *How can you use drama teaching to enhance the quality of children's writing?*

» *How can drama provide an audience and purpose for children's writing?*

» *How can drama be effective for both fiction and non-fiction writing?*

Activity 1: Your experience of writing lessons

» *Make a note of some of the writing lessons you have recently observed or taught. These shall be returned to later.*

Introduction

It is now accepted that children, and indeed all writers, need to have a sense of audience and purpose to write effectively. Pupils cannot be motivated by always having to write simply for the teacher. Bunting (1998) describes how '*writers need a sense of audience because the audience influences the tone, nature and form of the writing*' (p 9). The National Curriculum in England Programme of Study for English (DfE, 2013) requires that children:

> write clearly, accurately and coherently, adapting their language and style in and for a range of contexts, purposes and audiences.
>
> (DfE, 2013, p 13)

Ideally, the audience and purpose should be real and as a teacher you should be very creative in searching out real purposes for writing. This is not always possible, however, and here is where drama steps in. By becoming involved in various drama activities, children are able to suspend disbelief and immerse themselves in experiences and worlds that, for a while, are real to them. As McNaughton (1997, p 82) maintains:

> During drama the children try to create situations 'as if they were real life'. Their first-hand involvement in situations may fix the incidents in their minds and give them a more direct experience to write about.

Clipson-Boyles (1998, p 4), too, argues:

> Drama puts language into action in ways with which children can identify, respond and learn. It brings language alive by providing meaningful contexts. These include

roles, purposes and audiences, all of which give the language authenticity in the eyes of the children.

This chapter considers ways in which drama can be used to enhance children's writing, before, during and after the drama, looking at both fiction and non-fiction writing. Opportunities for writing are explored within process drama, but script writing is also considered.

Background to the teaching of drama

As with most areas of the curriculum, the teaching of drama has changed over the years and has been the centre of many debates. One relates to the relative importance of the process of drama as opposed to the final product (the performance). You will see how this debate is very similar to the process and product approaches to the teaching of writing. Czerniewska (1992) describes how a process approach to the teaching of writing involves drafting and redrafting, whereas a product approach focuses on a correct final result. Currently, drama consists mainly of process drama (often known as *drama in education*), but there is certainly a place for performance drama.

Another debate concerns drama being used as a vehicle for teaching other subjects. Purists will argue that drama is a subject in its own right and should be protected as such. Others see the value of using drama to teach many different aspects of the curriculum. Again, there is now more of a balance between the two views and, certainly in this chapter, drama is described as a very valuable way of enhancing children's writing in many different subject areas.

Drama and writing

By being involved in drama activities, children share ideas and are motivated to write. They see a purpose for their writing and will have an audience. Because of this, they will see a reason for drafting and redrafting their writing. It has also been found that through drama children are able to explore language and use more imaginative vocabulary (Bearne et al, 2003).

Clipson-Boyles (2012, p 83) describes how children can be encouraged to '*write before the drama*', '*write during the drama*' and '*write after the drama*'. In other words, children can write a note or create a message that sets up a drama; they can write as the drama is developing, usually as one of the characters; or can write reflectively after the drama. McNaughton (1997, pp 82–3) describes how children's writing can be enhanced following a drama activity:

> *– after drama they have a memory of that situation. I suggest that this memory allows them to choose more appropriate language and to write at greater length and in more detail about the experience.*

Crumpler (2005, p 359) believes that writing during the drama is more effective than writing after the drama:

> – *that the texts which the children create are a component of the drama work and not separate from it. – If writing is viewed as a separate, more serious activity that children complete after the drama is over rather than as a feature of the drama work, the imaginative energy created from moving back and forth from the real to the fictional is diluted, and possibly lost altogether.*

Drama can be used to enhance children's writing of both fiction and non-fiction texts. The generic and language features of non-fiction texts can seem more relevant if they are tools in a drama activity. The following case study illustrates how persuasive writing can be taught through drama.

CASE STUDY

Developing persuasive writing

The children's attention, at the beginning of the week, was drawn to different examples of persuasive text. They were asked to think about what was common to all the texts. The teacher, Sue, drew their attention to how, at the beginning of each piece of writing, there was a strong opening statement. Various points were then made to support the statement. Finally, the argument was summed up. Instead of immediately asking the children to write a piece of persuasive text, Sue decided to use a drama activity to motivate the children and provide them with a purpose and audience. Various roles were given to the children; they were all villagers. Some were shopkeepers, some were parents, some nurses and doctors from a local hospital, some fire officers. In role, Sue, as a local councillor, called a meeting of the villagers and told them that she had heard that a road was going to be rerouted through the village, bringing heavy traffic with it. After hearing concerns from the villagers, they decided to put together a strong persuasive letter to the local authority asking them to reconsider. The children as villagers felt very strongly that the road should not go ahead, and with Sue as scribe, still in role, the class composed a piece of shared persuasive writing:

Sunny Village

Dear Mr Smith

We have heard that there is a plan to reroute a road through our beautiful village. This will be a very busy road. We have had a meeting and we are all very concerned. First of all, the road will be near the local primary school and there could be accidents. The fire brigade and the ambulance people are all worried that they will not be able to get their vehicles to fires or to hospitals in time. This might mean that some people might die. That would be terrible! In addition, shopkeepers think that people will not be able to park near their shops because of traffic and so they will lose trade.

In summary, the road should not come anywhere near the village. We hope that you will listen to our concerns.

Yours sincerely

The villagers of Sunny Village

The pupils produced interesting and relevant writing following this dramatic activity, probably more than if they had simply been told to write after a discussion. In their specific roles they really thought about the implications of a road coming through the village. The features of persuasive writing became obvious to the children as they gathered their thoughts together.

FOCUS ON RESEARCH

The effect of drama on writing

McNaughton (1997) carried out research to examine the effect that drama has on the development of children's writing. In what she describes as '*quasi-experimental*' (p 57) research, she looked at the imaginative writing of two groups of children: Group A experienced drama before writing, whereas Group B was prepared for the writing by taking part in discussion. The drama lessons consisted of improvisation, mime, tableaux, hot seating and teacher in role. McNaughton found that the children who had taken part in the drama activities were, in their writing, more able to describe the emotions of the characters and reflect different opinions and points of view, using more natural speech patterns. Their vocabulary choices were also more appropriate and adventurous and they used more dialogue in their writing.

McNaughton concludes that both discussion and drama can improve children's subsequent writing; however, drama seems to add "something extra" (p 85). The following case study built on the work of McNaughton.

CASE STUDY

Developing imaginative writing using the first person

In his undergraduate dissertation, Alex looked at the possible effects that drama might have upon writing quality in a Key Stage 2 classroom. The children produced two pieces of writing: one before the drama activities and one after. For both pieces of writing, pupils wrote in the first person as they were learning about first person accounts.

Pupils first learned about evacuees through the use of *traditional teaching*. This *traditional teaching* used discussions and visual media as a form of teaching, with pupils discussing what they felt it would have been like to be an evacuee. They were then given examples of real accounts by evacuees and the class discussed the texts before writing their own accounts.

Drama based on evacuees was then employed, both through the use of *hot seating* and the creation of a scene based on their hot seating answers. Pupils played the roles of the evacuee children and were asked questions such as:

* *Are you scared?*

* *Why are you being evacuated?*

* *Do you like the family you are with?*

* *How long are you there for?*

These open questions not only allowed for pupils to develop their understanding and empathy about evacuees but also provided them with a basis of what to write about when it came to producing an account.

To further develop their understanding, the children created scenes that would develop ideas for writing. Examples of these were:

* the evacuees saying goodbye to their families;

* the evacuees meeting their new families;

* the evacuees working on a farm.

Once this drama session had ended, pupils wrote a second account about being an evacuee.

Alex found that use of drama produced a significant change in compositional ability and performance, with pupils having greater diversity of ideas than was usual in their writing. What was most interesting was that all ability groups improved their compositional ability. Children sustained the use of the first person throughout their writing.

Drama techniques

In this section some drama techniques are described in terms of the development of both fiction and non-fiction writing. Different genres, including non-fiction, are referred to, but detailed definitions of the genres are described later in Chapter 6. Case studies are used to exemplify some of the techniques.

Hot seating

This is one of the simplest techniques to use with children and one which teachers new to drama will find very easy to control. A pupil or teacher, in role, sits in the *hot seat* and is asked questions by the rest of the class. The character can be fictitious or real. Hot seating is an excellent technique for encouraging children to examine motives or think beyond the literal. A successful model for the teaching of writing is to draw children's attention to the text and language features of a particular aspect or genre by reading examples, before asking them to use what they have learned to produce their own piece of writing. In the following case study, children were taught to write character studies. Descriptions of characters were read to them and then the children produced their own character studies. This is a common enough model of teaching children to write in a particular way. What is a little different is the way in which hot seating was used to make the writing more effective.

CASE STUDY

Writing simple character studies

In a whole class lesson, a Year 1 class was read the story of *Cinderella*. The children were asked to identify the main characters in the story: Cinderella, the two step sisters, the fairy godmother and the prince. They were asked to choose adjectives to describe those characters. These could be literally taken from the text or inferred from actions, pictures or comments from other characters in the story. Children had to justify their choice of adjectives.

Before the children were asked to use these adjectives in simple character studies, hot seating was used to probe motivation and find out a little more about the characters. For example, children asked the hot seated step sisters to explain why they were so hard on Cinderella. One of the sisters said that she did not like the way in which Cinderella and her father had come into their lives.

After the hot seating session, the children were asked to play a *Guess who* game. On their whiteboards they had to write a sentence describing one of the characters without giving away the character's name. They had to draw on the adjectives already suggested or use something that had come out of the drama. They were all asked to write in the present tense. So, sentences that were created included:

She has the smallest feet. *Guess who?*

He is very rich. *Guess who?*

They make their step sister do all the hard work. *Guess who?*

They are lazy. *Guess who?*

She has magical powers. *Guess who?*

They were not happy about having a new sister. *Guess who?*

After the guessing game, the teacher gathered the sentences and, as a whole (shared) class activity the teacher and children wrote a paragraph to describe each of the characters. They discussed the use of pronouns so that each sentence would not start with the character's name. The use of appropriate conjunctions was also encouraged. The study of the step sisters read as follows:

The step sisters were very ugly. They were cruel to their sister, Cinderella, and made her do all of the hard work. They said that was because she had upset their family. The sisters went to the ball and left Cinderella behind. They were very annoyed when the prince married Cinderella but they knew that there were many princes around.

The simple character studies were enhanced by the use of hot seating, particularly when thinking beyond what was in the actual story. The other characters were described in similar ways; for example, the Fairy Godmother had been asked, when hot seated, about other magical tricks that she had performed and that was also reproduced in the final piece of writing.

Activity 2: The Highwayman

» *Read* The Highwayman *by Alfred Noyes. If you were to hot seat the ostler after the killing of the highwayman, what questions do you think the children (as journalists after the event) would ask him?*

Freeze frame

In freeze frame a given moment in a story or account is frozen by a pair or group of pupils. For example, the scene in *Alice in Wonderland* where Alice comes across the tea party will have the Mad Hatter, the Dormouse and the March Hare gathered together over tea. Alice looks on and the image is frozen. A narrator could, perhaps, speak over the frame.

There was a table set out under a tree in front of the house and the March Hare and the Hatter were having tea at it: a Dormouse was sitting between them, fast asleep, and the other two were using it as a cushion, resting their elbows on it, and talking over its head.

Other key scenes from the story could be used to focus the children's attention on the characters and the plot. This in itself is important for writing, but if *thought tracking* is added to the freeze frames then writing will become even more creative.

Thought tracking

Children in role in the freeze frame or other children in the class are asked what the characters might be thinking. Using the same frozen image of the Mad Hatter's tea party, the children in their characters could be asked what they are thinking in that moment. This scene could then be described by the children, in writing, using the responses from the drama.

Discussion or conscience alley

In discussion/conscience alley, pupils use drama to explore a dilemma in a story or an issue. Usually, children are in two lines facing each other while one child walks down the middle of them. As he/she passes, each person in the line makes a comment. Those on one side support one point of view while those on the other present opposing arguments. The pupil walking down the *alley* will then decide on what action is to be taken. This technique is very useful for preparing children to write a discussion where different points of view have to be presented in a balanced way and then a conclusion drawn. (See Chapter 6 for details of the characteristics of a discussion.)

CASE STUDY

Imaginative writing based on a text and using conscience alley

Chris was a primary PGCE student. His topic for his mixed Year 3 and 4 class was Ancient Egypt and he decided to use drama as part of a series of lessons leading up to a piece of creative writing. The writing was to be about an Egyptian mummy awakening from a sarcophagus in the classroom, reacting to and interacting with the modern world.

The class were reading Jeremy Strong's *There's a Pharaoh in Our Bath* and they took inspiration from the first chapters in which an Egyptian pharaoh is resurrected. Chris used the drama to aid the children's creativity because he thought the children would be more creative if they imagined being a mummy themselves, rather than just thinking about what the mummy would do. The class had a range of abilities and some children struggled with creativity and expressing their thoughts. With the low-attaining children, Chris first did a hot seating activity in which the children imagined being a freshly awoken mummy in the classroom. The children in the hot seat had their thoughts and imagination scaffolded and prompted by other children in the class and by Chris himself. Progressing from this, Chris did a conscience alley activity in which he pretended to be a mummy. The children were organised into two lines. Those on one side had to say something positive to the mummy about twenty-first-century life, while those on the other side had to say something negative. Chris modelled some answers, suggesting they could say things about how the mummy moved or looked, or warn it about waking up in the modern world or about things with which he would not be familiar. Chris used props from around the classroom to aid the learning, for example turning on a tap and being shocked by the flowing water, and trying to walk through a clear window.

Both of these activities worked well with the lower-attaining children. Some of the children lacked confidence in the activities, but the tasks stirred some creativity and imagination. This imagination was evident in their written work, which was filled with the ideas explored during the drama activities.

Chris gave the higher-attaining children less structure. They worked with the teaching assistant during the lesson while Chris worked with his group. Before the groups split, Chris asked the higher attaining group to put their heads on their desks and close their eyes. Then, when they opened their eyes, they would be an Egyptian mummy waking up in the modern world, in a twenty-first-century classroom. These children worked well with the independence in the drama activity and in relation to the classroom. The children re-enacted their drama to

Chris when the whole class re-assembled, and the ideas the children explored ranged from unsuccessfully trying to get pens out of a see-through pencil case, to waving to their own reflection in the screen on a turned-off laptop, to getting a tissue and putting it on their head thinking it was a hat. These were ideas that Chris had not thought of himself. Again, as with Chris's lower attaining group, the high attaining group retained the ideas from the drama activity and their creative writing was filled with their dramatic experiences.

Chris's lesson is an interesting example of how children of all abilities can use drama to write more effectively.

Mantle of the expert

In this approach, the participants in the drama take on the role of the expert. This is effective for developing both fiction and non-fiction writing. The drama can take place after they have studied, for example, aspects of World War II. Children could be given reports from the front (written by the teacher) and then be asked, as a committee of journalists (the experts), to put together a newspaper. The children take on the mantle of the expert and make decisions about what should and should not be included. They might even be asked to consider what needs to be hidden from the readers in a time of war. The writing that comes from this activity will have a *real* audience and purpose.

Teacher in role

Teacher in role is one of the most useful approaches to teaching drama. In role, you, as the teacher, have control of the drama. The roles adopted are often known as *high status* (where the teacher in role is a leader) or *low status* (where the teacher calls on the expertise of the class members). In a high status role the teacher, for example, might enter the classroom and say '*Well thank you everyone for coming this evening. As you know, I am your local councillor and I've come to hear your concerns about the playground in the local park. Now what do you have to tell me?*' As the drama progresses the children, as villagers, put their concerns and then they decide to write to their member of parliament. This letter can be written as a piece of persuasive writing (see Chapter 6). The writing will be completed inside the drama. If the teacher has a low status role, he or she will look to the pupils for help. For example, the pupils could set themselves up as market stall holders, thinking about the sort of market stall they would like to have. Time should be spent establishing these roles. Posters advertising the market or individual stalls could be created, with the teacher in role arriving as a newcomer to the market. *What does she need to know? What are the rules of the market? What is the best way to attract customers?* As a whole group, the children will discuss and then prepare a manual for the newcomer (instructional text) (see Chapter 6).

It should be made clear to the children when you are in role; this can be done simply by wearing a hat or a scarf.

Questioning is extremely important if you are in role so that the drama can be moved along. A question is important at the beginning of the drama to set the context and establish the roles. As the drama progresses, questions keep the children focused and, after the drama, children will be questioned as they reflect on their experience. As Parsons maintained:

> *When children develop a deep belief in their roles they can accept the challenges from the teacher-in-role as a natural part of the drama, can think more deeply about issues, respond appropriately and extend their use of expressive language. Involvement and commitment spur their efforts to communicate their intentions and opinions to others within the dramatic fiction.*
>
> (1991, p 107)

Activity 3: Pirates

» *Imagine the scene where a pirate's crew is setting off to look for buried treasure. You are in role as the pirate captain. What writing activities could be developed before, during or after this drama?*

Script writing

Most of this chapter has been concerned with process drama and the ways in which it can help children develop their writing skills. However, there is a place for the more traditional approach to drama and the reading and writing of scripts. Woolland (2008) argues that play-writing and process drama can work hand in hand:

> – *playwriting can be seen as an extension of writing in role, writing which arises out of a dramatic fiction and feeds back into it, encouraging active reflection. It is not a big jump to move from writing in role (adopting an appropriate voice, tone, register and vocabulary) to writing dialogue, assigning words to people.*
>
> (Woolland, 2008, pp 5–6)

In writing play scripts children will work as they do when introduced to any new genre: they will be presented by the teacher with a number of diverse scripts; they will look carefully at the common features and then they will attempt, first through shared and guided writing sessions, and then, working in pairs or as individuals, producing their own writing. When reading play scripts, children's attention will be drawn to the main differences between scripts and straightforward narratives. Some of these differences are:

* the development of the plot through dialogue;
* the way dialogue is set out;
* the use of a narrator;
* the development of character through speech;
* the use of stage directions.

As Woolland (2008) argues, it is not a big leap to go from process drama to script writing. The most successful scripts often come out of role play. Mike Leigh, a successful film and theatre director, is well known for using improvisation techniques to develop characterisation before he writes his scripts. This can work equally well in the classroom. If we go back to the example of the Mad Hatter's tea party, then the dialogue that was produced through *thought tracking* would work well as a short script. For example:

Mad Hatter (to Alice): What are you doing here, there's no room?

Alice: There's plenty of room. I'd like some tea.

Dormouse: What's that noise; I'm trying to sleep?

March Hare: Have some wine.

Short interludes like this are a good beginning for younger children attempting to write scripts for the first time.

Of course, the chapter 'A Mad Tea-Party' in *Alice's Adventures in Wonderland* consists mainly of dialogue and older children could easily convert this into a play script.

Children can get used to writing dialogue by drawing comic strips. The key moments in well-known stories can be drawn and dialogue added in speech bubbles. These bubbles would then be written as traditional scripts.

Play scripts do not have to result in public performances, but children will often want to share their work with other members of the class. Recordings of plays can also be successful, especially as imaginative sound effects can be added.

Activity 4: Revisiting writing lessons

» *Go back to the notes you made for Activity 1. Describe how some of these writing lessons could have been made more effective by using drama activities.*

FOCUS ON RESEARCH

Teachers' observations

Winston (2004) worked with classteachers on drama activities and pulled together the teachers' observations relating to the positive effects they had seen drama have on their children's writing:

- *It motivated more children to want to write;*

- *It provided more children with substantial ideas and experiences so that they had something to write about;*

- *Each child could draw individual responses from the drama. Consequently, despite the structure of a writing frame individual pieces of writing were different and reflective of the child's rather than the teacher's thinking;*

- *Children generally wrote more and in a shorter period of time;*

- *Children's vocabulary and sentence structure were noticeably richer when their writing emerged from drama work;*

- *More children demonstrated a clearer sense of audience in their writing;*

- *More children demonstrated empathy for those whom they wrote about;*

- *Some children's writing could be seen to have benefited from the input that the visual qualities of drama had to offer.*

(Winston, 2004, p 26)

Conclusion

Winston's research sums up many of the reasons why we should all try to incorporate drama activities into our lessons. Techniques have been described that are simple to carry out, even for a teacher new to drama teaching. It has been shown how *real* audiences and purposes can be created in drama to give pupils the opportunity to delve into their imaginations, empathise with characters (both real and fictional) and, thus, enhance the quality of their writing.

Critical points

» *Drama activities can provide children with real audiences and purposes for their writing.*

» *Very simple drama techniques, such as hot seating, can be used to develop children's understanding of characters and their motivation; this will be reflected in their writing.*

» *Drama is equally effective in developing fiction and non-fiction writing.*

Critical reflections

» *Think about how your pupils' writing can be enhanced by using drama techniques. When you do not have a real audience and purpose how can role play be used instead? Remember that drama activities can be used to develop writing in different genres; the requirements of the genre, both in terms of linguistic and structural features, will be seen by the children as being necessary rather than simply an academic exercise.*

Taking it further

English, E (2014) Is There a Place for Drama?, in Waugh, D, Jolliffe, W and Allott, K (eds) *Primary English for Trainee Teachers*. London: Sage.

This chapter looks at the place of drama in the English National Curriculum in all curriculum areas.

Glazzard, J and Palmer, J (2015) *Enriching Primary English*. Northwich: Critical Publishing.

This text provides ideas for trainees and teachers to extend both their own teaching and their pupils' learning in primary English through creative approaches and enrichment strategies to promote best practice and outstanding teaching.

Winston, J (2004) *Drama and English at the Heart of the Curriculum*. London: David Fulton.

This is a very accessible book that describes the importance of drama in the classroom, giving many practical examples.

Waugh, D and Jolliffe, W (2013) *English 5–11*. London: Routledge.

See Chapter 14 'Drama' for practical ideas and an exploration of the place of drama in schools.

Woolland, B (2008) *Pupils as Playwrights*, Stoke-on-Trent, Staffs: Trentham Books Ltd.

The book gives many examples of script writing projects for different year groups.

References

Bearne, E, Dombey, H and Grainger, T (2003) *Classroom Interactions in Literacy*. Maidenhead, Berkshire: Open University Press.

Bunting, R (1998) Process, Genre, Strategy, Framework: Three Decades of Development in the Teaching of Reading, in Graham, J and Kelly, A (ed) *Writing Under Control*. London: David Fulton, pp 7–18.

Carroll, L (1992, first published 1865) *The Adventures of Alice in Wonderland and Through the Looking Glass*. New York: Yearling, Random House.

Clipson-Boyles, S (1998) *Drama in Primary English Teaching*. London: David Fulton.

Clipson-Boyles, S (2012) *Teaching Primary English Through Drama*. London: David Fulton.

Crumpler, T P (2005) The Role of Educational Drama in the Composing Processes of Young Writers. *Research in Drama Education*, 10(3): 357–63.

Czerniewska, P (1992) *Learning About Writing*. Oxford, UK and Cambridge, MA: Blackwell.

DfE (2013) *The National Curriculum in England Key Stages 1 and 2 Framework Document*. London: DfE.

McMaster, J C (1998) Doing Literature: Using Drama to Build Literacy. *The Reading Teacher*, 51(7): 574–84.

McNaughton, M J (1997) Drama and Children's Writing: A Study of the Influence of Drama on the Imaginative Writing of Primary School. *Research in Drama Education: The Journal of Applied Theatre and Performance*, 2(1): 55–86.

Noyes, A (1981) *The Highwayman*. Oxford: Oxford University Press.

Parsons, B (1991) Story-making and Drama for Children 5–8 Years, in Wright, S (ed) *The Arts in Early Childhood*. Sydney, Australia: Prentice Hall.

Winston, J (2004) *Drama and English at the Heart of the Curriculum*. London: David Fulton.

Woolland, B (2008) *Pupils as Playwrights*. Stoke on Trent, Staffs: Trentham Books Ltd.

5 Writing poetry

ADAM BUSHNELL, SALLY NEAUM AND DAVID WAUGH

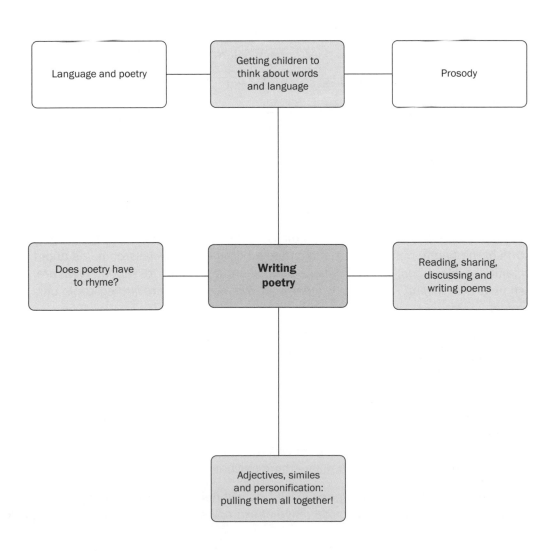

Teachers' Standards

3 Demonstrate good subject and curriculum knowledge

- have a secure knowledge of the relevant subject(s) and curriculum areas, foster and maintain pupils' interest in the subject, and address misunderstandings

- demonstrate an understanding of and take responsibility for promoting high standards of literacy, articulacy and the correct use of standard English, whatever the teacher's specialist subject

- if teaching early reading, demonstrate a clear understanding of systematic synthetic phonics

Critical questions

» *How can we engage children's interest in poetry?*

» *How strong is your own knowledge of poetry?*

» *What experiences do children need to have before they can write poetry?*

» *What can we do to support children's writing of poetry?*

» *Does poetry have to rhyme?*

» *What kinds of poetry might we ask children to write?*

Introduction

When he was Children's Laureate, Michael Rosen developed the Poetry-Friendly Classroom project, designed to help teachers interest children in poetry. He stated:

> *Teachers sometimes ask me, 'what's the best way to get children writing poems?' One of the first things I suggest is to create a poetry-friendly classroom. It's about making a classroom a place where poems are welcome. It's about pleasure, stimulation, feeling, curiosity, wonder and fun and children finding their own voice.*

In this chapter, you will find ideas for making your classroom poetry-friendly and strategies for teaching a range of poetic forms. You will consider what is meant by poetic experience and how you can develop children's ability to write poetry in which they express their ideas clearly, concisely and well.

Ofsted (2007) found one pupil who said about writing poetry: '*You are controlling the pen. You can make up your own rules ... poetry's not like normal writing*' (Ofsted, 2007, p 7). In this chapter you will consider the extent to which children need to be aware of rules when writing poetry and how you might stimulate them to want to share their ideas.

If you are to help children to write poetry well, you will need an understanding of different poetic forms and a knowledge of a wide range of examples of these. Typically, when we ask children to write we show them examples of the type of writing we want them to produce, then model this type of writing through shared writing before guiding them in their independent or shared attempts at independent work. However, research has shown that teachers sometimes lack the necessary knowledge and understanding to do this effectively.

FOCUS ON RESEARCH

What do teachers know about children's poetry?

Cremin (2011) drew upon the first phases of a UK Literacy Association (UKLA) project *Teachers as Readers: Building Communities of Readers Phase I* (2006–07), which involved a survey of 1200 teachers' reading habits and their knowledge and use of children's literature. She maintained: *'In relation to poetry, the results ... represent a cause for concern'*.

* *58% (of teachers surveyed) named one, two or no poets;*
* *22% named no poets;*
* *10% named 6 poets.*

The top five poets who all received over 100 mentions included:

* *Michael Rosen (452);*
* *Allan Ahlberg (207);*
* *Roger McGough (197);*
* *Roald Dahl (165);*
* *Spike Milligan (159);*
* *Benjamin Zephaniah (131).*

After these, three poets were mentioned more than 50 times:

* *Edward Lear (85);*
* *Ted Hughes (58);*
* *A A Milne (57).*

The data for poetry indicate that the teachers in the survey leant towards the more humorous or light hearted poets (eg, Rosen or Milligan) or towards the work of particular poets whose work may well be studied under the ... category of classic poetry (eg, Causley, Lear, Stephenson or Milne).

In the sample of 1200, very few women poets were mentioned; the highest numbers were:

* *Grace Nicholls (16), Christina Rossetti (11), Eleanor Farjeon (9), Judith Nicholls (8), Pam Ayres (5), Floella Benjamin (3), Sandy Brownjohn (3), Sharon Creech (3), Carol Ann Duffy (3), Jill Murphy (3), Jackie Kay (2), Valerie Bloom (2) and Wendy Cope (1).'*

Cremin concluded:

> *The apparent lack of knowledge of poets may indicate that teachers tend to select poetry for its capacity to teach about literary language rather than enjoying it for its own sake. Ofsted (2007), in tune with this research, also suggest that teachers, both primary and secondary, tend to rely upon a narrow range of poems, many of which they were taught in school.*

Activity 1: Your knowledge of poetry

» *Look at the names of the poets most often cited by teachers in Cremin's study. How many of them do you know?*

» *Which other poets do you know besides those mentioned?*

» *Do you feel that your knowledge of poetry is limited to humorous poems and classic poems which you had to study at school?*

Getting children to think about words and language

It is said that Ernest Hemingway made a ten-dollar bet that he could write a story in six words. He won the bet with:

For sale. Baby shoes. Never worn.

Notice what you think and feel when you read these words. What story do they create in your mind? Which emotions do they evoke? Notice how these six words have the power to set the brain ticking and the heart knocking (Doonan, 1993). As readers or listeners, we immediately engage with the story at both a cognitive and an affective (emotional) level. This is clearly evident, year on year, in the collective *Ohhh* when we read the story to trainees.

This immediate and powerful response is not happenstance. It is achieved through meticulous choice of words and purposeful attention to how they are combined. Notice how Hemingway's skilled use of language and metre creates a world in a moment. Notice how it resonates with all of us, and yet remains equivocal, how it gives voice to each of our inner realities.

Hemingway wrote this piece as a story. However, it could also be read as poetry – free verse. Language in poetry distils meaning to awaken our senses and to elicit an interpretative engagement from the reader. Hemingway's *story* does exactly this; his precise and economical use of language and attention to form (repeated two-word phrases) combine to evoke a powerful response in the reader – a deep experience in a moment.

Language and poetry

This careful, evocative use of language is the essence of poetry writing. To write poetry effectively we need to be alive to language. We need to be able to use language to give shape to our experiences, and to express this in ways that connect with the reader, or listener. Words in poems need to be used with precision; each word a contribution to communicating meaning. Words and language in poetry are often chosen to lead the reader, or listener, to a response but without telling them what to feel. Therefore, the precision in language is not only about the choice and phrasing of language but also about what is not said – language that leaves things unsaid, hinted at, or is equivocal. As poet *Samuel Taylor Coleridge* said, poetry is: '*the best words in the best order*'.

Prosody

Writing poetry also requires attention to prosody of language. Prosody is the '*music*' of language; it is the pitch, volume, tempo, rhythm and stresses we use to communicate meaning effectively, and in a nuanced way. Prosodic structure of language can create a powerful poetic effect. Read this opening verse of Robert Louis Stevenson's poem *Windy Nights* out loud. Notice how the tempo, rhythm and stresses contribute to the experience of the poem.

Windy Nights

Whenever the moon and stars and set

Whenever the wind is high,

All night long in the dark and wet,

A man goes riding by.

Late in the night when the fires are out,

Why does he gallop and gallop about?

Writing poetry also requires that we think and use language to synthesise ideas – to see and express things in different, perhaps unusual, ways. For example, Carol Anne Duffy opens her poem *The Dresses* thus:

The Dresses

I like your rain dress,

Its strange sad colour,

Its small buttons like tears.

She writes of a fog dress and a snow dress before finishing with:

But I love your thunderstorm dress,

Its huge, dark petticoats,

Its silver stitching flashing as you run away.

Notice how she combines different ideas to poetic affect. Notice how she uses the same patterns and themes in her synthesis of ideas. Notice the images and feelings it evokes for you.

Activity 2: Choose your words

»   *Read Wilfred Owen's poem* Futility:

Futility

Move him into the sun-

Gently its touch awoke him once,

At home, whispering of fields unsown.

Always it woke him, even in France,

Until this morning, and this snow.

If anything might rouse him now

The kind old sun will know

Think how it wakes the seeds,-

Woke, once, the clays of a cold star.

Are limbs, so dear-achieved, are sides,

Full-nerved- still warm- too hard to stir?

Was it or this the clay grew tall?

-Oh what made fatuous sunbeams toil

To break earth's sleep at all?

Below are some examples of Owen's drafts of a section of the poem.

»   *Compare the two.*

So dear achieved, are
Are limbs ~~perfect at last, and~~ sides

Full
Warm – nerved –still warm, – too hard to stir?
Rich

                  bled
Are limbs, ~~pricked~~ with a little sword,

Yet limbs –still warm –too hard to stir?

> *Are limbs, so ready for life, full grown,*
>
> *Nerved and still warm –too hard to stir?*

» *Consider the alternatives and the words that Owen eventually used.*

- *How do the words chosen and rejected alter the meaning in the poem for you?*

- *How do the words chosen and rejected change the metre in the poem?*

- *Which would you have chosen?*

- *Explain why.*

The language of poetry is different from everyday speech. It uses much of the language of speech but in particular ways – ways that Goodwyn (2011) argues we need to practise in order to become skilled. So to enable children to find writing poetry engaging and enjoyable, as well as hearing poetry, they need opportunities to become alive to language. They need opportunities to play with language; to be attentive to their choice of words and expression; to understand how language and prosody can be used effectively; to explore meaning in language; and to recognise how we can bring ideas, language and prosody together to create effect.

The case study below shows how a teacher uses Hemingway's model of six powerful words to draw children's attention to language use and to explore how meaning is created and interpreted.

CASE STUDY

Six-word poems

Hannah, a third-year trainee, knew from discussions with her classteacher that many of the children in her Year 4 class found writing poetry difficult. Despite the children's good effort at the tasks given, the teacher was aware that much of the poetry written used limited language and expression. In response to this she had decided to focus the children's attention on language to build their confidence and ability to express their ideas using precise and effective language. Hannah planned a series of lessons to teach this.

Hannah recalled the six-word stories that she had heard at university, and the experience of writing her own. She remembered how precise the language and expression had to be to write the stories and decided to adapt this idea as the starting point for her lessons.

The overall aim of her lessons was to get the children to describe themselves in six words, which would be read to the class as a prompt to discussions about language and interpretation. Hannah was aware that she had to approach this in a sequential way, enabling the children to engage with language and meaning to write their descriptions and to be able to listen to, and discuss, the language in other children's work.

The lessons and activity sequence was as follows:

- Introduce the idea of the six-word description using examples from the BBC's *Life in six words.*

- Get the children to write a description of themselves – initially using around 20 words.

- Work at reducing this to six words – identifying the most important aspects of who they are and finding accurate and precise words to describe these characteristics.

- Put these up anonymously in the classroom for the children to read.

- Read a few of the descriptions to the class each morning and identify the child. Focus the discussion on the language used.

- Why were these words effective in describing the child?

- Which other words could be used that kept the essence of the description?

- Which other words would the rest of the class use to describe the person?

- Why do we choose different words?

- Which words are right? Why?

Alongside these focused activities, where possible she used poetry in other lessons across the curriculum and read poetry to the class for them to listen to and enjoy.

The lessons and activities proved to be very successful in drawing children's attention to how we use words and language. It also opened up important discussions about selecting words and the different interpretations that we have of some words.

Hannah intended to build on this knowledge and skill in the poetry writing lessons that followed.

Activity 3

» *Why did Hannah move away from writing poetry as the introduction to lessons on poetry writing?*

» *What was the focus of Hannah's lesson?*

» *How may this enable the children to write more effective poetry?*

» *In what ways did Hannah adapt the six-word story idea?*

» *Why do you think she decided to make these adaptations?*

» *What would you plan next for these children to enable them to be more successful at poetry writing?*

Reading, sharing, discussing and writing poems

One teacher, who went on to write for children, commented:

> *Before I started writing for a living, I attended a creative writing course. My tutor was a poet and made me write poetry. I didn't want to. I've always been a lover of words in the form of stories but not much poetry. She made me write poems because it forced me to choose my words more carefully; to be sparse with language and not to waste words. I'm not sure it worked entirely but it certainly took me on a journey to love poetry.*

Children begin in the early years listening to books being read to them. These books contain repetitive language, rhyme and rhythm, all of which feature heavily in poetry.

The Gruffalo, for example, can be shared as a story, sung as a song or read as a poem. You can read editions in French, Italian, Polish, German and even Latin, and there is even a *Gruffalo in Scots* and the sequel *The Gruffalo's Wean*, which includes:

> *A moose took a dauner through the deep, mirk widd. A tod saw the moose and the moose looked guid.*

This is an excellent book to share aloud in Key Stages 1 and 2 when examining accent, dialect or seeking local identity.

Yet this passion for poetic form is not always continued as we extend children *beyond* early years and through the next stages of their school career. In the following case study, Adam Bushnell describes the effect of finding a topic which engages children's interest.

CASE STUDY

Zombies

I once met a Year 6 class that was so disaffected that the mere suggestion of writing a poem would send up a cacophony of deafening noise complete with the odd flying chair in frustration.

So, I asked this class what they were interested in and there was one resounding answer ... zombies. This class was obsessed with zombies.

I managed to find a huge range of literature to support our zombie-writing topic. There are many zombie parody books including *The Zombie Night before Christmas* and a picture book called *The Very Hungry Zombie*. There is even a flipbook called *10,000 Zombies* where you can make not only 10,000 zombie illustrations but also create over 10,000 zombie story creations. The images are truly gruesome and I would seriously check this book out and discuss with other teachers before you use it in school, but it really worked with this particular class.

We made our own class zombie flipbook, action stories with cliff-hangers and non-chronological reports on how to look after a pet zombie after reading the book *How to Speak Zombie*.

There are books of zombie poetry that even your most hardened Year 6 class will enjoy. We used *Zombie Haiku: Good Poetry For Your ... Brains*.

The next thing we knew the pupils were churning out perfects haikus with a zombie twist.

> One thing on my mind
>
> you are there in front of me
>
> I will eat you now!

By asking for pupils' areas of interest, *any* writing can be made exciting to *any* class. There are resources to complement all forms of writing. Identifying that interest is the first step in finding them. The whole zombie-writing topic could easily be transferred to any other area of interest – from football to fairies, from dinosaurs to dragons, from hip hop to Harry Potter.

There are poems out there to suit everyone. The more we talk about poems in the classroom, the more variety of poetry we share; the more we discuss poetic form then, the more poetry will be written.

CASE STUDY

Year 2 class looking at adverbs

Asif asked his Year 2 class if they knew what a verb was. Most did and some examples were written on the board as they were shared.

He then asked what an adverb was. The class did not know, so Asif began to move his pen through the air. He explained that an adverb describes the verb. He asked the pupils to describe how the pen was moving.

The answer was *slowly* and Asif explained that *slowly* was an adverb.

He then changed the pace of the pen's movement and the class chorused, '*It's moving fastly!*' Asif told the Year 2 class that *fastly* was not a word and asked if they could think of other examples. Eventually, *quickly*, *rapidly* and *speedily* were among the answers. The class then stood on the carpet and began walking on the spot.

Asif called out adverbs to describe how they should walk and the class physically acted these out. Having walked *sneakily, tiredly, happily and grumpily*, Asif then asked the class what most adverbs ended in. The answer '*ly*' was instantly reached.

The children then worked in talk partners writing examples of adverbs onto whiteboards and shared their favourites with the class.

They worked on sheets filling in the blanks to describe verbs with adverbs.

The children finally came back to the carpet and listened to *Up, Up and Away* by Ruth Heller, a book built around adverbs.

The lesson in the case study is a good introduction to adverbs that can lead on to adverbial phrases and eventually writing poems including these techniques. The physical process of acting out the adverb helps children to retain the meaning of the word and its applicable uses. This is using actions that lead to understanding to lead to application into writing (see Chapter 4).

This might be developed in the following ways:

- drawing a fairy, witch or monster etc and labelling it with verbs such as flying, roaring, laughing etc;

- then making these verbs into adverbial phrases by adding adverbs so flying becomes flying quickly, roaring becomes roaring loudly, laughing becomes laughing quietly etc;

- giving the pupils a poetry template; they can then add their adverbial phrases to fill in the blanks, for example,

I Am a Monster

I am a monster and I am ... flying quickly

I am a monster and I am ... roaring loudly

I am a monster and I am ... laughing quietly

I am a monster and I am ... etc.

Once this three-part structure is followed, then pupils could create their own piece of poetry based on a different subject, such as an animal, robot or alien.

CASE STUDY

Developing language use for poetry writing

Year 1: looking at adjectives

Sarah, a Year 1 teacher, decided to explore adjectives with her class. She showed them a picture of a dragon on the interactive whiteboard and asked them for adjectives to describe the dragon. Children suggested *scary, fiery, red, scaly, pointy* etc. Children then worked in small groups to write lists of words, helping each other to sound them out.

Each group created their own word bank of adjectives. These were then shared and discussed. They wrote a class poem called '*Dragon is …*':

Dragon is … scary

Dragon is … fiery

Dragon is … red

Dragon is … scaly

Dragon is … pointy

The children then wrote their own versions of the class poem using their word banks to help and adding any other adjectives they thought applied.

Year 2: looking at similes

Ngozi gave each of her pupils a pebble from the beach. She described her own pebble as being '*as smooth as …*', but then she explained that she could not think of a word to complete her description. The children offered suggestions such as *ice*, *glass* and *a desk*.

Ngozi explained that this descriptive technique of comparing one thing to something else was called similes. Ngozi then asked the children for adjectives to describe the pebbles other than *smooth*. They had answers such as *grey*, *hard* and *cold*. The children then completed the descriptions by making similes such as *as grey as an elephant*, *as hard as metal* and *as cold as snow*. The children then took their pebbles to their desks and wrote simile sentences about them, some using tablet computers.

Year 3: looking at personification

Michael, a final year trainee, held a water bottle up to his class seated on the carpet. He said that he would describe it as a *happy water bottle*. He then dropped it and said that it was *a sad water bottle*. He shook it and said it was *a frightened water bottle*. He slammed it onto his desk and said it was *an angry water bottle*. The class discussed why this sounded strange.

Michael explained that this type of description was called *personification* and said that it made objects or nouns that were not people sound like they had the emotions of people. They then completed worksheets labelling objects such as eyes or gloves or plants with sentences such as *The excited eyes looked at the present* or *The kind gloves kept out the cold* or *The happy plant sunbathed in the light*.

Activity 4

»   *Look at some collections of poems, for both adults and children.*

»   *As you read them notice the poet's use of adjectives, similes and personification.*

» *Think about why they are effective.*

» *Start your own teaching resource by collecting together some of the ones that you think are most effective.*

Adjectives, similes and personification: pulling them all together!

The lessons in these case studies introduced poetic writing techniques at a young age. But the more they are repeated and extended throughout pupils' school careers, the more they become writing habits. The more they are used then the more they are understood.

These can all be developed in the following ways.

• In Year 4 and beyond, these children who have looked at adjectives, similes and personification should be offered multiple opportunities to practise using them in their work. They can use them when labelling settings, characters and objects across all subject areas.

• They can write poems that alternate the techniques on every three lines. For example:

Gandalf the Wizard is magic,

Gandalf the Wizard is as wise as an owl,

Gandalf the Wizard has a compassionate staff

• Poetic language can be used incorporating all three techniques into one line. For example,

The dinner plate was a battlefield, as messy as a landfill site and covered in cruel flies.

• Children could go on to explore metaphor and other writing techniques.

Children need ideas for the content of their poems if they are to use the above techniques effectively – their poetry needs both form and content.

FOCUS ON RESEARCH

Form and content

Wilson discusses the prerequisites for enabling children to write poetry, referring to *content space* and *rhetorical space* (see Sharples, 1999 and Chapter 2).

Content space refers to what we want to say or write and the rhetorical space to how we say/ write it.

If the content space is not sufficiently stimulated, there may result poetry writing which is lacklustre: the child's interests, beliefs, experiences or values may simply not have been aroused. If the rhetorical space is not provided with sufficient information about how to structure the writing there may result poems which express great interest but shut the reader out because of their lack of shape or coherence. If on the other hand the rhetorical information is provided at the expense of arousing children's interest there may result poems which dutifully jump through 'poetic hoops' but give no real sense of 'life'.

(Sharples, 1999, p 21)

Operating in both spheres, he says, is important to transform knowledge and experience, a key feature of poetic writing.

Activity 5

Thinking about content space and rhetorical space:

» *Complete the limerick below.*

» *Consider what you need to know in order to complete the limerick.*

There was a young lady from Crewe

Who didn't know quite what to do

She went here and there.

» *List the things that you need to know to complete the limerick – think about content space and rhetorical space.*

» *How could you teach this? Think more broadly than a lesson plan. How could you ensure that children are alive to language, that they can draw on topics for the content space and that their knowledge of poetry is good enough to inform the rhetorical space?*

Does poetry have to rhyme?

Look at the limerick activity above. Limericks often feature towns in the first line. Crewe is a good choice because there are lots of words which can be used to rhyme with it in the second and fifth lines. York, Leeds, Hull and Kent would also be good selections, but how many words could you find to rhyme with Middlesbrough?

Milton said '*rhyming causes vexation, hinderance and constraint in expression*'. If one of the greatest poets found rhyme a challenge, think how hard it must be for inexperienced writers to make their poems rhyme. Teachers often notice that rhymes make poems nonsensical or do not allow children to express what they actually want to say. They become preoccupied with the form at the expense of the content.

A good start to rhyming can be to discuss the kind of vocabulary which might be used in a poem and to create a word bank of possibilities; to this can be added a selection of words which rhyme with those in the word bank. This can be an excellent opportunity to discuss spelling possibilities and some of the quirks of the English alphabetic system (eg, bear, hair, their, there, fare all rhyme but the rhyming sound is spelled in different ways). This activity can also help children consider which words might be best suited to being placed at the ends of lines and which would be better elsewhere because there are few words which rhyme with them.

Rap music and Hip Hop in general rely heavily on rhyme, but it can often be a relaxed verse using more half rhymes and playing with sounds. This form of performance poetry can really allow children to have fun while expressing themselves using the written word.

The poet Adisa states in *What Is Poetry?*

> *Poetry is everywhere*
>
> *Poetry is music to my ear*
>
> *Poetry is a grateful dancer with elegance and flair*
>
> *Poetry has many shapes and forms but poetry is not square*
>
> *Poetry is written on paper but poetry doesn't live there*
>
> *For poetry is in your eyes in your smile and even in your tears.*

Performing a poem can bring it to life, giving a new direction to the words selected. Recording a poem means that this performance can be newly discovered again and again. There is certainly a place for rhyming poetry in children's writing, but free verse can also be a useful option which can allow them to express ideas with fewer restrictions.

FOCUS ON RESEARCH

Poetry and digital media

Hughes (2007, p 3) argues that digital media offer a new way in which poetry can be explored and created:

> *Poetry is meant to be lifted from the printed page and explored in multimodal ways (visually, gesturally, aurally). The use of new digital media for reading, writing, and representing poetry encourages an exploration of the relationship between text and image and how images and sound might be used to mediate meaning-making. New media have an immersive and performative potential that encourages students to get inside a poem and play with it. Giving students opportunities to create poems or respond to and annotate existing poems using new media provides them with opportunities to use the technology in meaningful ways.*

Conclusion

This chapter has emphasised the importance of developing the language and techniques of poetry writing. Case studies illustrate how this can be achieved in practice. A key message is that teachers need to have a wide knowledge of poetry and poetic techniques if they are to engage children's interest in both reading and writing poetry.

Critical points

»   *There are many ways in which we can engage children's interest in poetry.*

»   *Our own knowledge of poetry is an important factor here.*

»   *Children need to have stimulating experiences before they can write poetry.*

»   *We can support children's writing of poetry in various ways, including through modelling, sharing poems, creating word banks and rhyming banks.*

»   *Poetry does not have to rhyme, but where children are asked to produce rhymes we should support them in doing so.*

»   *Children should be exposed to a wide range of poetry including free verse, classical, narrative, structured and humorous.*

Critical reflections

»   *Reflect upon the critical points above and consider a poetry lesson you have taught or observed. In light of what you have read, how could this lesson have been improved?*

Taking it further

You can find out more about a range of poetry writing by familiarising yourself with the following styles. There are many websites which provide examples and lesson ideas, and some of these are listed too.

•   Writing structured poems – haiku, cinquains, triolets, limericks, kennings etc

•   Writing free verse

•   Rhymes used to remember things (mnemonics): *30 Days Hath September* and *Never Eat Shredded Wheat*.

•   Nursery rhymes can be looked at by young children and learned by heart as well as by older children who might explore the hidden meanings behind some of them, for example, *Ring o' Roses* and *the Plague*.

•   The lyrics of songs, including hymns, which can sometimes be difficult for children to understand.

•   Jingles used in advertising: children could write their own to advertise school and local events.

- Rhymes in greetings cards: many tend to be trite and children could be asked to try to improve upon existing ones.

- Short comic verse such as that written by Spike Milligan.

- Longer comic verse, for example Roald Dahl's *Revolting Rhymes* (2001), and poems by Pam Ayres, Allan Ahlberg, Michael Rosen, Roger McGough and Kit Wright.

- Ballads and narrative poems.

- Free verse without rhyme.

- Nonsense poems.

- Poems written by children.

- Extracts from descriptive *adult* poetry, such as *Ode to Autumn* by John Keats, the Witches' Brew in *Macbeth* by Shakespeare and *Daffodils* by William Wordsworth.

- Poems from different cultures.

References

Cremin, T (2011) Reading Teachers/Teaching Readers Why Teachers Who Read Make Good Teachers of Reading. *English Drama Media*, February 2011(19): 11–18.

Doonan, J (1993) *Looking at Pictures in Picture Books*. Stroud: The Thimble Press.

Duffy, C A (2007) *The Hat*. London: Faber and Faber.

Goodwyn, A (2011) Literacy Reading: The Challenge of Getting Young People to Experience Poetry, in Lockwood, M (ed) *Bringing Poetry Alive*. London. Sage.

Hughes, J (2007) Poetry: A Powerful Medium for Literacy and Technology Development. *What Works? Research into Practice*. A research-into-practice series produced by a partnership between the Literacy and Numeracy Secretariat and the Ontario Association of Deans of Education. Research Monograph no.7. [online] Available at: www.edu.gov.on.ca/eng/literacynumeracy/inspire/research/hughes.pdf (accessed 12 February 2015).

Lewis, C D (ed) (1966) *The Collected Poems of Wilfred Owen*. London: Chatto & Windus.

Ofsted (2007) *Poetry in Schools: A survey of practice, 2006/2007*. [online] Available at: http://dera.ioe.ac.uk/7075/2/Poetry_in_schools_%28PDF_format%29.pdf (accessed 12 February 2015).

Sharples, M (1999) *How We Write: Writing as Creative Design*. London: Routledge.

Wilson, A (2005) The Best Forms in the Best Order? Current Poetry Writing Pedagogy at KS2. *English in Education*, 39(3): 19–31

Websites

Poetry line

www.poetryline.org.uk/research-and-publications

BBC six-word memoir

www.bbc.co.uk/radio4/today/reports/misc/sixwordlife_20080205.shtml#

Literacy shed – the poetry shed

www.literacyshed.com/the-poetry-shed.html

Poetry archive

www.poetryarchive.org/

For background reading on poetry and a glossary of poetic terminology, see:

Waugh, D, Neaum, S and Waugh, R (2013) *Children's Literature in Primary Schools*. London: Sage.

6 Non-fiction writing

KATE ALLOTT

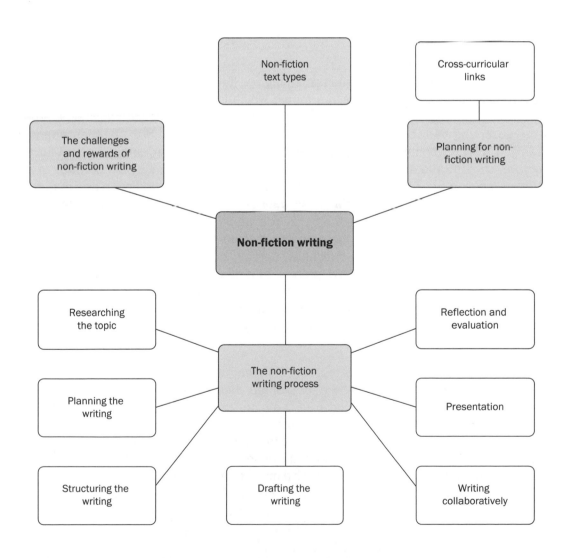

Teachers' Standards

3 Demonstrate good subject and curriculum knowledge

- have a secure knowledge of the relevant subject(s) and curriculum areas; foster and maintain pupils' interest in the subject and address misunderstandings

- demonstrate an understanding of and take responsibility for promoting high standards of literacy

Critical questions

» *What are the potential rewards and difficulties of non-fiction writing?*

» *What text types should be taught?*

» *How do we teach children to become successful writers of non-fiction texts?*

» *How should non-fiction writing be planned for and assessed?*

Introduction

Imagine you have been asked to write something you have not written before. As a student teacher it might be an assignment in a format which is new to you; as a newly qualified teacher perhaps school reports for your class; or as a more experienced teacher, a report for the governing body on an initiative you have led. What do you do? As an experienced writer, you would probably first ask for examples you could look at, and get a feel for the structure, content and style. You would have a clear understanding of the purpose of the writing: the governors, for example, may have put money into your initiative and may want to know whether it has had an impact. You would gather the information you planned to include and have a go at drafting the work. You would have in mind, as you wrote, the people who would be reading it – the parent might be very anxious about her child's progress, or she might have reading difficulties herself, or might even be another primary teacher. How can what you write be appropriate for all of these potential audiences? You would be very likely to ask for informal feedback at this stage, from whoever asked you to do the writing, and you might then redraft your work in light of the comments. Before it was finally handed over, you would check it very carefully and possibly ask one or two others to check it for you.

Teaching non-fiction writing involves teaching children this process, and all the skills which as experienced writers we tend to take for granted. Non-fiction writing is hugely varied in form, but there are some widely recognised common text types, and teaching also involves familiarising children with these so that they have the confidence and skills to produce them independently. Non-fiction writing matters because children's success in education will largely depend on their ability to show what they know and understand through writing, and for many of them their careers will also involve many forms of writing.

The challenges and rewards of non-fiction writing

Non-fiction writing is not simply a useful skill: for many children it is an opportunity to write about subjects that they are fascinated by and knowledgeable about, and the desire to share their enthusiasms and expertise is often very strong. It also offers the opportunity to be highly creative. The decisions writers make – *What shall I put in? How shall I organise it? How shall I present it? How shall I connect the elements? How shall I begin and end it?* – allow them to adopt an individual approach, and both the process and the outcome can give very deep satisfaction. There is also a pleasure in mastering the different text types and learning the tricks of the trade. Indeed, older writers are often confident enough to be able to subvert the genre with *spoof* non-fiction texts similar to *Dr Xargle's Book of Earthlets*, and to have a lot of fun doing it.

However, all of these aspects of non-fiction writing can challenge less confident writers. They may find it difficult to decide what is relevant to include and worry that they have left out something important. Organising the content, when there is not a simple chronological sequence to follow, can be challenging, and when text is handwritten, moving elements around is a cumbersome business. Style can also pose difficulties: when children are struggling to find their own voices as writers, some non-fiction texts require a more adult voice, and formal writing can be particularly challenging. Specialised vocabulary may be needed. Writing effective introductions and conclusions can be difficult even for experienced writers. Children who do not read widely are at a particular disadvantage, but even those who do may read mostly fiction and be relatively unfamiliar with the structures and language of non-fiction writing. Corbett and Strong (2011, p 2) say that '*children's writing will be an echo of their reading*', and without wide reading of appropriate non-fiction models, writing non-fiction may be something they do reluctantly, badly or both.

Activity 1: Analysing a writing sample

» *Read Figure 6.1 (overleaf), a piece of writing by a Year 3 pupil, Maryam. As you can see, it is an information leaflet for her local park. Both the research and the writing were carried out completely independently. What do you think are the strengths of this writing, and what aspects do you think could be developed in future teaching?*

While some children seem able to absorb almost effortlessly from their reading the knowledge and understanding needed to write in the forms they read, and Maryam is probably such a reader and writer, others, even when they do read quite widely, find it difficult to apply their understanding of what they read to their own writing. For these children, systematic and well-focused teaching is essential. This teaching has two strands: the process of writing non-fiction, and the characteristics of different non-fiction text types. The process will be discussed later, but look first at the main non-fiction text types.

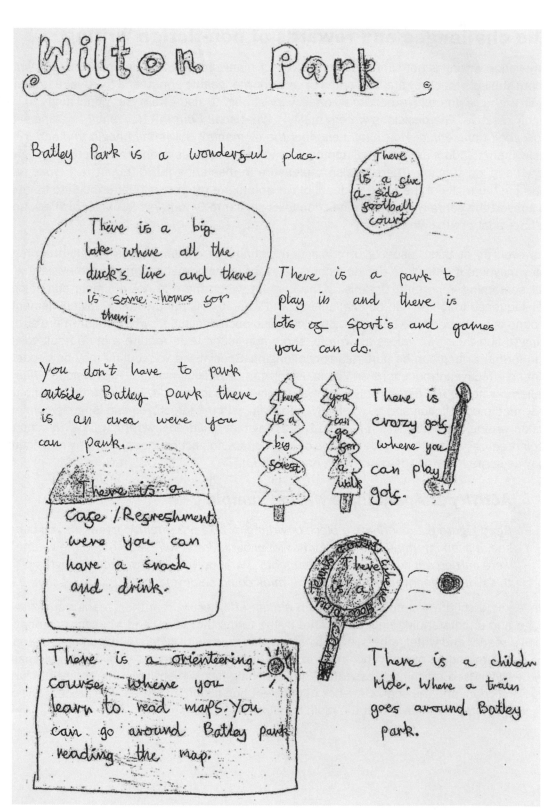

Wilton Park

Batley Park is a wonderful place.

There is a big lake where all the duck's live and there is some homes for them.

There is a five a-side football court

There is a park to play is and there is lots of sport's and games you can do.

You don't have to park outside Batley park there is an area were you can park.

There is a big forest

you can go for a walk

There is crazy golf where you can play golf.

There is a cafe / Refreshments were you can have a snack and drink.

Tennis court where There is a

There is a children ride. Where a train goes around Batley park.

There is a orienteering course where you learn to read maps. You can go around Batley park reading the map.

Figure 6.1 *A piece of writing by a Year 3 pupil, Maryam*

Non-fiction text types

It is important to recognise that non-fiction writing covers a huge range of text types, from the brief slogan, note or list to the dissertation or textbook. It would not be helpful or easy, however, to teach such a number of text types to children, and so teaching in primary schools usually introduces six main non-fiction text types. Merchant and Thomas (2001) give a useful explanation of *genre theory* and how the National Literacy Strategy adopted and popularised this approach to non-fiction writing. Once children are familiar with basic text types, they can recognise that diaries, journals, biographies and autobiographies are all recounts, for example. Note that the 2014 national curriculum programme of study does not explicitly list text types to be taught, but the six which were introduced by the National Literacy Strategy in 1998 are well embedded in practice and are unlikely to be abandoned.

Table 6.1 *The six basic non-fiction text types*

Recount Purpose: to re-tell events. • An opening which sets the scene • A recount of what happened, in chronological order • A conclusion which may comment on the events • Written in the past tense, often with time connectives (*many years later, soon afterwards*)	**Non-chronological report** Purpose: to give information about a topic. • An opening which introduces the subject • Information about the subject, organised into sections • Usually in the present tense • A conclusion which draws the report together
Explanation Purpose: to explain how something works. • An introduction to the topic • A step-by-step explanation of how the process works • Usually written in the present tense • Often uses time connectives and/or causal connectives	**Instructions** Purpose: to explain how to do something. • The aim of the activity • Materials/equipment needed • Steps needed to achieve the goal, in chronological order, with numbered steps, or bullet points, or time connectives • Written in the imperative
Persuasion Purpose: to argue for a point of view or course of action • Thesis – an opening which hooks the reader in and explains the purpose of the writing • Arguments – often in the form of point and elaboration • Reiteration – summary and restatement of the argument	**Discussion** Purpose: to present different points of view about an issue. • Statement of the issue • Arguments for, with supporting evidence • Arguments against, with evidence (these can be alternated with the arguments for) • Summary and conclusion • Connectives such as *however, therefore, although*

Activity 2: Non-fiction text types

» *First, read the descriptions of the six basic text types given in Table 6.1, and then try to match the texts below to the types.*

A A superb property of a type which rarely comes onto the market. Treated in recent years to an extensive programme of modernisation, the house still retains some charming period features, yet with a highly contemporary feel.	**B** Florence Nightingale was born in 1820. In 1853 the Crimean War started. Florence was asked to go to the Crimea to help the soldiers who had been hurt. She worked at the Barrack Hospital at Scutari. Florence died at the age of 90.
C Knucklebones was played in Roman times with small bones, pebbles or lumps of clay. How to play: • Hold all the stones in the palm of the hand. • Throw them up and catch them on the back of the hand. • If you catch them all, throw them up again and catch them in the palm. • If you drop any, put all but one down, and throw that one up, picking up the dropped ones one by one while catching the one thrown up each time.	**D** Honeybees live in colonies of thousands of bees, co-operating to give the colony as a whole the best chance of survival. Individual bees cannot survive unless the colony survives. There are three castes of honeybee: • Queens: there is only one in each colony, and the queen lays the eggs. • Drones, which are males: there are several hundred in each colony. • Workers, which carry out all the tasks, including foraging for food and rearing larvae.
E Some children come to school by car, while others walk or ride their bikes. Each type of transport has different advantages and disadvantages. Travelling by car is quick and you stay dry and warm whatever the weather. However, cars are expensive, and they pollute the air and add to global warming. Walking or riding bicycles helps to keep you fit. They are quiet forms of transport and they do not cause pollution. However, they can be less safe and you can get cold and wet. Also walking can be very slow. How people come to school may depend on how far away they live. I would conclude that it would be best if most children walked to school or rode their bikes, as they do in other countries.	**F** The stones probably come from a place nine miles away. Even the smallest stone weighs more than 25 tons. Each stone would have been put on a sledge and pulled along a wooden track by a team of about 200 men, using wood fibre ropes. As the sledge moved along, wood from behind would be picked up and put at the front. It is thought that it would have taken six months to move the stones nine miles. At the site, holes would have been dug for the stones. They would be dragged to the hole, slid down a slope and then pulled upright.

Based on Module 6 of the National Literacy Strategy's training pack (1998).

Of course, many texts do not conform fully to the descriptions given – a non-chronological report about a history topic such as Viking houses would be in the past tense, for example – and many texts are a mixture of types: a book on hamsters is likely to combine instructions for looking after hamsters with interesting facts about them. However, having an understanding of the basic types is important, and children can learn to adapt them to match the purpose of their writing. The Primary National Strategy *Support for Writing* materials (DCSF, 2008) provide a wealth of useful information about the text types.

The non-fiction writing process

The National Literacy Strategy (DfEE, 1998) established a model for the teaching of writing generally, which begins with reading a number of examples of a text type and identifying key features. The teacher then demonstrates writing the text type to the whole class, and may also do some shared writing in which the children contribute ideas while the teacher scribes. Modelling is an important way of teaching children about every stage of the writing process, because it is showing rather than telling – and more than this, because as you demonstrate you are also providing a commentary on what you are doing and thinking: *I'm not sure how to begin this, but that's fine – I'll start with the first point and add the introduction later ... let me read it through ... how does that sound?* As the children begin to write independently, they may be supported in different ways – by an adult, in guided writing; by a writing frame which provides a structure for the writing; or by writing collaboratively with another child. If they encounter difficulties they may look at more examples, or they may use the checklist of key features identified during the reading phase. Non-fiction writing, however, is often a rather more complicated process, because reading is not only a way of finding out about the text type but is very often also the way of gathering information which will provide material for the writing.

The beginning of the writing process might therefore look like this.

* Read several information texts on life in Viking times, thus gathering possible content and also an understanding of the features of such texts, in order to produce a class book on the topic.

* Read information texts on Victorian slums and also persuasive letters on a range of topics, in order to write letters to the prime minister of the time asking him to take action.

* Read persuasive writing from opposing viewpoints on whether the town centre should be pedestrianised; also read examples of discussions, in order to write a balanced discussion of the issue.

We read in a very different way when we are researching a subject we plan to write about: we are looking for what is relevant to our topic, and for answers to questions we have. Good research skills are therefore crucial to good writing, as content is as important as structure and style.

FOCUS ON RESEARCH

The EXEL project

The Exeter Extending Literacy (EXEL) project, reported by Wray and Lewis (1997), was very influential in the teaching of non-fiction reading and writing in primary schools. The National Literacy Strategy's (1998) training materials for non-fiction were based on its work. The project was a response to concerns about how well non-fiction reading and writing were being taught, and the researchers developed the EXIT (Extending Interactions with Texts) model to support children's reading of non-fiction texts, and writing frames, which support children's non-fiction writing. The model presented a systematic process for researching topics, with clear purposes and questions in mind, and adopting a critical approach to the texts used. Writing frames have become very widely used, and this will be discussed later.

Researching the topic

The first step when gathering information or ideas on a topic is to check what is already known – *activating prior knowledge*, in the EXIT model terminology. Children then need to identify questions to research, consider what sources they might use to find information and make notes on what they find out.

CASE STUDY

Activating prior knowledge

Jessica was introducing a history topic to her Year 4 class. She began by asking all the children to write down at least one thing they knew about the Romans on a sticky note. These were collated on the board, and even when there was evidence of misconceptions Jessica did not challenge the children's contributions, as she did not want them to worry about being wrong, and she also wanted them to realise the need to check what we think we know. Every child's contribution was put on the board, even when several had written the same piece of information, but as she put them up Jessica modelled sorting them into different aspects of the subject, and even re-sorting as more information was added. She also modelled asking questions based on the information gathered, to fill in gaps and develop understanding of the topic. Children all then contributed a question, and these formed the basis of the research activity which followed.

The initial gathering of ideas may quite naturally generate questions, and it is important that children have identified questions to be answered before they begin to research the topic. Wray and Lewis (1997) suggest alternative ways of recording this stage of the process – the KWL grid (What do I **K**now? What do I **W**ant to find out? What did I **L**earn?) or the QADS grid (question-answer-details-source) (see Tables 6.2 and 6.3). This second grid allows for a brief answer and also a more detailed one, and develops the invaluable habit of noting where the information came from. Material for non-fiction writing may come from a range of sources: ideas for persuasive and discursive writing are likely to come largely from discussion, for example.

Table 6.2 KWL grid

What do I **Know**?	What do I **Want** to find out?	What did I **Learn**?
Birds can fly.	Are there any types of birds which cannot fly?	About 40 types of bird cannot fly. Ostriches, emus and penguins cannot fly. Chickens and ducks kept for food cannot fly.

Table 6.3 QADS grid

Question	Answer	Details	Source
Why haven't I ever seen a hedgehog?	They like to hide	They live in places where there are plants to hide among. They hibernate in the winter. They are nocturnal.	*Hedgehog* by Louise and Richard Spilsburg

Planning the writing

It is crucial that children have a clear sense of the audience for their writing and its purpose. Without this understanding it can be very difficult to make decisions about what to include and what style would be appropriate. A struggling Year 4 writer, writing postcards to his grandparents and his best friend, included very different information for the different audiences, knowing that something which would make his best friend laugh (*'I ate six ice-creams and I was sick in the sea'*) would produce only shock and disapproval from his grandparents.

As far as possible, the writing also needs a real purpose. Instructions, for example, should be for something the reader is not already able to do. Who really needs instructions for making a jam sandwich or a cup of tea? Many of us, however, would need instructions in order to grow tomatoes or make gingerbread men. It is more motivating to have a genuine purpose for writing, and it matters then that the instructions work. Once audience and purpose are clear, it is much easier to judge what structure and style is appropriate. Good instructions are concise and straightforward. For example, numbered instructions are easier to follow (*'I've just done 5 – let me look at 6 now'*) than ones using bullet points and time connectives (*'Am I on* after that *or* next?'). There is certainly no need to use more than one of these organising devices in any set of instructions. No need either to worry about exciting vocabulary or similes – just keep it simple. And it is easy to check whether the writing has achieved its purpose: ask someone to try out the instructions.

With audience and purpose clearly established, selection of content also becomes easier, as the writer can refer back continually to questions such as *What does my audience need to know?* or *What would my audience find interesting?* Writers may find it difficult to leave out information which is not really relevant to the topic, but it is important that they learn to select – relevant or not relevant? interesting or not interesting? important or not important? What to put in and what to leave out is a particular difficulty in recounts of children's experiences. Teachers will be familiar with the recount of the school trip which includes details of the coach trip, toilet breaks, lunch and shop, while failing to include any of the fascinating information and experiences which were the reason for the trip in the first place. Having an audience in mind – someone who did not go on the trip but is interested in it – perhaps the headteacher, or a teaching assistant who was not able to accompany the children, or parents reading a newsletter is a good way of helping to judge what is appropriate content. While thank you letters are a good idea, writing to the staff of the place visited causes some difficulties if it is intended to provide a reason for writing about the visit, as they do not need to be told all about the place where they spend their working lives.

Structuring the writing

Once the content has been selected, it will need to be organised. Children's understanding of the structure of a text type should come from their reading and analysis of a number of examples, so that they come to see what the examples have in common, and how they all work. Teaching them this process is more useful than simply teaching them structures, as it can then be applied to any text type they wish to write – helping them to become independent. However, in the early stages some support may be helpful. Planning structures such as Sue Palmer's *Writing Skeletons* (Palmer, 2001) provide very helpful visual representations of the structure of the different text types.

Writing frames were proposed by Wray and Lewis (1997) as a way of supporting children in structuring their non-fiction writing. Writing frames provide a series of prompts or sentence starters which provide a framework for a piece of writing; they can be very helpful if used flexibly. There are many photocopiable writing frames available for different text types, giving either subheadings or sentence starters to support writing. But to work well they need to be used thoughtfully. For a start, it is best if the class develops a frame for a particular piece of writing together, based on the models they have read and analysed, rather than being presented with a *ready-made* one. Once children have done this a number of times, they can see that they can develop their own frames for any text type. They also need to see the frame being used flexibly. Frames which have prompts such as *One reason why … Another reason is … A final reason is …* can suggest to some children that they must come up with not five, not two but three reasons because that is what the frame demands. Teachers should also model changing subheadings and sentence starters to fit what they want to say, particularly as some children find it very difficult to make their writing follow on from a sentence starter.

Writing frames are intended as a temporary support; as soon as children have internalised the structure of the text, they do not need a frame.

Structuring recounts and instructions is relatively straightforward, since they are chronologically organised, and explanations have a logical sequence, but even so children may have difficulties, as the explanation text in Figure 6.2 by a Year 3 writer shows.

How is coffee farmed?

When they turn red they are ripe. The cherries grow on bushes and they pick the ripe ones every few days.

There are two seeds in the cherry and they are the coffee beans.

They spread the cherries out in the sun to dry and rake them to turn them over. If it rains they have to cover them up.

The bushes take five years to grow. They grow in hot countries near the Equator in the mountains.

Figure 6.2 *Example explanation text*

The difficulty may have been deciding where to start in explaining the process, or the writing may have been done without any planning, and with facts simply written down as they were recalled. Note that as readers we have to work out for ourselves who or what *they* refers to, suggesting the writer has little sense of the needs of the audience.

Non-chronological texts such as reports, discussions and persuasive writing give more freedom in terms of organisation. Discussions, for example, can be simply structured with all the arguments on one side first, followed by all the opposing arguments; however, a more sophisticated writer may choose to pair up matching points on each side, so that the writing becomes more like a tennis match with the argument being batted to and fro. The writer may also consider how to use the ammunition of the *killer* point – whether to use it at the beginning, so that the argument is weighted throughout in favour of one side or to save it to the end so that what seemed a finely balanced argument is suddenly tipped. Non-chronological reports, apart from the introduction and conclusion which any information writing is likely to need, can often be structured in several different ways, as the following activity demonstrates.

Activity 3: Organising information

» *Consider this set of notes on the topic of the Stone Age and identify sections into which the final piece of writing could be divided. You may also identify a good introductory statement and conclusion.*

People ground wheat and barley between two stones to make flour.	Stone Age people lived many thousands of years ago.	People made tools out of stone. They knocked bits off flints to make hand axes.	During the Stone Age people started to grow crops and keep animals.
People began to make stone houses instead of living in tents.	People painted pictures of animals on the walls of caves.	The Stone Age ended when people learned to make bronze.	People made stone circles but we do not know why. There are lots in Britain.
People made henges which are circular ditches and banks. The biggest one is 400 metres across.	Stone Age people were hunters who caught animals for food, and also ate berries and nuts.	People wore clothes made of animal skins held together with bone pins.	Stone circles and henges may have been used for worshipping gods.

The process of organising information into sections and then within sections, and sequencing the sections, can be practised using sets of cards or strips of paper, each containing one piece of information, on a particular topic. Moving the cards around to group and sequence them is an effective physical representation for children of the mental process.

Drafting the writing

It is very difficult to imagine writing the end of a novel before the beginning, but one of the freedoms of non-fiction writing is the freedom to write sections in any order, not the order in which they may finally appear. Using the Stone Age information shown earlier, a writer might choose to work on any of the sections first, and indeed the writing could be done successfully with different authors writing different sections. An introduction, just as much as a conclusion, is often best written when the main part of the writing is complete: after all, how can the writer introduce the reader to something not yet produced?

It is at this stage that style becomes a consideration and, again, getting this right depends very much on having read a number of models (possibly including one or two not very good ones) and also having a clear sense of who the writing is for. Analysis of examples should give children an idea of language features of the text type, such as tense, person, length and structure of sentences, and vocabulary. As with writing frames, success criteria are best arrived at by the children discussing what makes a good news report, or advertisement, or diary entry, and producing their own criteria, rather than being presented with pre-prepared ones which sometimes seem to inhibit rather than support writing. For example, although it is true that explanations and discussions are likely to contain causal connectives, making the use of them a criterion for success is a back to front approach to writing: their use will occur quite naturally if writers are writing about '*causes, consequences, conjecture*' (Murray, 1822, p 129). Murray described connectives as '*hinges, tacks and pins*' which hold together words, phrases or sentences, and just as hinges, tacks and pins are not simply attached to a piece of wood for no purpose, so connectives cannot be added to a piece of writing if they are not necessary or meaningful.

Writing collaboratively

In the adult world, writing is often a collaborative process, particularly for writing at work (although even poets sometimes have help: Wordsworth in his old age said that the two best lines in *Daffodils* were written by his wife, Mary). Even if one person in a team takes the main responsibility for a report, for example, the draft is likely to be sent around the team for comments and amendments. Collaborative writing makes the writing process much more transparent to young writers, as they work together, share ideas and discuss their work.

CASE STUDY

Writing a discussion

Megan planned to ask her Year 6 class to write about whether parents should be allowed to take children out of school to go on holiday, a topic which had been attracting media interest. She adopted the role of permanent secretary at the Department for Education, with the class as her civil servants, and said that the education secretary had asked for a discussion paper outlining the arguments and making a recommendation to her. The children formed teams and were provided with material such as government statements on the policy, news reports and comments from parents' groups.

They were given time to discuss what they had read and their own ideas, and to list arguments on both sides. Each team then wrote a paper. Megan as permanent secretary shared all the drafts with the class, using the visualiser, and they discussed the strengths of each and how they could be combined to produce the best possible paper. At this point both the arguments and the style were reviewed; the children were very aware that they needed a fairly formal tone for this writing – though Megan emphasised that it should be clear and easy to understand. The final version was proofread by all the class before being sent to the education secretary. A week later Megan shared a response she had written, outlining how the law was to be changed in the light of the arguments the children had produced. Megan felt that working together had been of great benefit to the children, as they had discussed so many aspects of the writing during the process.

FOCUS ON RESEARCH

Argumentation

In a review of international research into the effective teaching of non-fiction writing, and particularly what was labelled *argumentation*, Andrews et al (2009) concluded that children need to be taught the process of planning, drafting, editing and revising their writing, with very clear explanations of the process and coaching through the various stages. The evidence suggested that self-motivation and personal target setting were also important, and that peer collaboration in writing was a useful strategy, because discussion about the writing was eventually internalised, so writers were able to talk themselves through the process. Research also indicated that teacher modelling was helpful and that children needed to know the purpose and audience for their writing.

Presentation

Non-fiction texts are often multimodal, conveying meaning through images, diagrams, tables and so on, as well as through written text. Children often very much enjoy these aspects of composition, but they do need to be thought through just as much as the writing.

CASE STUDY

Presenting a report

Joseph asked his Year 5 class to research different countries competing in the football World Cup and to present their information in a poster format. The children were so enthusiastic about the idea of designing a poster that they rushed the research stage and did not stop to plan the layout, but started to make their posters almost immediately. Joseph realised at the end of the first lesson that he had not really presented them with an idea of who might read the poster, and therefore what they would be interested in about *their* country, or what might make a poster effective in attracting attention and conveying information. In the next lesson he therefore began by explaining that the posters would be displayed in the corridor, where other staff and classes could read them. The children then discussed in groups what they would like to find out about a country they knew nothing about, and the class collated a list of key facts to research. They also sorted the facts into sections such as geography and footballing history. With this preparation, the research became much more purposeful. Once the children had gathered their information they looked at some posters and evaluated them. Joseph spent some time asking them to consider the needs of the reader – how big should the writing be? How high on the wall might the posters be placed? Would a common format be useful? Could some information be conveyed through pictures, diagrams or tables? How much information was anyone likely to read? It was agreed to have a world map as the centrepiece of the display, so the countries could be located on it. When the display had been mounted Joseph passed on positive comments to the class.

Reflection and evaluation

Although reflection and evaluation are often seen as the last stage in the writing process, they are likely to happen at every stage, as children share and discuss their plans and drafts.

The key question should always be: *Have I conveyed the information or ideas I wanted to convey?*

Planning for non-fiction writing

Schools need a clear overview of the writing curriculum, so that different text types are revisited over time, not simply for revision but to build on and develop children's knowledge and skills. You need to be aware that you may not always have time to follow the non-fiction writing process from start to finish, but you may need to focus on parts of it which children are finding particularly difficult and practise these. Children need to see the relevance of such activities to the process as a whole. For example, many writers, including students in higher education, lack confidence in planning and structuring their writing. More teaching of and practice in structuring different text types, including essays, should address this issue.

Cross-curricular links

Teaching time is always at a premium in schools. It makes sense therefore to link non-fiction reading and writing with curriculum areas other than English. What children are studying in, for example, history or science, can provide the material for their non-fiction writing. The skills they learn in English lessons can be applied in other curriculum areas. There is, of course, a danger with this approach that the skills are assumed rather than explicitly taught – in the writing sample about coffee seen earlier, for example, the writer did not have the knowledge and skills to structure the work appropriately. There is also a danger that every subject becomes simply a vehicle for teaching writing skills. You need to be very clear about the main focus of your lesson.

Conclusion

Being able to write non-fiction texts well is important in education and, for many of us, in our working lives. The craft of non-fiction writing can be taught, and children who are taught effectively will gain confidence and pleasure as well as academic success from developing these skills. The aim is to equip children with the knowledge and skills to become independent writers of high quality texts.

Critical points

» *Children need to know about different text types and also understand the writing process involved.*

» *Children need to explore and analyse examples of a text type before being expected to produce their own.*

» *Teachers need a good understanding of the characteristics of high quality non-fiction writing in order to teach effectively.*

Critical reflections

» *Do you feel you have the knowledge and understanding to teach non-fiction writing successfully? Do you feel that you can assess children's non-fiction writing and identify appropriate targets to support their writing development? There is a wide range of support material available which will help you develop your subject knowledge in this area.*

Taking it further

For a wealth of practical guidance and ideas for classroom activities, try:

Merchant, G and Thomas, H (2001) *Non-Fiction for the Literacy Hour: Classroom Activities for Primary Teachers*. London: David Fulton.

Palmer, S (2001) *How to Teach Writing Across the Curriculum at Key Stage 2*. London: David Fulton.

References

Andrews, R, Torgerson, C, Low, G and McGuinn, N (2009) Teaching Writing to 7–14 Year-Olds: An International Review of the Evidence of Successful Practice. *Cambridge Journal of Education*, 39:3.

Clark, C (2013) *Children and Young People's Writing in 2012: Findings from the National Literacy Trust's Annual Literacy Survey*. London: National Literacy Trust.

Corbett, P and Strong, J (2011) *Talk for Writing Across the Curriculum: How to Teach Non-fiction Writing to 5–12 Year Olds*. Maidenhead: Open University Press.

DCSF (2008) Support for Writing. [online] Available at: www.teachfind.com/national-strategies/primary-framework-literacy-text-types (accessed 11 February 2015).

DfEE (1998) *The National Literacy Strategy: Literacy Training Pack*. London: DfEE.

Merchant, G and Thomas, H (2001) *Non-Fiction for the Literacy Hour: Classroom Activities for Primary Teachers*. London: David Fulton.

Murray, L (1822) *English Grammar Adapted to the Different Classes*. York: Wilson & Sons.

Palmer, S (2001) *How to Teach Writing Across the Curriculum at Key Stage 2*. London: David Fulton.

Spilsburg, L and Spilsburg, R (2003) *Hedgehog*. Oxford: Harcourt Education Ltd.

Willis, J (1988) *Dr Xargle's Book of Earthlets*. London: Random House.

Wray, D and Lewis, M (1997) *Extending Literacy: Children Reading and Writing Non-fiction*. London: Routledge.

Answers

Activity 1: Analysing a writing sample

Maryam has selected relevant information to include in her leaflet: as far as we are aware, she has included all the main attractions and facilities of the park. The information is concisely presented in clear and accessible language. Maryam has made clever use of visual aspects of the leaflet, as the text boxes which keep each section separate, making information easy to locate, often reflect the topic of the section – the café section shaped as a building, the tennis section as a tennis racquet, the football section as a ball and so on.

To develop her writing, Maryam might compare her leaflet with a collection of leaflets from visitor attractions, and perhaps redraft her work in light of this: Could her leaflet do more to sell the park, for example, through the language used? She might also try the leaflet out on its potential audience. Is there anything else visitors might want to know? What most attracts them to the park?

Activity 2: Non-fiction text types

A: persuasion

B: recount

C: instructions

D: non-chronological report

E: discussion

F: explanation

Activity 3: Organising information

The information could be sorted into sections on:

* What was stone used for in the Stone Age?
* What did people eat in the Stone Age?
* Life in the Stone Age (wall paintings, clothes).

A good introductory statement would be: Stone Age people lived many thousands of years ago.

A good conclusion would be: The Stone Age ended when people learnt to make bronze.

7 Beyond text: using visual imagery and film to enhance children's writing

ROB SMITH

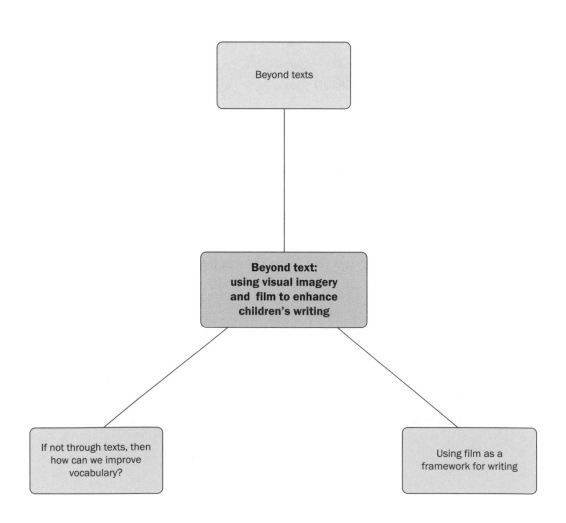

Teachers' Standards

1. Set high expectations which inspire, motivate and challenge pupils

• set goals that stretch and challenge pupils of all backgrounds, abilities and dispositions

3. Demonstrate good subject knowledge and curriculum knowledge

• demonstrate an understanding of and take responsibility for promoting high standards of literacy, articulacy and the correct use of standard English

4. Plan and teach well-structured lessons

• promote a love of learning and students' intellectual curiosity

5. Adapt teaching to respond to the strengths and needs of all pupils

Critical questions

» *What is visual literacy?*

» *How does visual literacy scaffold the writing process?*

» *How can vocabulary improve through using image and film stimuli?*

Introduction

Visual Literacy is the ability to interpret and make meaning from information presented in the form of an image or film – put simply: the ability to read an image or film.

To be visually literate, a child will need to be able to:

• analyse the image in a literal sense;

• analyse the intent and purpose of the image;

• use inference and deduction skills to deepen the sense of understanding of the content.

Being visually literate will allow children to make sense of the world around them. Even very young children are able to become literate in image and film. How many times have parents heard their children burst into songs like *Let It Go* or *Under the Sea* that they have learnt from repeated watching of films?

For many parents, children's repeated watching of films can be a source of frustration, but it shows us how much even the very young enjoy the stimulation of film. As teachers, we are able to utilise these skills as learning tools as soon as children begin school. Jenkin (2008) suggests that even though young people learn more than half of what they know from visual information, few schools have an explicit visual literacy curriculum. The National Literacy Strategy made tentative steps to combat this by incorporating film units into the framework, including *The Shirt Machine* in Year 4 and *The Piano* in Year 5. However, no mention of using film is made in the 2013 national curriculum (DfE, 2013).

FOCUS ON RESEARCH

Children's engagement with text

Is reading a panacea for all of our literacy needs? The National Literacy Trust reading survey (Clark, 2014) has shown that only 53.3 per cent of children enjoy reading. This would imply that 46.7 per cent of children are not engaged, enthused or enjoying their learning when reading is involved.

Even if we can engage our pupils in reading sessions, often a habitual cycle of reading is not adopted by the children. Clark (2013) suggests that fewer than one in three children (28 per cent) read at home every day. If we asked our pupils how many of them watch TV or film each day, we might assume that the number would be touching 100 per cent. Most children would not mind admitting to watching TV each day, but Clark's research shows that almost one in five children '*would be embarrassed if their friends saw them reading*' (Clark, 2013, p 10).

The new national curriculum states that reading '*widely and often increases students' vocabulary because they encounter words they would rarely hear or use in everyday speech*' (DfE, 2013, p 15). However, children with small or inadequate vocabularies will often comprehend less, and this may also lead to them choosing to read less and may set them on a path of perpetual failure as a reader. It is important that children have a level of functioning vocabulary that will allow them to read at the expected level. Often, in order for this to happen, direct instruction needs to take place. Biemiller and Boote (2006) suggest that children need to acquire 10–12 new meanings of words per week, and this is possible through direct instruction of around 20 meanings per week.

Biemiller and Boote (2006) also recommend the use of '*orally presented texts and explanations of word meanings in context*'. It is important to remember that, in 2006, the use of film in the primary classroom was less prevalent than it is today and was overlooked as a source of vocabulary development.

In the introduction to the 2013 primary national curriculum, teachers are told to encourage their pupils to read widely in order to '*develop their knowledge of themselves and the world in which they live, to establish an appreciation and love of reading, and to gain knowledge across the curriculum*' (DfE, 2013, p 15). It also asserts that reading '*feeds pupils' imagination and opens up a treasure – house of wonder and joy for curious young minds*'. So how can the image in our head become the writing on the page?

Imagine reading a description of a setting or a character in a novel, then being asked what you had imagined. It is likely that you will come up with a different image from somebody else who was asked to do the same thing. If you were then asked to write a description, it would be sourced from the image in your head, which you then transfer to the page. As adults, with wide-ranging life experiences, it is relatively easy to form images in our heads, based on real life experiences or virtual experiences from film or images we have seen. For example, the description below is based on a scene from a film:

A tiny girl wanders through a crowd of dishevelled people dressed in drab grey, a factory owner and his lover watch the girl dart between a group of adults to a soundtrack of gunshots, shouting and the howling of attack dogs. The girl is wearing a red coat, the only speck of colour in a sea of grey.

This scene is a powerful piece of cinematography – a scene from *Schindler's List*. Oskar Schindler is watching the liquidation of the ghettoes and he sees a small Jewish girl, in a red coat, amid the carnage. Without watching the film, it would be very difficult to write this scene as it is completely outside our own experiences, either real or virtual.

This scene also appears in the novel *Schindler's Ark*. The author talks about a *scarlet girl*. However, this girl is lost in the description of a riot of destruction and, while the extract is brutal, it seems to lack something that the immersive film experience brings.

Teachers often ask children to imagine things outside their own life experiences. For example, a teacher asking children to write about the beach may be surprised to learn how many children have not set foot on sand. One answer to this is providing the children with an image, or a film scene, to stimulate their imagination, and then get them to write their ideas on paper.

In the extract above, the sounds are described. Without watching the film, children may not think to add sounds, such as the dogs barking or the gunshots firing. With this in mind, we need to consider the balance of text and media that we offer to our pupils: we need to offer children rich texts, but we also need to supplement these texts with images or film, especially if we want them to write well. Starting with an image or film can give pupils the experiences they need to stimulate their imagination and curiosity and use this in their writing.

FOCUS ON RESEARCH

Ways of looking at images

Nodelman (1988) argues that pictures are subtle, complex forms of communication. They therefore have the potential for different types and levels of engagement as we look and seek to understand the image. The Booktrust identifies five different ways of looking. They describe how, as children develop cognitively, they increasingly begin to understand images, and to create meanings that are increasingly more fantastical, wittier, richer with information and more paradoxical. These ways of looking are not hierarchical in the sense that they replace one another. Being able to see rich and complex meanings in images does not preclude the possibility of looking at pictures for pleasure. Older children (and adults) are able to see images in different ways and with different levels of understanding. Indeed, we may engage with a picture in all the different ways at the same time.

Way of looking at pictures	Stage of development
1. Looking for pleasure	Sensory and concrete learning
2. Inspiring fantasy	Imaginative and fantasy
3. Stimulating curiosity	Broadening horizons
4. Understanding others	Developing empathy and personal understanding
5. Exploring the making of art and stories	Higher cognitive thinking

1. Initially, young children will look at images for pleasure –to seek out familiar things, to make links between objects, events and language, and to enjoy the sensory pleasure of engaging with images.

2. From the age of three children begin to engage with, and enjoy, imagining characters, places, stories, people and events. Their imaginations can be stimulated and they can engage in creative thinking.

3. Images, like pictures in galleries, can stimulate curiosity. Pictures can act as a provocation to a range of questions. As children develop cognitively and begin to seek to understand and make meaning in their world, pictures can be part of children's fascination with who, what, why and how.

4. Empathy enables children to understand other people. Images have an immediacy that text lacks, which enables us to tune into feelings and experiences. They encourage us to imagine *what if?*, to engage with feelings and situations beyond ourselves.

5. Older children are able use their cognitive skills to analyse and interpret pictures for their meaning. They are able to understand how metaphorical images are used and created, and how pictures can have multiple meanings. They are able to engage with abstract ideas and concepts embedded in images.

Adapted from Booktrust www.booktrust.org.uk

This taxonomy demonstrates the power of images as a stimulus to imagination, curiosity, empathy and cognitive thinking, all of which are essential to creative and imaginative writing.

Beyond texts

They were looking down upon a lovely valley. There were green meadows on either side of the valley, and along the bottom of it there flowed a great brown river. What is more, there was a tremendous waterfall halfway along the river – a steep cliff over which the water curled and rolled in a solid sheet, and then went crashing down into a boiling churning whirlpool of froth and spray.

*Below the waterfall (and this was the most astonishing sight of all), a whole mass of enormous glass pipes were dangling down into the river from somewhere high up in the ceiling! They really were **enormous**, those pipes. There must have been a dozen of them at least, and they were sucking up the brownish muddy water from the river and carrying it away to goodness knows where.*

(Dahl, 1964)

'*It is all chocolate*' cries Mr Wonka; this extract is the first glimpse of the chocolate room in Mr Willy Wonka's factory. Is the extract above a vivid description? If we ask children to read this extract and then create their own description of a land made of chocolate, what elements could they *magpie*, as in steal, from this extract?

Look at the verbs used: *looking, flowed, curled, rolled, crashing, boiling, churning, dangling*. If we asked pupils to write a description of their own chocolate landscape it would probably result in a selection (box) of Dahl's original description, rearranged with varying degrees of success. Children could also unpick the descriptive language that Dahl uses: *lovely valley, great brown river, tremendous waterfall, enormous ... pipes, brownish muddy water* – language that we, as teachers, could ask pupils to develop and improve.

However, perhaps this extract is not the best place to start. Perhaps there are different starting points to inspire creative writing that has flair and descriptive originality. Maybe a picture of a fantasy land filled with chocolate trees, candy cottages and marshmallow clouds would have been a more appropriate starting place.

It is often said that reading ability has a direct and almost immediate influence on a child's ability to write, and therefore many teachers continue to expect children to unconsciously absorb the author's flair for language. However, this may not always be the best way to help children to write creatively. There are many alternative strategies that we can employ.

FOCUS ON RESEARCH

The relationship between reading and writing

The National Literacy Trust's annual survey (Clark, 2013) highlights the dangers of relying on reading to inspire children to write. Data from the 2012 survey show that of those pupils reading at above their expected level, only 40 per cent were also writing at above the expected level. The correlation is weak at best but may be present where pupils have been taught to consciously lift sentence structure and vocabulary from texts.

If not through texts, then how can we improve vocabulary?

As a teacher you should be providing your pupils with a rich stream of vocabulary. However, unless you then teach them to consciously adopt this vocabulary, and use it first in their speech and then in their writing, it may be falling on deaf ears.

Activities that promote the use of rich and varied vocabulary are essential in the development of a child's working vocabulary. The following two case studies show two different ways that we can use multisensory approaches to improve children's vocabulary for writing.

CASE STUDY

Using multisensory experiences to develop children's vocabulary

A group of Year 4 children entered their classroom to the sound of the seaside. Bubbles were floating around from a hidden bubble machine. They sat in their normal places on the carpet as Guvinder, their teacher, told them to close their eyes and listen. Silently, they sat as Guvinder went on to lead them on a *guided discovery*. She asked them to imagine what they could see. As the pupils looked around, Guvinder asked '*What is in the sky?*' The children looked up.

Moving on to other senses, Guvinder asked the children to imagine the smells that could be present. She suggested that perhaps they could feel something with their hands or beneath their feet. The children became immersed in the scene and discussed the image in their heads, aided by the sound prompts. Guvinder then asked the children to collect sticky notes and felt tips to write down descriptive phrases.

The children then added their sticky notes to the class vocabulary track (see Figure 7.1).

They were then asked to read every other child's contribution. They chose their favourite and sat next to it. The pupils then took turns to walk down the vocabulary track while their peers read their favourite sticky note. So even if the pupils' reading ability could exclude them from the activity, they could still access all of the phrases by listening. The children then wrote a description using favourite phrases that they had either heard or read during the vocabulary track activity.

The class had created their own bank of descriptive phrases that were later discussed, improved and embedded into their writing.

The descriptions written were full of the language from the vocabulary track both of their own creation and those constructed by their peers. Their teacher encouraged the children to consciously analyse the words, judge them and steal ideas to use for their own purposes. This is not something that happens naturally when children read. As a teacher, you must actively encourage this to happen.

The method in the case study can be used across the curriculum to immerse the children in a setting.

Figure 7.1 *A vocabulary track*

Activity 1

» *Consider how you could help children to develop their setting descriptions.*

» *Consider how you could do the same thing with a forest or a cave or the beach.*

» *How could you use this teaching technique in a different curriculum area?*

CASE STUDY

Using film as a provocation for vocabulary development: Chaperon Rouge (Little Red Riding Hood)

The film *Chaperon Rouge* (https://www.youtube.com/watch?v=XyTDRzV9IcM) is a dystopian version of the classic Grimm tale, *Little Red Riding Hood*. As with the original, the setting in the film is a forest, but there are also ruined buildings and bridges. The intention is for the children to write a description of the setting, while dropping hints that all is not as it seems, and to give the reader clues that something *bad* is going to happen.

Step one: play the film's soundtrack without letting the children see what is on the screen. The easiest way is to turn off the classroom projector. Ask the children to close their eyes and imagine where they are. Once they have listened to the soundtrack, up to the point where the heroine closes her eyes, pause and replay it, but this time use prompts, for example:

- What can you see above you?

- How do you know where you are?

- What does it smell like?

- How are you feeling?

- What things can you see in the distance?

Allow the children time to become immersed in the setting. Following this immersion, replay the film, allowing the pupils to watch what is going on. When the setting is revealed, discuss whether it was expected or unexpected. Do they see what they thought they would?

Then ask the children to write descriptive sentences on sticky notes. They can only write one sentence on each sticky note and not a descriptive paragraph. Further constraints may be added, such as asking the children to include an adverb or verb starter or a simile.

Children then place their contributions onto the language track, and read all the ideas. They then choose one which they find most effective, which can be read out loud, and reasons are given for why they find it effective. This allows the children to read work that they may not have thought of themselves, and takes away the pressure of reading their own work which they may feel self-conscious about.

As we want children to be able to use a range of the ideas in their writing, we can also record them using a voice recorder. This can then be played to children, who can write down their favourite phrases. This resource can then be used at a later date by those who may need reinforcement and reminding.

When this activity was used with pupils in Year 6 they came up with these examples:

Darkness fell and the wind screamed through the trees, feeling every branch and leaf.

Slowly wandering through the depths of the overgrown forest, the wanderer came to an abandoned city.

Following these initial activities we can then model the writing of a setting. A range of other devices must be called upon to create an effective piece of writing, for example, similes, metaphors, personification, and alliteration, to create an effective description.

Once the pupils have completed their descriptions, the writing can be further developed. In the film *Chaperon Rouge,* the story becomes very tense when the heroine is chased by a pack of ethereal wolves. Below is an example, based on the film, that can be analysed by the pupils:

There was a cool breeze as she wandered between the tall trunks of the trees in the forest on the way to her Grandmother's house. She wrapped her scarlet cloak tightly around her and pulled up her hood before quickening her pace. It was slowly going dark; it was never a good idea to be out in the woods in the darkness. She heard footsteps behind her. She stopped. She listened. They had stopped too. She continued on her journey to her grandmother's house with the basket of treats for the old lady. There it was again ... footsteps. She hurried. There was rustling to her left. She ran. Something followed. She tripped. It was on top of her. Snarling. Growling. A wolf.

(Smith, 2014)

If you used this text, you could discuss how the pace is important while building tension; how short, snappy sentences build up a sense of panic or energy; and how three-, two- or even one-word sentences increase speed. You can show them how short sentences build tension, and longer ones relax it, allowing time for readers to catch their breath.

This case study shows how, with activities at each stage to help children to develop their vocabulary for writing, children's writing can be scaffolded from the initial description activity, into a sophisticated narrative.

Using film as a framework for writing

In the case study above, on the seaside, the stimulus was a soundtrack without images. The seaside is somewhere that the children may have visited or perhaps seen in film. The second case study uses film as the stimulus to writing, providing visual and auditory experiences as stimuli to writing. However, we sometimes ask children to write about things that many have not experienced. Many Year 6 teachers will recall an end of key stage assessment where the writing task was entitled: *How to look after a Miptor*. The task of writing an explanation of how to look after an imaginary creature may be challenging for many. To complete this task, children would first need to picture the creature in their heads, then imagine how to look after it, including habitat, daily routines etc, before thinking about how to write an explanation. For many children, this is a complex series of processes to go through, and they need to know how to approach these writing tasks. The case study below is not untypical of the tasks that are often given to children, and highlights the importance of teaching children how to approach writing tasks, to enable them to produce work that reflects their ability.

CASE STUDY

Story openers

Stephen, a Year 5 teacher, asked the children to write the opening to a narrative, adding in some of the features that they had been taught previously. The task instructions and success criteria were vague: *Write a story opening; set in the desert; it starts with someone chasing you.*

Stephen then gave the children five minutes thinking time and five minutes writing time.

One pupil wrote:

'Help,' I shouted as I was running from the bogie man. I was screaming it was me and my team mate but he died because the bogie man killed him because of his heavy bogies squashing him to death.

Activity 2

» *This piece of writing is not what you would expect from an average nine-year-old. Why do you think this is?*

» *How might the teacher improve the lesson to enable the child to write more imaginatively?*

To improve the lesson above, and give children the opportunity to demonstrate what they are capable of, you could ask the children to consider the following:

• What is it like in the desert?

• What could be chasing me?

• How do I set out the opening of a narrative?

• What vocabulary will be most effective?

• Shall I reveal what is chasing me or leave it until later?

• Am I writing in the first or third person?

• What punctuation do I need to use?

• Which connectives should I be using?

• How much does the teacher want me to write?

• What is the person next to me writing?

• How long do we have left to do this?

All of these questions need to be considered and discussed as part of the writing process. In a typical lesson, children may have quite a short time to answer all of those questions, formulate a response and then write. However, if we omit this process then the writing suffers considerably, as can be seen in the case study above.

One solution could be to spend time reading extracts from similar narratives that have similar openings; extracts that pupils could consciously magpie, that is, deliberately use ideas from. However, this solution is certainly costly in terms of time. It may, perhaps, require 2–3 hour sessions analysing the text with children, discussing how the author includes tension, uses sentence structure for pace, and ends on a cliff-hanger. And, where do we find these extracts? Teachers can recommend texts to each other in the staffroom, read blogs by other teachers, read the bibliographies in books such as this one or in other academic books. Or perhaps we can also use extracts from film. The case study below shows how effective this can be.

CASE STUDY

Replay

Sarah, a Year 2 teacher, showed the class the opening 20 seconds of a beautiful French animated film by Anthony Voisin called *Replay* (https://vimeo.com/4427887).

In this section of film, the children could see an unidentified figure running across a desert. The figure is breathing heavily. She runs towards a door of a bunker and opens it with an airlock. The figure shuts the door behind her and removes a gas mask, once an all-clear light flashes. All of this takes 20 seconds.

After the children had watched this film, Sarah asked them to write a description of the scene that they had seen.

One pupil wrote:

Running for her life the figure was. Her oxygen mask was going from her dark dirty mask. It started beeping then she could hear rustling in the trees braskling in the bracken. Her footsteps were getting louder and louder then she opened the big heavy metal door.

While this was perhaps not the best piece of writing in the class, it was the most that this pupil had written all term. The child not only wrote more than he usually did, but he also gained confidence as a writer. The reason for this is perhaps that the film answers these three main questions: Where is the setting? Who is the character? What is happening?

Activity 3

» *Why do you think that providing these starting points helped this child's writing?*

» *How could you build on this to support children's confidence in their ability to write?*

» *What other resources could you use?*

The case study shows how film can eliminate some key questions that the children may have, and help them to focus on what is important; so the learner has a framework to build their language around. They are then able to focus on the sentence structures and vocabulary. In this short piece, the writer has been able to introduce the following:

• a verb opener (Running ...);

• attempted use of the passive voice (running for her life the figure was);

- repetition of comparative adjectives (louder and louder);

- an increased number of adjectives, from one to five;

- a change to it being written in the third person – the writer has visualised the events happening to someone else;

- use of an expanded noun (big heavy metal door) and adverbial phrases (running for her life).

Watching a film can have an immediate impact on writers. It gives them a mental model on which they can build their own language. It delivers a structure that can easily be built upon by any writer. The use of film in this way ensures the task is accessible to all and not dependent on writers' reading ability or wider experiences.

Activity 4: Writing an opener

» *Watch an appropriate film and copy this method of describing the scene.*

» *Write your own opener.*

» *Use this in your teaching to model writing an opener using this technique. The children could then use the list of key questions to improve your description.*

Conclusion

As with every task you set in class, you need to ask yourself: What am I asking the children to do? What do I want them to be able to do at the end of it?

If it is to be able to write a description, some dialogue or a news report, then perhaps a piece of text is not always the best starting piece. If a child is spending 30 minutes decoding a text or highlighting key phrases or analysing the structure in order to write a piece of narrative, then this can be rather frustrating and time consuming. Perhaps film or an image can be a more immediate alternative. Another advantage of this is that it does not limit children's creativity. If the trigger is an image or a piece of film, then children have no written model to imitate; they can find their own writing style. Film and image is therefore an important tool in any teacher's classroom to inspire writing of all kinds.

Critical points

» *Visual literacy is the ability to interpret and make meaning from information presented in the form of an image or film – put simply: the ability to read an image or film.*

» *Films and images allow the pupils to become immersed in the experience, which then allows them to draw upon it for their writing.*

» *Children will not be exposed to new vocabulary in the same way that they are when reading a text. However, with modelling by the teacher and sharing new vocabulary, pupils will develop a more advanced working vocabulary and a more advanced writing style. In other words, it will take them beyond early writing.*

Critical reflections

» *This chapter does not argue that using film and image is a more effective tool for teaching writing than the traditional text-based methods. However, it is another tool to add to your toolbox of teaching strategies. The major differences are the level of engagement for all pupils and those children with a lower level of decoding ability, who are also not excluded from the task. Film and image get children engaged and hooked on a topic. They become enthused and they want to write. It is experiencing children's desire to write that is most enjoyable to see as a teacher in the classroom.*

» *Think about where you could use visual imagery and film in your teaching. Think cross-curricular. How could this support children who have difficulties accessing text? How could you use this strategy to stretch more able children's learning?*

Taking it further

The following texts provide ideas for working with digital and graphic texts:

Athique, A (2013) *Digital Media and Society an Introduction*. Cambridge: Polity Press.

Bakis, M (2012) *The Graphic Novel Classroom*. London: Corwin Books.

Dearne, E and Wolstenoroft, H (2007) *Visual Approaches to Teaching Writing*. London: Sage

BFI (2003) Look Again. A Teaching Guide to Using Film and Television with 3–11 Year Olds. [online] Available at: www.bfi.org.uk/sites/bfi.org.uk/files/downloads/bfi-education-look-again-teaching-guide-to-film-and-tv-2013-03.pdf (accessed 23 November 2014).

Lankshear, C and Knobel, M (2009) *New Literacies: Everyday Practices and Classroom Learning*, 2nd Edn. Oxford: Oxford University Press.

Literacy Shed Film Extracts. [online] Available at: www.literacyshed.com/ (accessed 23 November 2014).

References

Biemiller, A and Boote, C (2006) An Effective Method for Building Meaning Vocabulary in Primary Grades. *Journal of Educational Psychology*, 98: 44–62.

Clark, C (2014) Children's and Young People's Reading 2013. Findings from the 2013 National Literacy Trust's Annual Survey. National Literacy Trust. [online] Available at: www.literacytrust.org.uk (accessed 23 November 2014).

Clark, C (2013) Children's and Young People's Reading 2013. Findings from the 2012 National Literacy Trust's Annual Survey. [online] Available at: www.literacytrust.org.uk (accessed 23 November 2014).

Dahl, R (1964) *Charlie and the Chocolate Factory*. New York: Alfred A Kopf, Inc.

Department for Education (2013) *The National Curriculum in England Framework Document: For Teaching*. London: DfE.

Jenkins, R (2008) Visual Literacy. *Teaching and Learning*, 30 July/August: 4–8. [online] Available at: www.teachingexpertise.com/articles/visual-literacy-3961 (accessed 12 February 2015).

Nodelman, P (1988) *Words about Pictures. The Narrative Art of Children's Picture Books*. London: University of Georgia Press.

Smith, R (2014) The Literacy Shed. [online] Available at: www.literacyshed.com/ (accessed 23 November 2014).

8 Grammar and punctuation through writing

DAVID WAUGH

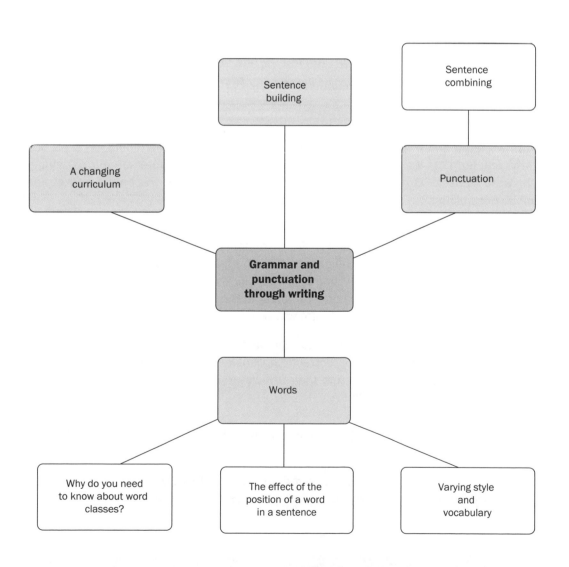

Teachers' Standards

3 Demonstrate good subject and curriculum knowledge

- have a secure knowledge of the relevant subject(s) and curriculum areas, foster and maintain pupils' interest in the subject, and address misunderstandings

- demonstrate an understanding of and take responsibility for promoting high standards of literacy, articulacy and the correct use of standard English, whatever the teacher's specialist subject

- if teaching early reading, demonstrate a clear understanding of systematic synthetic phonics

Critical questions

» *How can you engage children's interest in grammar?*

» *How can you develop children's grammatical understanding through writing?*

» *What is your role in developing grammar through writing?*

» *How can you help children to understand appropriate grammatical terminology?*

Introduction

How do we learn about grammar? Is it through formal lessons which focus on a particular grammatical term? Is it through exercises which invite us to complete sentences using particular word classes? Or is it through using grammatical features in context and exploring linguistic possibilities?

In this chapter, it is argued that grammatical terminology is best understood through purposeful activity which involves engaging with grammatical features through talking, reading and writing. This writing can often be shared, with the teacher modelling, inviting children's ideas, and drafting, editing and revising text. You will read examples of teachers who have taught grammar successfully by making it integral to their writing lessons. As the influential *Grammar for Writing* (DfEE, 2000, p 7) stated:

> the purpose of teaching grammar is not simply the naming of parts of speech, nor is it to provide arbitrary rules for 'correct' English. It is about making children aware of key grammatical principles and their effects, to increase the range of choices open to them when they write.

Activity 1: What do you remember about learning grammar at school?

» *Do you remember being taught about grammar at school? Was this done as part of general literacy work or did you have discrete lessons on grammar?*

FOCUS ON RESEARCH

Giving a purpose for grammatical knowledge

Myhill et al (2012) examined ways of developing children's writing and discovered that actively engaging children with grammar through writing was more effective than teaching grammar as a separate topic. They found that children were less likely to see the purpose of grammatical knowledge when it was taught out of the context of actual writing, and asserted that children can become more aware of the *infinite possibilities* of the English language through studying how language works, and that this can enable them to evaluate others' language use. They suggest that:

> ... a writing curriculum which draws attention to the grammar of writing in an embedded and purposeful way at relevant points in the learning is a more positive way forward. In this way, young writers are introduced to what we have called 'a repertoire of infinite possibilities', explicitly showing them how different ways of shaping sentences or texts, and ... different choices of words can generate different possibilities for meaning-making.
>
> (2012, p 3)

This view was outlined in *Grammar for Writing* (DfEE, 2000, p 12) which stated:

> Teaching at the point of writing ... focuses on demonstrating and exploring the decisions that writers make in the process of composition. Once embarked on, it soon becomes clear that the writing process model is not linear at all but iterative. Drafting, revising and sometimes the presentation of the text are all aspects of a common process involving constant rereading and improvement. Writers rarely draft without rereading and revising as they go.

A changing curriculum

Whenever a new curriculum initiative is taken, there is a tendency for the media to focus on some aspects without giving sufficient attention to the initiative as a whole. For the *Rose Review of Early Reading* (Rose, 2006) systematic synthetic phonics was the aspect which was given most prominence, while for the new *National Curriculum for English* (DfE, 2013) spelling, grammar and punctuation were focused upon. However, Rose stressed that children should learn to read within a language-rich curriculum and emphasised the importance of sharing literature with them. The national curriculum may devote a lot of space to spelling, punctuation and grammar, but it also stresses the value of sharing books and reading for pleasure. It also emphasises the importance of learning being integral rather than having necessarily discrete grammar lessons on terminology:

> Throughout the programmes of study, teachers should teach pupils the vocabulary they need to discuss their reading, writing and spoken language. It is important that pupils learn the correct grammatical terms in English and that these terms are integrated within teaching.
>
> (DfE, 2013, p 15)

The English national curriculum (DfE, 2013) places considerable emphasis on grammar and grammatical terminology, but makes it clear that much learning can occur through speaking, reading and writing:

> *The grammar of our first language is learnt naturally and implicitly through interactions with other speakers and from reading. Explicit knowledge of grammar is, however, very important, as it gives us more conscious control and choice in our language. Building this knowledge is best achieved through a focus on grammar within the teaching of reading, writing and speaking. Once pupils are familiar with a grammatical concept (for example 'modal verb'), they should be encouraged to apply and explore this concept in the grammar of their own speech and writing and to note where it is used by others. Young pupils, in particular, use more complex language in speech than in writing, and teachers should build on this, aiming for a smooth transition to sophisticated writing.*
>
> (DfE, 2013, p 66)

If you share a range of high quality texts with them, children can see what is possible: different ways of phrasing, interesting uses of language, authors' manipulation of language and even their creation of new words (look at Dahl's *The BFG*, for example).

Talk for Writing (DCSF, 2008) describes a teaching sequence for writing. This model shows how you should look at text, enjoy it, discuss the use of language, model writing, support and guide children as they attempt to replicate the genre in their own writing and lead them towards independent writing. This process will involve the use of grammatical terminology when discussing texts, and this terminology will be more readily acquired and better understood if it becomes part of the vocabulary of reading and writing. Consider, for a moment, a footballer who joins an English Premier League club from abroad. He may have no understanding of English, but he will quickly learn the English names for various aspects of football because he will hear words like *corner, penalty, off-side, foul* and *dive* in the context of the game. Every activity we undertake has a metalanguage and this is best learnt within the context of the activity – learning grammatical terminology is no different. Look at the example below.

Example: prepositional phrases

Do you understand what is meant by a prepositional phrase? Children are expected to know about prepositions from Year 3 and prepositional phrases are mentioned in the national curriculum from Year 4. Learned in isolation, the term might appear daunting, but if we start from a piece of text it soon becomes clear that we all use prepositional phrases, even though we may not know that that is what we are doing. In the following case study, you can see how a teacher introduced the idea of prepositional phrases to his class.

CASE STUDY

Prepositional phrases

Curtis wanted his Year 4 class to write simple poems which followed a pattern, with four lines of each verse being prepositional phrases and the final line identifying what was being described. He began by playing a video of *Inside, Outside, Upside Down* by Stan and Jan Berenstain in which a bear climbs into a box and has an adventure which involves being upside down, inside a box etc. Curtis asked the children what all the phrases in the video told them, and they talked about the way in which they all informed them about the bear's position.

Next, Curtis wrote a short poem on the board and read it to and then with the class.

Far away from here

Between Africa and America

Beneath the crashing waves

Deep under the sea

Lies a rotting ship

He asked the children to discuss the poem and to think about how the last line was different from the others. He then asked them to help him to write the next verse about the rotting ship. Curtis asked for suggestions for the different objects they might see, and he wrote some of their ideas on the board. These included: *a treasure chest, a cargo of gold, some mysterious boxes* and, gruesomely, *the bones of an old pirate*.

Children used mini-whiteboards to try out phrases which might describe the position of their chosen items, and discussed, in pairs, ways of developing and improving their writing. They then shared their ideas with the class and Curtis wrote some of the verses on the board. Some were incomplete and he used this as an opportunity to invite others to suggest how they might be finished. It was at this point that he began to use the term prepositional phrases to describe the phrases and he asked children to say what these might be and how they could define them.

A display of the children's verses was put up with the heading *Prepositional Phrases*, and Curtis ensured that this was referred to whenever such a phrase appeared in a child's writing or a story or poem.

Words

Part of your role in teaching writing involves helping children to understand words and how to use them. They need to understand that some words are useful and usable in most contexts, but that some are more or less appropriate when writing certain genres. Corbett and

Strong (2011) state that it is vital that children understand what words mean, if they are to be able to understand text. They describe *generative grammar* as '*the underlying principle that informs "talking the text". It is the brain's extraordinary ability to internalise underlying patterns of language through the constant experience of hearing sentences and then to use those patterns to create new utterances*' (p 9). So if you draw upon a teaching sequence for writing to structure your work with children, it is important that when you talk with them about different genres or text types you enable them to understand key vocabulary. Delahunty and Garvey (2010) have considered the use of words in context.

FOCUS ON RESEARCH

Registers and words

Although most of the words we use every day can be used in almost any context, many words of the language are restricted to uses in certain fields, disciplines, professions, or activities, ie, **registers***. For example, the word phoneme is restricted to the linguistic domain. Interestingly, some words may be used in several domains with a different meaning in each, though these meanings may be a specific version of a more general meaning. For example, the word morphology is used in linguistics to refer to the study of the internal structure of words and their derivational relationships; in botany to refer to the forms of plants; in geology to refer to rock formations. The general, abstract meaning underlying these specific meanings is the study of form.*

(Delahunty and Garvey, 2010, p 138)

Varying style and vocabulary

What does this mean when you are teaching writing? You need to discuss different genres with children and show them how style and vocabulary vary according to the text type they are using (see Chapter 3). The 2013 national curriculum for England mentions *audience* several times. A key aim in the national curriculum is to ensure that all pupils:

*   write clearly, accurately and coherently, adapting their language and style in and for a range of contexts, purposes and audiences

You should, therefore, constantly seek opportunities to talk about words and their meanings. This includes looking at how words are used in context and at ways in which they can be modified according to how they are used. For example, look at the sentence below:

Rachel was happy.

You can change the meaning of the sentence by adding one morpheme – in this case the prefix un-:

Rachel was unhappy.

If you were to focus on this prefix with children you might go on to look at other words which can be modified by adding *un-* (*lucky, fortunate, kind* etc). If you do this orally and then in writing, you can reinforce children's understanding of how words are constructed and help them to read unfamiliar words which begin with *un-*. You can do the same thing with other prefixes and might even give some children the task of changing sentences to an opposite meaning, using a range of different prefixes *(im-, in-, ir-, dis-)*. You can also explore suffixes and the effect they have upon words, for example: *hope* and *hopeful, love* and *lovable, like* and *likeness*.

Through talking about language and listening to language, children develop the *generative grammar* Corbett described earlier. By articulating our own thought processes during shared writing, we can further embed this. For example, you might take the sentence *Rachel was unhappy* and say:

> *Now, Rachel* was *unhappy, which means that she might not be now. What shall I do to show that she still is unhappy? I know, I'll change* was *to is* and get *Rachel is* unhappy. *But what if I knew that something good was about to happen, what would I write then? I know, I'll change* is *to will be* and *unhappy to happy, and I might even add a word to show when she will be happy. I could use* soon *or* tomorrow *or* next week*, or even add an extra phrase or clause like* when her dad comes back from Leeds.

Why do you need to know about word classes?

When discussing texts, it is useful to have a language for discussion. It becomes simpler to talk about the way in which an author uses adjectives rather than *describing words*, especially as adjectives are not the only type of describing words.

A shared vocabulary or metalanguage can also be useful when you want to set targets for children's writing such as:

> *Ensure you make use of adverbs to show how different actions were performed, or Try to avoid repeating a person's name too often by using pronouns instead sometimes.*

When we learn a second language, we usually find that this involves using the names of word classes. In most other countries in Europe children learn these terms in primary school and are able to talk about language in an informed way. Horton and Bingle (2014, p 17) argue that terminology should be introduced when children are exploring and using language:

> *You would not teach children to swim without introducing terms such as breast stroke, front crawl and sculling in order to communicate precise meaning and it is more than likely that you would do this whilst swimming. It is no different from teaching children about language: terms such as adverbial, subordinate clause and collective noun can all be used effectively whilst engaged in a writing activity. The use of a metalanguage will give children the tools with which to discuss choices and manipulate language confidently and powerfully.*

The effect of the position of a word in a sentence

Many English words can belong to more than one word class, depending upon how they are used or where they are placed in a sentence. This can be very confusing for children, but if you model writing and talk about the way in which you use words, you can help them to understand.

For instance, compare:

I swim every day

and

On Mondays I go for a swim

It is easy to see that the word *swim* is a verb in the first sentence (it is preceded by a subject). If you were to substitute this word with another, you would have to choose another verb, for example, *walk, skip, steal, drive.*

In the second example, however, the word *swim* is preceded by a determiner, *a*, and is an object following the verb *go*. If you substituted another word it would have to be a noun or noun phrase, such as *coffee, pint, meal, nap, ride on my bike, lie down in a darkened room.*

Words which can be used in more than one class are sometimes called *open-class items*, while those which can be used in only one class are known as *closed-class items*.

Just to add to any confusion, new usages often use a verb as a noun, for example:

It's a big ask. (instead of *demand*)

or a noun as a verb:

Please text me. (instead of *send me a text*)

This is nothing new: Shakespeare not only invented many new words, such as *bedroom, assassination* and *uneducated*, but also changed usages, as in the Duke of York's: *Tut, tut, **grace** me no grace, nor **uncle** me no uncle!* (from Richard II).

Activity 2: Word classes

» *Lots of English words can belong to more than one class. Look at the words below and try using them in sentences to see how many different word classes they could each belong to:*

   – *light*

   – *stream*

   – *fast*

   – *play*

   – *chair*

Sentence building

All of this may seem very simple and obvious, but it is a vital part of children's language development and shows them how the grammar of our language works in action. You can use terms like *past* and *present tense* and *future*. You can talk about *happy* being an adjective and you can say that *was, is* and *will be* are verbs. If you use those terms as you model and articulate our writing, they will be much more meaningful to children than if you tried to give them definitions and exercises to check that they could remember them.

In the following case study this way of working is developed further.

CASE STUDY

Random sentence creation

Grace wanted to encourage her Year 3 class to think about sentence construction while becoming familiar with some key word classes. She made sets of word cards which included nouns, verbs, adjectives, adverbs, prepositions, conjunctions and determiners. Grace was mindful that some of the words could belong to more than one word class, depending upon how they were used, and she considered using different coloured card for each word class, but decided that this might lead to later misconceptions. Children were given mini-whiteboards and pens, in pairs.

Grace explained to the class that they were going to play a game in which they would build sentences, and asked one child to choose a word from the pile of nouns, hold it up and read it to the class. Marc picked up a card which had the word *house* on it. Grace then invited the pairs of children to think of any adjectives which could go with the noun and to write them on their whiteboards. She asked children to read their adjectives out to the class and these included: *old, large, beautiful, small, pretty* and *mysterious*. She then asked Jade to choose a card from the determiners pile and she chose *that*. Grace asked the children to put the word *that* before their adjectives and wrote some examples on the board, including:

That old house

That dark house

That beautiful house

Grace asked the children if these were sentences, and they agreed that something else was needed to make them complete. Geeta suggested that the phrases needed verbs to become sentences, and when asked to suggest some verbs which could be added, she suggested *That old house smells*. The pairs were asked to make suggestions on their whiteboards and Grace shared these with the class.

Grace followed this up in subsequent lessons with differentiated activities, preceded by shared writing, in which some children completed sentences using various word classes; some added phrases and clauses; and some wrote part-sentences for each other to complete.

Activity 3: Terminology for Year 3

In Year 3 children are expected to know the following terms: adverb, preposition conjunction, prefix, clause, subordinate clause. How could you help children to understand these terms through meaningful activities such as those used by Grace in the case study?

You can, then, look at words with children to explore their meanings and to see how they can be used within text to convey meaning. In the following case study a teacher devises an activity which might be used with different age groups to look at words and sentences.

CASE STUDY

Sentence Countdown

Sidra discovered that many of the children in her Year 5 class enjoyed the TV programme *Countdown*, especially the *Word games* in which people take letters and then have to make the longest word possible using as many of the letters as possible.

Sidra decided to try a variation on the game using words instead of letters. She created two sets of word cards; one which included several words from the national curriculum spelling list for Years 5–6, and another which comprised all of the 100 most common words.

Table 8.1 *The 100 most common words in the English language, in order of frequency (Masterson et al, 2003)*

the	are	Do	About	And
up	me	Got	A	Had
down	their	To	my	Dad
people	said	her	big	Your
in	what	when	put	He
there	it's	could	I	Out
see	house	of	this	Looked
old	it	have	very	Too
was	went	look	by	You
be	don't	day	they	Like
come	made	on	some	Will

time	she	so	into	I'm
is	not	back	if	For
then	from	help	at	Were
children	Mrs	his	go	Him
called	but	little	Mr	Here
that	as	get	off	With
no	just	asked	all	Mum
now	saw	we	one	came
make	can	them	oh	an

In the *Countdown* game contestants choose either consonants or vowels. Sidra explained that the children were going to choose either common words or spelling list words, but that they would need to choose from both piles.

She tried the activity with a small group first, asking each child to make eight choices from word piles which were turned face down. Once everyone had a set of eight words, children had to rearrange them to make the longest possible sentence using as many of the words as possible. Sidra encouraged the children to spread the words out, read them carefully and ask for help if they were unsure about meanings, and to experiment with different orders. She found that children were quite competitive and that there were some arguments over who *owned* which word, so she decided to modify the game by getting children to work in pairs to create sentences and then ask other pairs on each table of six to help them to add words or rephrase where possible. She then made the game a competition between tables rather than individuals and this led to a more co-operative and much more productive lesson.

Children were asked to write their sentences down as a record of what they had done and to help them learn and remember spellings.

Sidra's activity not only focused children's attention on some of the spellings they would need to learn from the Year 5–6 spelling list, but it also allowed them to focus on features of sentence construction and word order.

Punctuation

Let's eat Granny!

Let's eat, Granny!

If you can see the difference placing a comma between eat and Granny has upon the meaning of the above sentences, you understand the importance of punctuation. Yet punctuation presents a hurdle for writers which some never quite seem to surmount, and this is evident in shops, streets and even students' essays.

Activity 4: Punctuation

»   *Look at the examples below and punctuate them so that they make more sense:*

–   *Thank you! Your donation just helped someone. Get a job!*

–   *My hobbies are cooking my family and my dog.*

–   *Gate in constant use illegally parked cars will be clamped.*

The way in which we punctuate has changed over many centuries. In fact, many early texts did not use punctuation and did not have spaces between words. It was only after the invention of printing in the fifteenth century that punctuation was gradually standardised. It was not until the eighteenth century that punctuation began to look as it does today, and even then there were examples which we might now find confusing.

Bunting (1997, p 44) maintained that '*We need to recognise that there are two main aspects of punctuation: rules which must be used and conventions which are more open to interpretation*'. She gave examples of rules including:

•   capital letters at the beginning of sentences;

•   full stops at the end of sentences;

•   question marks at the end of sentences which are questions;

•   apostrophes to mark elision (*don't*) and possession (*John's*) (*its* is the possessive exception).

However, some uses of punctuation can be more flexible and authors may choose, for example, to use exclamation marks for emphasis rather than full stops, or they might use dashes rather than brackets to separate a subordinate clause or phrase. Some writers use more commas than others, while colons and semi-colons are often used rather than full stops when authors wish to link clauses. Punctuation is often thought to be a device for separating items in sentences and paragraphs, but it can also be used to draw things together. This can be the case when we combine sentences to link items and to help our writing to flow. A key part of shared writing should be to show children how they can reshape their writing using conjunctions and punctuation.

Sentence combining

Sentence combining

Andrews et al (2004, p 2) concluded, from a study on sentence-combining:

Taking into account the results and conclusions of the accompanying in-depth review on the teaching of formal grammar (Andrews et al., 2004), the main implication for policy of the current review is that the national curriculum in England and accompanying guidance needs to be revised to take into account the findings of research: that the teaching of formal grammar (and its derivatives) is ineffective; and the teaching of sentence combining is one (of probably a number of) method(s) that is effective.

In the following case study, you can see how a teacher drew upon sentence combining to address children's punctuation problems, while encouraging them to look carefully at different ways of presenting information.

CASE STUDY

Sentence combining

Ella's Year 6 class included several children who often used commas to link sentences where colons or semi-colons would be correct. Once SATs were over, the children were going on a residential visit to Whitby on the North Yorkshire Coast and some of their literacy work was focused on preparations for this. Ella decided to make use of the things children were discovering from internet searches, leaflets, brochures and books to model sentence combining and to encourage children to draw similar items together, while separating others.

She began a shared writing session by asking each pair of children to prepare two interesting *facts* they had discovered about Whitby and to write these on mini-whiteboards to share with the class. Ella then asked one pair to share one fact and wrote this on the board:

Whitby is a fishing port.

She then asked if anyone else had information about Whitby as a fishing port and wrote on the board:

There is a fish market next to the harbour.

Cod and haddock are caught within 19 kilometres of the coast at Whitby.

There are lots of excellent fish and chip shops in Whitby.

From May to August, salmon can be caught from small boats in the River Esk and near Whitby harbour.

Lobsters and brown and velvet crabs are important to Whitby's fishing industry.

Ella explained that while a single sentence which combined all of the facts might be challenging for readers, it would be possible to combine some of the sentences and to save words and avoid repetition. She modelled this by taking some of the facts and combining them into longer sentences:

Whitby, which has lots of excellent fish and chip shops, is a fishing port with a fish market next to the harbour.

Cod and haddock are caught within 19 kilometres of the coast, while from May to August, salmon can be caught from small boats in the River Esk and near the harbour.

Ella discussed the use of commas to separate the subordinate clauses in the above sentences and talked about ways in which conjunctions such as with and while can draw clauses together. She went on to look at the use of colons and semi-colons to link clauses and modelled some examples:

Whitby is a fishing port: cod, haddock, salmon, lobsters and brown and velvet crabs can all be found there.

There are lots of excellent fish and chip shops in Whitby; hardly surprising since so many kinds of fish are caught nearby.

By working with her class and modelling sentence combining and the manipulation of text, Ella helped them to understand conjunctions, clauses and subordinate clauses, and the functions of punctuation marks. She followed this up by encouraging them to look critically at examples of each other's writing and to suggest ways in which it might be developed and improved by using some of these devices. *Grammar for Writing* maintained that:

> *By structuring and restructuring ideas in writing, children extend their powers of imagination, learn to express increasingly complex, abstract and logical relationships, develop skills of reasoning and critical evaluation. This, in turn, feeds back into their competence as thinkers and speakers.*
>
> (DfEE, 2000, p 8)

Conclusion

Because many of us were either not taught about some aspects of grammar or were taught them badly, there can be a tendency to avoid these elements when we teach. However, quite apart from the demands made by the curriculum, there is an intrinsic value in understanding more about our language and being able to create a language for discussing it with the children you teach. If you make learning about grammar integral to children's reading and writing rather than separating it into discrete lessons, you will enable them to reflect upon their language usage and that of others.

Critical points

» *Children's grammatical understanding can be developed through writing if you make use of modelling and discussion.*

» *You can engage children's interest in grammar by providing meaningful activities.*

» *The teacher's role in developing grammar through writing includes modelling the writing process, talking about writing, prompting discussions and guiding children's writing.*

» *Children can be helped to understand appropriate grammatical terminology through meaningful activities which involve a range of language features and which lead naturally to discussion of grammatical terminology.*

Critical reflections

» *How secure do you feel about your own knowledge and understanding of punctuation and grammar? There are many excellent, readable texts which explain key aspects in an engaging way with lots of practical ideas. It is worth exploring some of those mentioned below, even if you feel quite confident, as they will help you to understand some misconceptions that children have.*

Taking it further

For practical ideas underpinned by research and linked to the national curriculum:

Horton, S and Bingle, B (2014) *Lessons in Teaching Grammar in Primary Schools*. London: Sage.

To develop your own subject knowledge and for lesson ideas:

Waugh, D, Allott, K, Waugh, R, English, E and Bulmer, E (2014) *The Spelling, Punctuation and Grammar App*. Morecambe: ChildrenCount. (Available through The App. Store)

For an entertaining and informative look at punctuation:

Truss, L (2009) *Eats, Shoots & Leaves: The Zero Tolerance Approach to Punctuation*. London: Profile Books.

To find out more about grammar, spelling and punctuation try:

Crystal, D (2005) *How Language Works*. London: Penguin

and

Horton, S and Bingle, B (2014) *Lessons in Teaching Grammar in Primary Schools*. London: Sage Learning Matters

and

Waugh, D, Warner, C and Waugh, R (2013) *Teaching Grammar, Punctuation and Spelling in Primary Schools.* London: Sage Learning Matters.

References

Andrews, R, Torgerson, C, Beverton, S, Freeman, A, Locke, T, Low, G, Robinson, A and Zhu, D (2004) *The Effect of Grammar Teaching (Sentence Combining) in English on 5 to 16 Year Olds' Accuracy and Quality in Written Composition. Review Written by the English Review Group. Eppi.* London: Social Science Research Unit, Institute of Education, University of London.

Berenstain, S and Berenstain, J (2014) Inside, Outside, Upside Down. [online] Available at: www.youtube.com/watch?v=UM4badeqfA4 (accessed 12 February 2015).

Bunting, R (1997) *Teaching about Language in the Primary Years.* London: David Fulton.

Corbett, P and Strong, J (2011) *Talk for Writing Across the Curriculum.* Maidenhead: Open University Press.

Delahunty, G P and Garvey, J J (2010). *The English Language: From Sound to Sense. Perspectives on Writing.* Fort Collins, CO: The WAC Clearinghouse and Parlor Press. [online] Available at: http://wac.colostate.edu/books/sound/ (accessed 12 February 2015).

DCSF (2008) *Talk for Writing.* London: DCSF.

DfE (2013) *The National Curriculum in England: Framework Document.* London: DfE.

DfEE (2000) *Grammar for Writing.* London: DfEE.

Horton, S and Bingle, B (2014) *Lessons in Teaching Grammar in Primary Schools.* London: Sage.

Masterson, J, Stuart, M, Dixon, M and Lovejoy, S (2003) *Children's Printed Word Database: Economic and Social Research CouncilF funded project* (Ref: R00023406). Nottingham: DCSF.

Myhill, D A, Jones, S M, Lines, H and Watson, A (2012) Re-Thinking Grammar: The Impact Of Embedded Grammar Teaching On Students' Writing And Students' Metalinguistic Understanding. *Research Papers in Education*, 27(2): 139–66.

Rose, J (2006) *The Independent Review of the Teaching of Early Reading: Final Report.* London: DfES.

Answers

Activity 2: Word classes

You were asked to look at the following words and try using them in sentences to see how many different word classes they could each belong to: light, stream, fast, play, chair.

Word	Possible uses
light	I decided to light the fire (verb) The car was light blue (adjective) I switched on the light (noun)

stream	The stream flowed rapidly (noun) The crowd began to stream out of the stadium (verb)
fast	I am going to fast this week (verb) I am going on a fast (noun) He drove a fast car (adjective) He ran fast (adverb)
play	We went to see a play at the theatre (noun) One day I will play for the Rovers (verb) The children had a play fight (adjective)
chair	She was chosen to chair the meeting (verb) The chair was brown (noun)

Activity 3: Terminology for Year 3

You were asked how you could help children to understand the following terms through meaningful activities: adverb, preposition conjunction, prefix, clause, subordinate clause, direct speech, inverted commas (or speech marks). There are many possibilities, but you will find one example for each below:

Term	Possible activities
adverb	Ask children to perform actions like walking or sitting in different ways – walk slowly, sit smartly etc.
preposition	Give children a soft toy or other item and a box and ask them to work together to find as many positions as possible for the toy and the box and to record them – on the box, in, under, inside, beneath, above etc.
conjunction	Ask children to write short sentences on mini-whiteboards and then give some children conjunctions to write on separate whiteboards. Get all the children with conjunctions to hold up their words and ask the others to suggest conjunctions which could join at least two of their sentences together.
prefix	Play a partner game. Give each child a card with a word which could be modified with a prefix. Give some children cards with prefixes and ask children to get into pairs with prefixes which could match the words.
clause	Provide sets of clauses on cards and ask children to explore different ways of combining them by using conjunctions and/or punctuation.
subordinate clause	Provide simple sentences and ask children to say more about the subjects. They can then construct subordinate clauses which can be inserted in the sentences.

Activity 4: Punctuation

The sentences make more sense if they are punctuated as follows:

Thank you! Your donation just helped someone get a job.

My hobbies are cooking, my family, and my dog.

Gate in constant use. Illegally parked cars will be clamped.

9 Handwriting: the mentality and physicality of longhand

CAROLINE WALKER AND ALAN GLEAVES

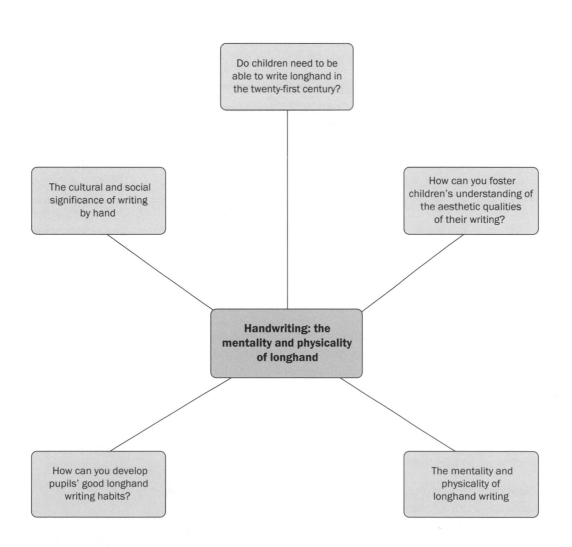

Teachers' Standards

5 Teaching to respond to the strengths and needs of all pupils

- know when and how to differentiate appropriately, using approaches which enable pupils to be taught effectively

- have a secure understanding of how a range of factors can inhibit pupils' ability to learn, and how best to overcome these

- demonstrate an awareness of the physical, social and intellectual development of children, and know how to adapt teaching to support pupils' education at different stages of development

- have a clear understanding of the needs of all pupils – including those with special educational needs, those of high ability, those with English as an additional language and those with disabilities – and be able to use and evaluate distinctive teaching approaches to engage and support them

Critical questions

» *What does the national curriculum say about children's handwriting development?*

» *Is writing by hand a culturally and socially significant activity?*

» *Do children need to be able to write longhand in the twenty-first century?*

» *How can teachers foster and develop children's understanding of the aesthetic qualities of their writing?*

» *How can teachers develop pupils' good longhand writing habits?*

» *What do teachers need to know and understand about the mentality and physicality of longhand writing from the perspective of individual pupils' capabilities?*

Introduction: handwriting and the primary national curriculum

The new primary national curriculum for England that appeared in 2013 contains explicit statements on inclusion, numeracy and mathematics, and language and literacy. Within the statement on language and literacy (Statement 6), the curriculum document states (2013, p 10):

> *Teachers should develop pupils' spoken language, reading, writing and vocabulary as integral aspects of the teaching of every subject.*

Expanding upon this theme, Paragraph 6.3 makes clear that:

> *Teachers should develop pupils' reading and writing in all subjects to support their acquisition of knowledge.*

And furthermore, that:

> *Pupils should develop the stamina and skills to write at length, with accurate spelling and punctuation.*

Before we even consider the research and practice-based issues related to children's writing, the curriculum alone makes it very clear that not only is handwriting a critical ability that all children should possess, but also that it should be viewed as a universal curriculum issue: that is, teachers should have expectations of children's handwriting proficiency across the whole curriculum. Aspects of handwriting skill and ability constitute statutory requirements in much of the national curriculum. For example, the Year 2 programme of study states that pupils should be taught to:

* form lower-case letters of the correct size relative to one another;

* start using some of the diagonal and horizontal strokes needed to join letters and understand which letters, when adjacent to one another, are best left unjoined;

* write capital letters and digits of the correct size, orientation and relationship to one another and to lower-case letters;

* use spacing between words that reflects the size of the letters.

The development of writing by hand runs through the primary national curriculum as a thread, and focuses strongly on presentation, legibility, speed and the unique qualities of the written word that differentiate it from the spoken word:

> *Writing also depends on fluent, legible and, eventually, speedy handwriting.*
>
> (2013, p 15)
>
> *… (Pupils need to) … develop the physical skill needed for handwriting …*
>
> (p 19)
>
> *… (Pupils should be) … establishing good handwriting habits from the beginning.*
>
> (p 26)
>
> *… Joined handwriting should be the norm; pupils should be able to use it fast enough to keep pace with what they want to say.*
>
> (p 33)

But there is something very interesting and important about the way that the national curriculum makes its statutory statement on handwriting, and this is in the use of the phrase 'pupils should develop the stamina and skills to write at length …'. This asserts that not only are teachers responsible for the tangible outcomes of writing (the written product and its content), but also that teachers must foster and nurture specific elements of longhand writing that frequently act as impediments to children's development in this area, related equally to the emotional impact of *doing* handwriting, and the very physical and highly individual process of *doing* written work. Such matters form the basis of this chapter, *Handwriting: the mentality and physicality of longhand.*

The cultural and social significance of writing by hand

Long before the advent of digital devices, computers and smartphones, the novelist Ernest Hemingway, writing in the early to mid-twentieth century, was busy using technology to write his novels. According to a reporter in the *Los Angeles Times* (LA Times, 2011), Hemingway, long regarded as a novelist whose writing was grounded in escapade and experience, had two separate sides to his personality – a macho hard-living adventurer and a solitary recluse, spending weeks and months tapping away on his typewriter in his lodge in the American Mid-West. In fact, Hemingway's Swedish-made typewriter has become one of the most important literary relics of the twentieth century, and it was auctioned on Wednesday, 10 July 2013, selling for $65,000. Hemingway's predilection for typewriting was for a long time regarded as something of a contradiction, critics contrasting the artistic creativity of writing with the industrial productivity of typing.

With the passage of the mid- to late twentieth century, typing and, more recently, word-processing using desktop and laptop computers have become far less contentious as a means of expression, and for many writers and artists it is now commonplace as a means of writing. In fact, it is now longhand writing that has become highly unusual, and for many people, almost an anachronism! Roald Dahl, for example, has become famous for his stories that he wrote by hand in his garden shed, and J K Rowling well known for her handwritten notes penned while sitting in a café.

Longhand thus exerts a curious fascination that seems to go far beyond the immediately obvious aspects of writing that teachers seem to spend so much time on, that is, the planning, the structuring, the assembling content and the fine-tuning presentation. But it is the mixture of mentality and physicality of writing that is equally important; without understanding these elements of writing, teachers' work with children is ultimately less effective and meaningful. The ways in which children's ideas and language are converted into something as personal, unique and special as longhand writing thus merit a great deal of attention.

Do children need to be able to write longhand in the twenty-first century?

In an article published in the New York Review of Books blog, the poet Charles Simic (2011) proclaimed, '*writing with a pen or pencil on a piece of paper is becoming an infrequent activity*'. John McGregor (2012) agrees:

> *Pen and paper is always to hand. An idea or phrase can be grabbed and worked at while it's fresh. Writing on the page stays on the page, with its scribbles and rewrites and long arrows suggesting a sentence or paragraph be moved, and can be looked over and reconsidered. Writing on the screen is far more ephemeral – a sentence deleted can't be reconsidered.*

Well, most of us are completely familiar with the endless distractions of the internet, but does that mean children should only ever write using a pen and paper?

Many writers and educationalists have expressed the opinion that children do not really need to write longhand at all in the twenty-first century. They claim that the proliferation of digital devices, laptops and smartphones has replaced longhand writing, and that such gadgets and machines have made it easier for children to write better quality work (Chen, 2013; Hutchison et al, 2012; see also Chapter 13 of this book). According to these authors, taking away the personal physical interaction of the writing process releases pupils from the tyranny of writing and exposes greater possibilities for creative work (Eid et al, 2007). Not only that, but changing the primacy of expression from a bodily to a device-oriented approach, they argue, is more inclusive, creating a level playing field for children who, for cultural reasons, reasons of gender stereotyping and reasons of physical disability, supposedly cannot access manual writing in the same way as some other children. Sumner et al's (2014) work, for example, suggests that digital devices may offer a level of automatisation of writing for children with dyslexia that therefore allows more time for pupils to concentrate on spelling improvement.

However, recent research (James and Engelhardt, 2012) has shown that the act of writing causes us to engage more deeply with ideas and thus to remember more of what has been said or copied, since writing is not simply a physical process – it is what Berninger and Graham (1998) and Berninger and Amtmann (2004) term *language by hand*. Other research suggests that encouraging children to write with digital devices changes the emphasis of what is written to a more superficial emphasis on the presentation of visual ideas and extra features at the expense of their deeper significance for individual children, a process known as *feature overload* in general terms (Olchowka, 2014) and as cognitive redundancy in terms of the specific effects of particular media (Gleaves and Walker, 2013). Yet other research suggests that handwriting enables pupils to be more creative with their ideas, on the basis that with a digital device, children are hindered by the limitations of the software or the user-interface.

Notwithstanding the national curriculum, however, there are many reasons why children should write longhand wherever possible in the twenty-first century, and these will be developed through the course of this chapter, guiding teachers to consider these issues when engaging children in writing processes and tasks.

How can you foster children's understanding of the aesthetic qualities of their writing?

The experience of writing is not a one-dimensional process whose aim is merely to transmit knowledge and communicate effectively: it is far more than that; it is a sensual and visceral experience and the teaching of writing should emphasise this. In addition, teachers will find it helpful to foster in all children a gradual appreciation of the aesthetics of their writing as an inner reflection of what each child is capable of. This is ultimately an extremely significant diagnostic tool, not simply for writing development but also as a window into children's imaginative and emotional growth. The individuality of children writing with pens and paper is also an outlet for personalisation of creative expression and gives many children the opportunity to own and possess something that they do not necessarily have access to elsewhere in their lives.

In writing longhand, there is a unique relationship with the reader and between the reader and the writer. The stops and starts of the text, the blobs of ink as the writer writes furiously, the size of the writing, fluctuating between tiredness, passion, boredom, obligation and effort all conspire to making writing longhand an event of great intimacy and insight. The smell of the writer and their environment too is an insight into another world, the perfume, the dog, the tear marks, the lip-print: all of these are not possible in the realm of the digital writer, but it means that teachers should include these sensory elements of writing for all pupils.

A good place to start children's development of an appreciation of writing skill and practice is through the introduction of activities that are pleasurable for children, which give them an opportunity to produce objects and artefacts that give them a sense of accomplishment as well as effort and care.

CASE STUDY

Children's diaries and their personal writing diaries

A school in Yorkshire decided to give each child a diary which was theirs to decorate and use on a permanent and regular basis. This was felt to be a powerful way of letting children see the development of their own writing and relating it to a more multisensory approach to writing. This was especially important for very young children, where the use of pictures and drawings may complement short words or even individual letters in their diary. The staff decided it was critical to communicate to children two fundamental issues:

- First that the act of writing can be a joyful experience when it reflects a child's daily activities.

- Whether it is done on beautifully designed or recycled paper, the gradual changes in a children's writing are fascinating for children themselves, as they see shapes and sizes of letters and words transforming with time.

FOCUS ON RESEARCH

To have and to hold the handwritten word

For most people, acquiring and possessing objects that have some meaning to them, however small, is extremely important. A physical relationship between a person and an artefact appears to have more significance than we have hitherto realised, and this principle seems to apply to writing and reading. Rose (2011) suggests, for example, that readers of digital material are more distracted by surface features and less emotionally engaged with the ideas in the text. Similarly, writers of digital text (through keyboards or mobile devices such as tablets) are, according to Herring (2004) and Sefton-Green et al (2009), more detached from the written word, and less inclined to take ownership of its contents.

There are many possible reasons for this, such as the possibility that writing with a rapidly responsive digital device encourages writers to write in a more *pre-reflective* sense or that the multisensory nature of writing (movement, smell, unique appearance etc) adds an element of richness of meaning for both writer and reader. It seems that the proximity and intimacy of writing, where the pen is an extension of our body, somehow materialises the thoughts and ideas to a different level – a very visceral level that is simply not possible with a keyboard or a touch-sensitive device.

Activity 1: The sensuality of writing longhand

» *With a group of children, talk about letters and why people have written letters in the past and why they are still important today. Talk about the layout of letters and bring in examples of different kinds of letters, such as letters home from family members in the forces; love letters; letters to people in hospital; letters home from people in prison.*

» *Then lay out as many different kinds of paper as possible, in different textures, colours etc. In addition, set out multisensory objects that make each pupil's letter personal to them, such as perfume, little stickers, lipstick, furniture polish and so on.*

» *Ask each pupil to write a very short letter to anyone who they want to tell something to, choosing their own paper and extra effects. This activity works well for younger and older children, using either just words and pictures or longer pieces of text.*

How can you develop pupils' good longhand writing habits?

In terms of child development, children's capabilities expose themselves through a variety of tasks perceived in different ways according to the ethos of the classroom. In some classrooms, writing is a rite of passage, children's efforts only *earn* a place on the wall if they are of a particular standard or they conform to particular views of the appearance and quality of writing. For children whose esteem is low, or who, for whatever reason, have trouble forming and maintaining a consistent look of their writing, the physical expression becomes a traumatic experience, and the physical act of writing is therefore bound up with and related intrinsically to how they feel about themselves. The physical becomes the emotional, and feelings of anxiety pervade the physicality of writing so that possessing tools and even experimenting with them becomes a matter of anxiety, and children's resilience in handwriting may be eroded as a result. Therefore, happy and effective habits for good quality longhand writing are critical to the longer-term development of writing.

The physical act of writing is extremely demanding for many children, and a critical mass of imagination and creative capital can go some way toward facilitating children's development on these areas. One key issue for teachers to consider is, therefore, the relationship between drawing and writing by hand. For young children, especially, encouraging drawing using a range of pens and pencils is a good first step towards developing the confidence and capacity to engage in more sustained periods of writing.

CASE STUDY

Warming-up to write

In one school, the issue of longhand writing was addressed through periods of preparing to write. This took the form of an enjoyable process in the classroom, where children laid out their writing implements and then sat and did writing *warm-up* exercises to both strengthen their hands, warm them if they were cold and also help to emphasise the fact that writing is as much a physical as a mental process that can be improved through practice and the building of stamina. Warm-up exercises sometimes took the form of hand stretches and drawing shapes in the air, or more precise fine co-ordination activities, such as bead-threading, or ribbon or pipe-cleaner weaving, which also improve eye–hand co-ordination.

FOCUS ON RESEARCH

Handwriting automatically

Children's handwriting development begins in early infancy, in parallel with children's motor abilities and their predisposition to try and grasp objects and leave marks, or at least some evidence of their interaction with the concrete world. Despite this, however, neurological studies into child motor development have established that a child's cortico-spinal tract, which contains the major nerve fibres descending from the brain and extending to the tips of fingers, does not cease its development until the age of ten. Therefore, handwriting is not, and should therefore not be viewed as, a short-term skill that children must be taught and acquire, before moving on to other aspects of literacy (Medwell and Wray, 2007).

Indeed, handwriting is emerging as one of the most significant skills and abilities that any child possesses. A high level of what is known as *automaticity*, or the ability to have internalised the handwriting processes so that they are fluid and rapid, is one of the most significant factors in reducing a child's *cognitive load*. Cognitive load is, in turn, a critical factor in children's learning, since occupation with many mental activities means that children may not be able to devote conscious and subconscious effort to other skills, such as organisation, planning and, importantly, emotional regulation (Kellogg, 2001). A lack of emphasis on the fluency and automatic aspects of writing may inadvertently seriously disadvantage many children who are already struggling with other aspects of their learning development (Graham and Santangelo, 2012).

Activity 2

Children have varying ages at which they are ready to write longhand, and forming letters and words may take a great deal of time and effort. One important activity is to assist children in understanding what a good writing grip and position looks like.

» *To facilitate this, spend time in lessons modelling what a good pencil grip and pen grip looks like and helping children to develop self-assessment of their own writing process.*

» *Sit in front and to the side of children repeating the process slowly and steadily.*

» *Then engage the children in paired activities. Bring in mirrors for each pair of children and, for each pair, children can take it in turns to be the* helper *and the* helped: *helpers hold the mirror in front of partners for them to watch themselves writing to ensure that their pen holding position is good and their posture is good. Then children switch to being* helped.

The mentality and physicality of longhand writing

Children may have many reasons why they find the physical act of writing problematic, although their letter and writing production may be of high quality when they work slowly, closely and carefully. Conversely, children may have spatial difficulties when it comes to scaling letters and words appropriately on the page but may produce accurate and aesthetically beautiful writing for specific purposes. It is important to point out, therefore, that motor and spatial capability lie on a continuum of complexity and that there are many reasons why they predispose children to experiencing difficulty in particular areas.

For example, dyspraxia, dysgraphia, dyslexia, particular conditions affecting variously children's muscle tone and their visual conceptualisations of letter shape and their ability to represent text, may all contribute to a child's longhand writing capability, and teachers need to both foster and nurture approaches to writing that make a child's capability greater.

One very important consideration for teachers is the balance between clear longhand writing and children's individual creativity. Legibility is of course a key factor in the development of children's handwriting, but this should be facilitated while taking into account individual pupils' capabilities and their social and cultural backgrounds.

CASE STUDY

Creating a diverse and safe writing environment

In a culturally diverse school in the Midlands, children had differences in letter formation and traditions in writing that meant that their written work was different from some other children. In addition, many children had different abilities for different forms of writing – for example, some were good at copying letters but weaker at representing letters from their imaginations. In such cases, teachers used stencils of letters or all shapes and sizes, and children practised outlining the letters many times, with different pens and pencils, and from small movement writing using fine muscular control, to large-scale movement using whole arms and even walking around letters placed on the floor. Aside from developing children's ability to produce well-formed letters and handwriting, teachers also constructed a safe and happy writing environment, prioritising writing as a means to personal expression.

FOCUS ON RESEARCH

Handwriting and dyspraxia

Developmental dyspraxia is commonly known as a condition that is associated with the incomplete development of movement organisation in the brain and, as such, the brain does not process information in the fullest and most efficient way for other bodily systems, such as the nervous system, to adequately make sense of it (Dewey and Wilson, 2001). As a result of the interrupted neurological messages received by the muscles, many children with developmental dyspraxia find difficulty in planning, co-ordinating and controlling their movements, and what might be intended to be a very deliberate effort on the part of a child to write carefully may manifest itself in difficulties with legibility and consistency.

According to Dunford et al (2005), among the wider impact on children's daily lives, dyspraxia can often create difficulties in handwriting because the simultaneous perceptual and motor processes of carrying it out effectively and efficiently require such a significant cognitive investment that other aspects of writing (such as creativity, accuracy, imagination) may suffer. It is, therefore, tempting for teachers to consider that using a digital device to mechanise children's handwriting is an obvious and almost intuitive response to allowing children a level playing field, so that they can explore imaginative and creative writing. However, two problems stand behind such a strategy: first, is that longhand writing has been shown by some important studies to be a complex act, comprising mental representation, inner language organisation and motor skill, and so to imagine it as a lower level skill when compared with other supposed *higher order* activity such as creative writing, is a fallacy, and a serious one at that. Second, however difficult it may be for some children with developmental and learning difficulties to master longhand writing, the investment in pedagogic effort to develop it is a hugely significant step in their academic development and sense of well-being. Longhand writing is in fact a gatekeeper to many other areas of achievement and success in individuals' lives. As Conti (2012) puts it:

> *Illegible handwriting is a problem for a large number of children ... it can affect [children] not only personally (their self-esteem), but also academically, and their careers in the future. So, it's got a very long trajectory.*

Activity 3: Exploring writing with the body

» With a group of children, watch some film clips and read some stories about different ways of using the body (including hands, arms, mouth and feet) to write. After each story or clip, engage the children in writing in different ways and using different tools, such as a variety of pens, brushes and markers. Carry this activity out as a carousel and then put children in groups to produce posters on what they have learnt, focusing on the following questions:

  – Is it possible to write with any part of the body?

  – Can you learn to write in a different way?

  – Why would someone have to learn to write another way?

Conclusion

Not all children, even in highly developed economies, have access to devices that facilitate rapid, uniform and automatically corrected writing. It is critical that children learn to write longhand, to afford them personal rights, to create in them personal capital of a skill that is theirs to possess and to create in them a personal assurance and esteem that they can produce something of beauty that can be shared with others. In a world where children are assailed by information from every direction, and where the speed, brevity and convenience of digital writing seems to dominate, there is something quite special about manual writing: the slowness alone seems, for example, to be made for children who cannot perform tasks at speed; but for children who are withdrawn and find the school environment too bustling, the quietness of writing is reassuring. And for children who find the publicity of screens over-whelming, the privacy of writing is consoling: as Rourke (2011) asserts, 'Above all (...) writing longhand is a secretive pleasure'.

Critical points

» The English national curriculum makes specific requirements for children's handwriting.

» Writing by hand is a culturally and socially significant activity.

» Despite advances in digital technology, children still need to be able to write longhand in the twenty-first century.

» There are many strategies which you can use to foster and develop children's understanding of the aesthetic qualities of their writing and develop pupils' longhand writing habits.

» You need to know and understand about the mentality and physicality of longhand writing from the perspective of individual pupils' capabilities.

Critical reflections

»   *Literacy is a human and civil right and all pupils have a right to learn to read the written word and, in turn, to write words themselves. All children should have the possibility of expressing themselves through their own thoughts and words, in order to understand their lives and to act as informed citizens of their communities and wider society.*

Taking it further

Here are some significant research reviews and ideas that will be useful for a more detailed exploration of some of the ideas that we have discussed in this chapter:

1.   Handwriting without Tears: A Research Review. (2013) [online] Available at: www.hwtears.com/files/HWT%20Research%20Review.pdf (accessed 12 February 2015).

2.   Stevie Graham (2010) Want to Improve Children's Writing? Don't Neglect Their Handwriting. American Educator, Winter 2009/10/. [online] Available at: www.aft.org/sites/default/files/periodicals/graham.pdf (accessed 12 February 2015).

3.   The Importance of Teaching Handwriting in the 21st Century (2012) Hanover Research. [online] Available at: https://www.zaner-bloser.com/media/zb/zaner-bloser/pdf/hw_hanover.pdf (accessed 12 February 2015).

References

Berninger, V W and Amtmann, D (2004) Preventing Written Expression Disabilities through Early and Continuing Assessment and Intervention for Handwriting and/or Spelling Problems: Research into Practice, in Swanson, L, Harris, K and Graham, S (eds) *Handbook of Research on Learning Disabilities*. New York: Guilford Press, 345–63.

Berninger, V W and Graham, S (1998) Language by Hand: A Synthesis of a Decade of Research on Handwriting. *Handwriting Review*, 12: 11–25.

Chen, X (2013) Tablets for Informal Language Learning: Student Usage and Attitudes. *Language Learning and Technology*, 17(1): 18–26.

Conti, G (2012) Handwriting Characteristics and the Prediction of Illegibility in Third and Fifth Grade Students. Presented at Handwriting in the 21st Century?: An Educational Summit, Washington, D.C., 23 January.

Dewey, D and Wilson, B N (2001) Developmental Coordination Disorder: What Is It? *Physical and Occupational Therapy in Pediatrics*, 20: 5–27.

Dunford, C, Missiuna, C, Street, E and Sibert, J (2005) Children's Perceptions of the Impact of Developmental Coordination Disorder on Activities of Daily Living. *The British Journal of Occupational Therapy*, 68(5): 207–14.

Eid, M A, Mansour, M, Saddik, A H E and Iglesias, R (2007) A Haptic Multimedia Handwriting Learning System. Proceedings of the International Workshop on Educational Multimedia and Multimedia Education. Augsburg, Bavaria, Germany: ACM, 2007, 103–8.

Gleaves, A and Walker, C (2013) Richness, Redundancy or Relational Salience? A Comparison of the Effect of Textual and Aural Feedback Modes on Knowledge Elaboration in Higher Education Students' Work. *Computers & Education*, 62: 249–61.

Graham, S and Santangelo, T (2012) A Meta-Analysis of the Effectiveness of Teaching Handwriting. Presented at Handwriting in the 21st Century?: An Educational Summit, Washington, D.C., 23 January.

Herring, S C (2004) Slouching toward the Ordinary: Current Trends in Computer Mediated Communication. *New Media and Society*, 6(1): 26–33.

Hutchison, A, Bechorner, B and Schmidt-Crawford, D (2012) Exploring the Use of the iPad for Literacy Learning. *The Reading Teacher*, 66(1): 15–23.

James, K H and Engelhardt, L (2012) The Effects of Handwriting Experience on Functional Brain Development in Pre-literate Children. *Trends in Neuroscience and Education*, 1(1): 32–42.

Kellogg, R T (2001) Competition for Working Memory among Writing Processes. *American Journal of Psychology*, 114: 175–91.

LA Times (2011) Critic's Notebook: Under the Influence of Hemingway. *Los Angeles Times*. [online] Available at: http://articles.latimes.com/2011/jul/03/entertainment/la-ca-david-ulin-20110703 (accessed 12 February 2015).

McGregor, J. (2012) My Desktop. *The Guardian Newspaper*. [online] Available at: www.theguardian.com/books/2012/jun/20/jon-mcgregor-my-desktop-photos (accessed 12 February 2015).

Medwell, J and Wray, D (2007) Handwriting: What Do We Know and What Do We Need to Know? *Literacy*, 41(1): 10–15.

Olchowka, B (2014) Beware of Feature Overload. [online] Available at: www.uxmatters.com/mt/archives/2014/03/beware-of-feature-overload-a-case-study.php (accessed 12 February 2015).

Rose, E (2011) The Phenomenology of On-screen Reading: University Students' Lived Experience of Digitised Text. *British Journal of Educational Technology*, 42(3): 515–26.

Rourke, L (2011) Why Creative Writing Is Better with a Pen. *The Guardian Newspaper*. [online] Available at: www.theguardian.com/books/2011/nov/03/creative-writing-better-pen-longhand (accessed 12 February 2015).

Sefton-Green, J, Nixon, H and Erstad, O (2009) Reviewing Approaches and Perspectives on 'Digital Literacy'. *Pedagogies*, 4(2): 107–25.

Simic, C (2011) Take Care of Your Little Notebook. New York Book Review. [online] Available at: www.nybooks.com/blogs/nyrblog/2011/oct/12/take-care-your-little-notebook/ (accessed 12 February 2015).

Sumner, E, Connelly, V and Barnett, L (2014) The Influence of Spelling Ability on Handwriting Production: Children with and without Dyslexia. *Journal of Experimental Psychology: Learning, Memory, and Cognition*, 40(5): 1441–7.

10 Multimodal literacies can motivate boys to write

PETULA BHOJWANI

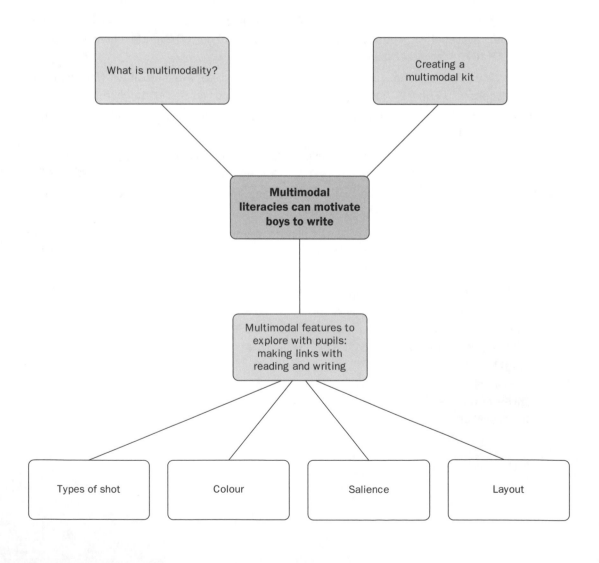

Teachers' Standards

1 Set high expectations which inspire, motivate and challenge pupils

- set goals that stretch and challenge all pupils

2 Promote good progress and outcomes by pupils

- guide pupils to reflect on their progress and their emerging needs

- encourage pupils to take a responsible and conscientious attitude to their own work and study.

4 Plan and teach well-structured lessons

- contribute to the design and provision of an engaging curriculum

5 Adapt teaching to respond to the strengths and needs of all pupils

- know when and how to differentiate appropriately, using approaches which enable pupils to be taught effectively

- have a secure understanding of how a range of factors can inhibit pupils' ability to learn, and how best to overcome these

- demonstrate an awareness of the physical, social and intellectual development of children, and how to adapt teaching to support pupils' education at different stages of development

- have a clear understanding of the need of all pupils – including those with special education needs (SEN), those of high ability, those with English as an Additional Language (EAL) and those with disabilities – and be able to use and evaluate distinctive teaching approaches to engage and support them

Critical questions

» *How do you recognise, value and build upon boys' wider literacy experiences?*

» *How do you develop boys' literacy knowledge and skills through a range of modes in printed and digital media?*

» *How do you encourage boys to see the point of writing?*

» *What role can technology play in the classroom to support boys in engaging with and producing multimodal texts?*

» *How do you motivate boys in progressively becoming expert readers/viewers and authors/writers of multimodal texts?*

Introduction

Over the years boys develop individually as listeners, watchers, speakers and doers, all of which are skills required in literacy, at whatever stage of learning. Their responses will often be diverse and expansive as they use gesture, image, written word and sound. As teachers you need to be alert and ready for each of these literacy opportunities to arise, for example recognising hybrid events as boys visually and freely enact adventures from home and popular culture worlds, a mode which sadly can be admonished or curbed in school. Millard (2003) referred to a *'transformative pedagogy of literacy fusion'* to describe how the two worlds of home and school can be fused in classroom practice. She explored the fusion of *popular culture* texts and *classic* texts and stressed the importance of developing strategies by means of which children's understanding and transformations of their preferred modes of narrative pleasures can be housed within a literacy framework. Other researchers have also highlighted the importance of new literacy frameworks when considering text production in digital environments such as social networking sites (Dowdall, 2009), identifying the significance for educators supporting children to construct texts in wider contexts (Merchant, 2007, and see Chapter 13 of this book). Recognising the diverse cultural spaces that children inhabit today sets the challenge of how to bring these together in the classroom.

This chapter draws on ways of building on children's wider experiences by highlighting the opportunities that a multimodal approach offers in engaging boys in writing in the classroom and beyond. Both writer and reader make meanings and so it is important that the young person is supported in understanding how the text works on the page to attempt to understand the writer's intentions. Equally, as readers, they will make their own interpretations and this is important. Multimodal activities, combined with adult support will hopefully encourage young readers to engage more confidently with texts and develop as writers as they learn to build upon their ideas, make informed choices and create texts to be proud of.

What is multimodality?

Figure 10.1 shows four main modes (sound, writing, image and movement: SWIM), which can combine to form a multimodal text. For example, a picture book might have photographs montaged with paintings and printed word in a variety of fonts and arrangements, it may make a noise when a button is pressed and may have a flap feature which provides movement in the form of a pop-up mechanism. The modes are carefully positioned and selected; for example, illustrators such as Dave McKeen and Lauren Child often combine photographs, sketches, paint and collage in their illustrations and use colour to depict mood. This chapter argues that if children can recognise how texts have been constructed by identifying the function of the modes used in a text then they can begin to apply this to their own writing and compositions.

Multimodality is commonly recognised through technology too. Texts in the twenty-first century are becoming increasingly screen based, not only through radio, television, DVD and

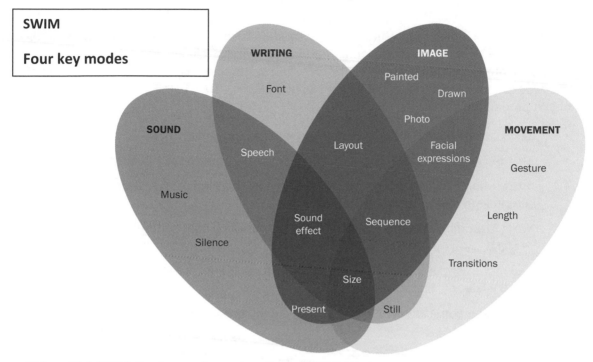

SWIM

Four key modes

Figure 10.1 *SWIM: the four main modes of a multimodal text*

cinema but also through presentations on computers and tablets, the ever growing possibilities of the internet, and not forgetting mobile phones and the world of gaming and console machines. Communication and meaning-making is becoming ever more mixed and re-mixed. Thus literacy is ever evolving.

Many texts that children enjoy outside the classroom are multimodal, combining the modes of sound, word, image and movement (SWIM). Multimodality can be understood by recognising the mixing or combining of modes. As Bearne and Wolstencroft (2007, p 2) argue,

> *Multimodality involves the complex interweaving of word, image, gesture and movement, and sound, including speech. These can be combined in different ways and presented through a range of media.*

FOCUS ON RESEARCH

The visual mode

The visual mode can be particularly appealing to boys and can contribute important meanings to a text. Kress and Van Leeuwen's (1996/2006) research, 'Reading Image: The Grammar of Visual Design', draws on a vast range of examples, including children's drawings and textbook illustrations to examine the ways in which images communicate meaning. They highlight structures which they identify as a *grammar* to identify the position and role of visual design such as framing and use of colour. Their research can be used to analyse children's work as they identify a systematic account and construction of a *langue* (a tool for describing the sign-making practices). They highlight the key principles of text production as follows.

- Texts can be read in more than one way.

- The design of the text by the author and/or publisher facilitates this process.

- The author/publisher may have indicated a particular 'hierarchy' by drawing attention to particular prominent features.

- What is prominent to the reader will be determined by both cultural factors and the design.

- The movement of the reader between 'salient' elements results in different paths eg circular, zig-zag, linear.

- Intended reading paths may be noticeable to different degrees.

(Kress and Van Leeuwen, 1996/2006)

Creating a multimodal kit

A multimodal kit is a good way of grouping resources to engage a child in literacy. Kits can be used to create opportunities for texts and ideas to travel from home to school rather than relying solely on the more traditional direction of school to home. For example, a digital camera can capture images from boys' home play or wider experiences such as a family outing which could develop into a text in school.

Suggested resources to include in a kit include:

- a digital camera and/or a tablet such as an iPad;

- 3–5 multi-layered picture books possibly around a theme, for example animals;

- some props to encourage small world play, for example a puppet to support a book;

- a talking photo album (an album with a simple recording device to allow narration to support insert pictures or writing).

With an emphasis on the resources travelling back and forth between home and school, the kit stems from the concept of '*funds of knowledge*' which recognises that children from diverse backgrounds bring diverse experiences. It is therefore important that you make time to listen to children's ideas as they respond to the resources and to provide support to help develop their sparks of interest and early plans in creating their own texts prompted by one of the resources or experiences. Our identities can be presented through the choices that we make, and so encouraging individual choice is important for ownership and authorship. Previous projects have also shown that by increasing children's understanding of the design of a text, they become more equipped and motivated to engage, build and share.

Activity 1: The relationship between words and pictures

» *Try covering pictures with a piece of paper and just reading the words on the page. Then reveal the image and see if it is what you expected.*

» *Through discussion with your colleagues or fellow students explore the role of words and images and how each shows messages to add meaning.*

Sometimes images are used to reinforce the text and show what is written but some authors and illustrators skilfully play with this and often give other messages in the pictures (eg, see picture books by Anthony Browne, Emily Gravett and Mini Grey).

Multimodal features to explore with pupils: making links with reading and writing

Layout

Conventional texts tend to use a single type of font and are written on the page in a uniform straight line from left to right. In picture books and graphic novels today more non-linear techniques are evident. These might include words positioned on top of illustrations, on wavy lines, different fonts for effect, pages or flaps that open out etc. Note how many different devices you can find as you read the texts in the kit.

Colour

The use of colour can include noting light and shade too. The mood can often change when dark shadows are included in contrast to brighter shades and can be tracked in both picture books and onscreen. Film makers and illustrators use these techniques to give clues to the reader or viewer to hint at what might happen next.

Salience

This term refers to the most prominent part of the page or screen. Think about where your eyes are drawn to after you have studied the text for a short time. Where does your vision land? This might be different to someone else as we all expect and see different things when we read as we bring our own experiences and interests to a text. Consider why you are drawn to the area on the page or screen; for example, it might be due to the author or illustrator's use of colour (perhaps a bold warm colour) or the large sized font. Why did they make this more salient? Is there an important message or meaning that you need in order to read on? This is a clever technique which would be powerful to include when the young person creates their own text.

Type of shot

Close, distant, side … This sort of language can be very specific and useful for understanding film. However, images on the page also require a language to help us understand the events and actions; for example, there might be a close up shot of the character's expression to alert the reader that he or she is frightened. A long-distant shot might show the setting.

Activity 2

Below is a list of some text types that you can easily find today.

»   *Consider what texts can be found in the home and school settings.*

»   *How many can be found in both settings?*

»   *Which texts do you think boys may prefer?*

»   *Observe and consider boys' responses to these texts. Which are favoured?*

»   *Where have you seen each type and are these texts evident in your school?*

»   *How are they multimodal?*

»   *What is the medium of communication (computer: internet information and software presentations; paper-based; sound and visual media: radio, television, videos and DVDs)?*

story books	*console games*
non-fiction books	*logos*
pop-up and lift the flap books	*songs*
web pages and web logs	*newspapers*
blogs	*card collections*
advertisements	*catalogues*
poetry	*posters*
magazines	*artwork*
comics	*texting*
take-away menus	*cartoons*
leaflets	*movies*
animated films	

In the following case study the boy engages with both paper and digital versions of a published text. He is encouraged by his teacher to identify the modes, and how they work or are positioned to convey messages and apply this to his own work.

CASE STUDY

Andrew, an 11-year-old boy

Andrew was part of a year-long home school multimodal project. The resources that he was given included an iPad and several multi-layered picture books. Andrew was drawn to the *Magic of Reality* (2011) by Professor Richard Dawkins which he read as an ebook app and a paperback book. With his teacher he explored the affordances of paper and screen by comparing the two versions. The book has quality pictures shaped alongside and around text to engage the reader but Andrew quickly identified the video clips and moving images in the ebook version which he recognised expanded on the printed text to inform further. This addition gave the reader wider content to support information as meanings were offered to the reader/viewer through the additional dimension of the screen, enabling Andrew to make decisions on how to navigate through the text. In addition to this, it was felt that in both versions the content of the text was appealing. The opposing views of reality and fantasy were presented, and he seemed to develop his own questioning tone when making his version. Andrew used the app Mofo to make a Sun character, and he spoke in first person to present his own version of the changing understanding of our Sun. In his recording which was written prior to his narration, it is clear that he is drawn to the scientific facts that he can present in a knowledgeable tone to the listener.

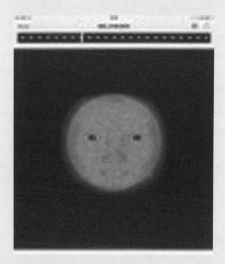

'Hi I am the Sun. Lots of things have been said about me for thousands of years while I have been shining up here in the sky. People wondered how I was made. What am I? There are two sides to my story myths and reality, and I will tell you both sides; the fun stories and the truth.

First some Myths, some people believed there was an Egyptian god Ra. When people worshiped him he would fly up high and he would go down when people stopped worshipping because they were tired. This happened every day. Another myth was that I was a Greek god called Helios who rode chariots across the sky.

We all know **now** that I do not move across the sky! I stay still and I fire gas and my core is molten metal. I am actually formed by large molecule clouds which started taking in stars. I have a very short life span because the bigger we are the quicker we die out but it will take billions of years for me to burn out and plus I can't be blown out like a candle. I am the hottest thing in our universe and I will be living a lot longer than you, so don't worry I will be looking after you for a few more billions of years.'

Presentation techniques and how to organise the content have been carefully considered in Andrew's work. Three clear sections show his ability to weave the facts through a first person account which informs the viewer as he adopts the role of the Sun. However, it is the recorded audio of his writing and the animation of the moving facial expressions that make further connections with the viewer as his communication includes direct expression as the powerful, animated face looks straight at the viewer. This is a successful multimodal text which is built using sound (narration), word (voiced pre-prepared text), image (portrayal of the sun as a face) and movement (animated face). It was highly motivating to complete, and Andrew was aware throughout that the screen based platform for his work meant that it would be viewed beyond the teacher.

Activity 3

» *Look out for digital versions, such as ebooks, of a popular text which appeals to boys; The Magic of Reality fascinates many boys since it is a science-based book with facts. Encourage the children to identify and explore the function of both digital and print-based modes.*

iPad apps such as Mofo can be quick to work through which allows momentum to be maintained for further editing and reworking. Seeing the characters come alive and rebuilt can be highly motivating and encourages authorship as decisions are made about the pitch of the voice, facial expressions, tone and content in making the recordings.

FOCUS ON RESEARCH

Boys' writing, popular culture and a third space

In Bhojwani's (2011) study of 6–7-year-old boys making meaning at home and at school, it was clear that popular culture was particularly evident in their text production. For example, they experimented with themes, discourse structures and styles using diverse cultural resources as they played out the villain and hero roles (Dyson, 1993). In composing each scene or story, the boys built imagined worlds which in fact showed how home and school literacy practice can intersect. Others have called this a third space (Bhabha, 2004; Moje et al, 2004), a theory which has been used within a variety of different disciplines to explore and understand the space *in between* (Bhabha, 2004, p 1). Of particular interest is the idea of developing literary identities, where several different *funds of knowledge* meet (Moll et al, 1992). Also an important concept of new literacy studies, it is argued that third space theory allows us to think about how children's meaning-making often lies between home and school (Cook, 2005; Levy, 2008). Third space is a place where the imagination has legitimacy because it is a space for agency and choice. This was visible when interviewing the boys and observing their imaginative play, but perhaps it is most noticeable in their sketch books, which they transferred between the home and school domains. The boys moved in and out of the third space with ease, for example, playing a Star Wars game on a console at home, in role as Darth Vader with peers in the playground and playing with Star Wars Lego with a relative at home. The relevance of third space to boys' literacy development is that it offers ways of thinking about a hybrid area which can bring together different modes of communication and also the virtual, the actual and the imaginative. The third space could be entered both at home and at school; from a teaching perspective, activities could be set up to encourage the boys to connect home and school in this way.

It is possible to study boys' personalities and curiosities in this third space, a place where identities can be formed (Pahl and Rowsell, 2005). A prominent finding was that this is a space where boys show agency and take risks; they learn to rehearse skills through play or in their imaginations and inhabit different identities to try out new roles and empathise with characters. The third space can also be understood as a place where the boys slip from the official school space into the unofficial one (Dyson, 2001). This can be evident when we observe them drawing from cultural symbols and practices in the ways of being a child in their homes to make meanings about being a child in school. Look out for unofficial and semi-official spaces '*revealing the children's powers of adaptation and improvisation*' (Dyson, 2001) as they can flexibly apply cultural resources to their text making.

The example below illustrates how finding the *right* text can make connections between boys' wider interests or worlds to encourage them to write and develop as meaning makers.

CASE STUDY

Michael, a ten year-old boy

Michael had a particular flair for drawing at both home and school but often seemed disconnected to literacy teaching in the classroom. When given *Stormbreaker* (2005) by Anthony Horowitz, he entered the world of the graphic novel and began to develop his connection with visual literacy. The text travelled from school to home, and within a week of receiving the book, he had not only read it but created his own text using some of the graphic devices illustrated in the novel. He also showed that he was happy for his work to be shared as he emailed his narrative to his classteacher for feedback. It could be argued that an opportunity had been created that had enabled Michael to adapt formats found in his reading of *Stormbreaker* and make meaning on paper from the fantasy world in his own mind.

Figure 10.2 Michael's work: text using graphic devices from Stormbreaker

Comment

Looking closely at Michael's work, Kress and Van Leeuwen (1996/2006) would highlight the significance of him choosing to stick the comic style drawings on three different coloured pieces of card, perhaps to emphasise the sections of the story. It is also interesting to see that he has consistently positioned written blocks of text down the right-hand side of the page. The action, movement and illustrated sound effects are largely evident in the bold drawings. This is an example of a paper multimodal text which is strongly influenced by a fantasy world fuelled by Michael's imagination and connection with narratives found in popular culture. It is multi-layered and complex, due to the non-linear designs that he has chosen to use and thus a sign of agency and confidence in the clear decisions he has made.

Michael went on to read the Manga Shakespeare series which his teacher felt was good preparation for his transition to Year 7. He used the Comic Life programme to create his own Manga characters and graphic text on screen. This transference meant that he could combine voice and sound effects to his text and images to add further meanings.

Activity 4

» *Consider a particular boy who you teach in the two settings of home and school. What roles do they undertake? (For example, captain of the school football team, avid reader, gamer, Spiderman or Star Wars fan).*

» *How could you use this knowledge to inform what you do in the classroom?*

» *What do you think are the benefits of starting from the child's interests, at home and school?*

In recognising boys' range of interests and roles across sites you may be surprised about the multiple identities they adopt (see Pahl and Rowsell (2005, 2006) for further reading). As teachers, this information can be applied in the classroom in the texts that we choose to use in literacy and the bridges that we can build between home and school.

Conclusion

It is important to develop your awareness of children's ability to employ a range of writing techniques across the domains of home and school.

One of the important challenges for teachers is to recognise that children will arrive in the classroom expecting more from a text than simply words on a page. Recent years of technological change are making an impact on an increasingly *digital* generation who expect greater choice through an array of platforms and modes, which prompt play and offer new opportunities for engagement and meaning-making (see Chapter 13). Their prior experience of the screen and interaction with many modes mean that children bring an expectation of multiple levels and pace from a text. It follows that they may also have higher expectations of what the texts they produce should look like.

In this chapter the emphasis is placed on the importance of boys having agency and choice about what they produce as a text and communicate as they become more competent at signing meanings.

> *A creatively constructed writing classroom recognises the authority and expertise of the teacher and will include explicit teaching of writing, but this occurs within an environment of democratic participation, where children's voices are heard, where they have ownership of their texts and their decision making, and where they can articulate with confidence their reasons for their writing choices.*
>
> (Cremin and Myhill, 2012, p 24).

The process of arriving at a text or what Kress and Van Leeuwen (1996/2006) would refer to as a *design* has implications for literacy practice today given that the visual mode is becoming more prominent on screen and paper; it follows that a more technical understanding is required. In particular, teachers need a language to discuss the texts the children produce and to help them identify the significance of signs and meanings in different modes to the overall development of literacy. The language and concepts explicated by Kress and Van Leeuwen's *The Grammar of Visual Design* (1996/2006) can be particularly supportive in attempting to trace boys' pathways in communicative practices.

'Pedagogy takes place beyond the classroom …. If learning is to be efficacious, then what a child does now must be connected in meaningful and motivated ways related to social practices' (Gee, 1996, p 4). It is therefore argued that the social practices of boys need to be better understood and may begin with establishing their interests.

Critical points

» *Creating opportunities to make home/school links is essential to gain an understanding of children's literacy interests, experiences and broader knowledge about texts, which can be built upon and incorporated into school writing.*

» *Increased literacy knowledge and a stronger sense of authorship and authorial intent can be achieved through understanding how modes can be combined for effect. This has resulted in enthusiasms for books, book making and screen text production.*

» *When there is a clear purpose and opportunity to showcase work, boys can take pride in their own compositions.*

» *A multimodal approach improves confidence and a can do belief enabling boys to become expert readers/viewers and authors/writers of multimodal texts.*

Critical reflections

» *Consider why popular culture and multimodal approaches can be so important to boys at school today.*

  Some schools see popular culture as related to the home rather than the classroom and so this notion challenges practice. However, reflecting on initiatives which provide wider opportunities to promote creating multimodal texts can open further avenues of discussion and reflection on how understanding boys' social worlds can contribute to their literacy development (Dyson, 2003).

» *What opportunities can you identify to help boys find their voices in writing and gain confidence in the multiple ways of communicating?*

Taking it further

The following reading is grounded in multimodal theory or illustrates practical activities and classroom research which shows how visual literacy and multimodal teaching and learning can increase engagement.

Bearne, E (2003) Ways of Knowing; Ways of Showing, in Styles, M and Bearne, E (eds) *Art, Narrative and Childhood*. Stoke-on-Trent: Trentham Books.

Bearne, E (2005) Multimodal Texts: What They Are and How Children Use Them, in Evans, J (ed) *Literacy Moves On: Using Popular Culture, New Technologies and Critical Literacy in the Primary Classroom*. London: David Fulton.

Bearne, E, Graham, L, and Marsh, J (2007) *Classroom Action Research in Literacy: a Guide to Practice*. Leicester: The United Kingdom Literacy Association.

Bearne, E and Wolstencroft, H (2007) *Visual Approaches to Teaching Writing*. London: Sage/UKLA.

Bhojwani, P, Lord, B and Wilkes, C (2007) *'I Know What to Write Now!' Engaging Boys (and Girls) through a Multimodal Approach*. Leicester: UKLA.

References

Bhabha, H (2004) *The Location of Culture*. London: Routledge.

Bhojwani, P L (2011) Multimodal Literacies: 6–7 Year-Old Boys Remembering, Redesigning and Remaking Meaning in Home and School. PhD Thesis, University of Nottingham.

Cook, M (2005) A Place of Their Own. *Literacy*, 35: 2.

Cremin, T and Myhill, D (2012) *Writing Voices: Creating Communities of Writers*. London: Routledge.

Dawkins, R (2011) *The Magic of Reality*. London: Brantam Press.

Dowdall, C (2009) Impressions, Improvisations and Compositions. *Literacy*, 43(2): 91–9.

Dyson, A H (1993) *The Social Worlds of Children Learning to Read and Write in an Urban Primary School*. New York: Teachers College Press.

Dyson, A H (2001) Where are the Childhoods in Childhood Literacy? An Exploration in (Outer) School Space. *Journal of Early Childhood Literacy*, 1(1): 9–40.

Dyson, A H (2003) *The Brothers and Sisters Learn to Write. Popular Literacies in Childhood and School Cultures*. New York: Teacher College Press.

Gee, J P (1996) *Social Linguistics and Literacies: Ideology in Discourses*, 2nd Edn. London: Falmer.

Horowitz, A (2005) *Stormbreaker*. London: Walker Books Ltd.

Kress, G and Van Leeuwen, T (1996/2006) *Reading Images: A Grammar of Visual Design*. London: Routledge.

Levy, R (2008) Third Spaces Are Interesting Places. *Journal of Early Childhood Literacy*, 8: 43.

Merchant, G (2007) Writing the Future in the Digital Age. *Literacy*, 41(3): 118–28.

Millard, E (2003) Transformative Pedagogy: Towards a Literacy of Fusion. *Reading, Literacy and Language*, 37(1): 3–9.

Moje, E, Ciechanowski, K M, Kramer, K, Ellis, L, Carrillo, R and Collazo, T (2004) Working towards Third Space in Content Area Literacy: An Examination of Everyday Funds of Knowledge and Discourse. *Reading Research Quarterly*, 39(1): 38–71.

Moll, L, Amanti, C, Neff, D and Gonzalez, N (1992) Funds of Knowledge for Teaching: Using a Qualitative Approach to Connect Homes and Classrooms. *Theory into Practice*, 31(2): 132–41.

Pahl, K and Rowsell, J (2005) *Literacy and Education: Understanding the New Literacy Studies in the Classroom*. London: Paul Chapman Publishers.

Pahl, K and Rowsell, J (2006) *Travel Notes from the New Literacy Studies*. Clevedon: Cromwell Press.

11 Writing with children who are dyslexic

CATHERINE HUNT

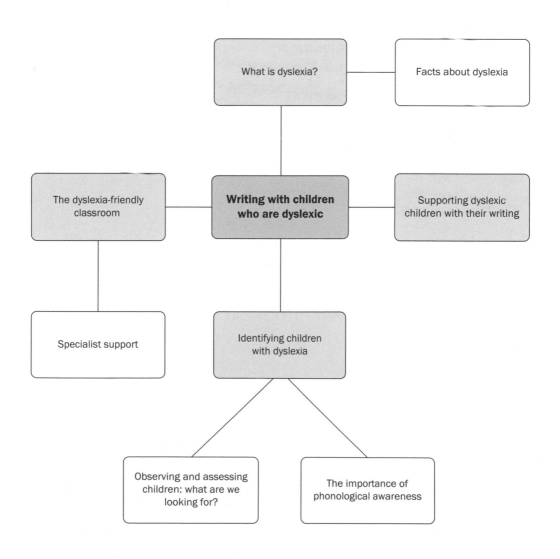

Teachers' Standards

1 Set high expectations which inspire, motivate and challenge pupils

- set goals that stretch and challenge pupils of all backgrounds, abilities and dispositions

2 Promote good progress and outcomes by pupils

- be aware of pupil's capabilities and their prior knowledge, and plan teaching to build on these

5 Adapt teaching to respond to the strengths and needs of all pupils

- know when and how to differentiate appropriately, using approaches which enable pupils to be taught effectively

- have a secure understanding of how a range of factors can inhibit pupils' ability to learn, and how best to overcome these

- have a clear understanding of the needs of all pupils – including those with special educational needs, those of high ability, those with English as an additional language and those with disabilities – and be able to use and evaluate distinctive teaching approaches to engage and support them

All teachers need to be teachers of dyslexia because 10 per cent of the population is dyslexic, meaning on average 3 children in a class of 30 have dyslexia.

www.bdadyslexia.org.uk

Critical questions

» *What is dyslexia?*

» *What are the indicators that a child may be dyslexic?*

» *How can you support dyslexic children with their writing?*

» *How do you create a dyslexic-friendly classroom?*

Introduction

In his book, *I Wonder What It Is Like to Be Dyslexic* Sam Barclay (2013) provides a beautifully realised series of prints that show how text can confound the dyslexic reader. In the prints, letters are half formed, they move across the page, swap places and morph into shapes. Barclay's aim is to enable the reader to get a sense of the confusion that people with dyslexia experience when faced with a page of text. Approximately 10% of the population are dyslexic, so it is highly likely that we will all, at some time, teach children who are dyslexic. Children with dyslexia will present with a range of difficulties but, in particular, difficulties with the acquisition of literacy; reading, writing and spelling. As literacy is vital to learning, it is important that you understand the difficulties that a child has, and the ways in which you can adapt your teaching, and your classroom, to ensure that you meet the needs of these children.

What is dyslexia?

The word *dyslexia* comes from Greek, meaning *difficulty with words*. The Rose Report (2009), which looks at the identification and teaching of children with dyslexia, defines dyslexia as '*a learning difficulty that primarily affects the skills involved in accurate and fluent word reading and spelling*' (p 31). The British Dyslexia Association states:

> *Dyslexia is an umbrella term and should be viewed as a continuum rather than a specific category. Children with the label 'dyslexia' may have different difficulties, which vary from slight to severe. Dyslexia is a neurological disorder, which is present from birth and is a life long condition. The cause of dyslexia has yet to be identified, but it is generally believed that the brain is 'wired' differently and this hinders the efficient development of language processing and literacy skills.*

> www.bdadyslexia.org.uk

Dyslexia is a specific learning difficulty (SpLD), which affects the acquisition of the skills of reading, spelling and writing. Many dyslexic children have weaknesses in language, memory, processing and sequencing. The problems often only become apparent when the child starts school and fails to acquire literacy skills, and sometimes numeracy skills, at the same rate as their peers. There is no cure for dyslexia so while the dyslexic child may have areas of weakness, it is also important to recognise their strengths and to nurture different styles of thinking and learning in order for them to be successful.

Facts about dyslexia

* *It affects about 10% of the population.*
* *Boys and girls are equally affected.*
* *Dyslexia occurs independently of intelligence.*
* *Most dyslexics have a family history of learning difficulties.*
* *Dyslexia often co-occurs with other specific learning difficulties such as DCD, Dyscalculia and Sensory Processing Disorder.*

(British Dyslexia Association (BDA))

The earlier a child with dyslexia is identified, the more effective the intervention will be. Identification can be difficult for parents and teachers as the signs are not always obvious, nor always consistent. The feeling that there is a discrepancy between intellectual potential and performance is a good indicator for further investigation, and when concerns about the child's progress continue, even after they have received additional support. Formal diagnosis requires an assessment by an educational psychologist or appropriately qualified dyslexia teacher. However, before formal assessment takes place, it is worthwhile investigating a child's

* vision – for short sightedness and tracking issues;
* hearing – for conditions such as glue ear;
* history of other difficulties such as speech and language acquisition.

Although there is no set age when it is appropriate to assess for dyslexia, some caution should be exercised about assessing very young children, as the outcome could be the result of immaturity rather than specific difficulties.

A formal assessment will identify a child's strengths and weaknesses and how to support them. An important, additional aim of the assessment is to improve the child's self-esteem by giving them an understanding of why they are experiencing difficulties. There may also be positive outcomes from the assessment as it will indicate where children have strengths in other areas such as verbal and/or spatial abilities. As Shaywitz (2005) observes, dyslexia should be evaluated as an asset, not just as a handicap.

FOCUS ON RESEARCH

The social and emotional needs of children with dyslexia

Casserley (2012) reports an intervention study to address socio-emotional needs of children with dyslexia. She argues that as well as good instruction in how to overcome children's literacy difficulties, it is also crucial to consider psychological aspects of having dyslexia.

Her research found that having dyslexia can have a negative impact on children's socio-emotional development which, in turn, can result in negative changes in behaviour. In the study, self-consciousness about their reading problems and inability to keep up with their peers was a prominent difficulty. Other manifestations identified as arising from the emotional effects of dyslexia were anxiety, task avoidance, lack of motivation and inattentiveness. Less prevalent, psychosomatic symptoms included irregular sleep patterns, feeling nauseous, withdrawing or becoming subdued before written tasks or assessments.

Casserley's (2012) study reported positive effects from an intervention programme to raise the children's socio-emotional levels and therefore concluded that greater emphasis needs to be placed on confidence and self-esteem building, in addition to curricular and environmental modifications, if children with dyslexia are to feel secure and positive in their learning abilities.

Identifying children with dyslexia

Once other reasons for a child's lack of progress in literacy have been investigated and discounted, an assessment of the child may be appropriate. When undertaking any assessment of a child, it is important that it is done in the spirit of the SEND Code of Practice (2014), which states that the purpose of identification is to work out what action the school needs to take, not to fit a pupil into a category.

Once assessment has been agreed as the best way forward, the initial step is to find out as much background information as possible. Where there are concerns about a child's literacy, it is important to find out about the child's broader development as well as specific issues with literacy. This should be the initial step in the assessment of a child whatever their age.

- Birth – were there any problems before, during or after the birth, for example a premature birth?

- Acquisition of speech – any delays or deficits in speech and language development?

- Acquisition of physical milestones, for example walking, talking.

- Vision – outcomes of any tests. Could vision be a reason, or a contributory factor in the child's lack of progress?

- Hearing – outcomes of any hearing tests. Has the child had persistent ear infections or glue ear?

- General health – outcomes of preschool checks.

- Family history of learning –Does anyone in the family have literacy difficulties and/or is dyslexic.

This background information may identify patterns in the child's development that are significant, and provide further evidence for or against the need for a formal assessment. For example, signs that the very young child may be dyslexic are:

- late talking;

- learning new words very slowly;

- difficulty with rhyming.

Once the child is of school age, the demands of schooling often mean that the signs become more apparent. One role of the classteacher is to understand the importance of identifying these children and providing for their needs. The classteacher is responsible for monitoring, assessing and recording the progress of all pupils. It is likely that standardised tests are carried out and it may be noticeable from these that there is a problem. As Rose states:

> It is generally agreed that the earlier dyslexic difficulties are identified the better the chances of putting children on the road to success. However, blanket screening for dyslexia of all children on entry to school is questionable, not least because screening tests for this purpose are as yet unreliable. A better way to identify children at risk of literacy difficulties and dyslexia is to closely observe and assess the responses to pre- and early reading activities in comparison to their typically developing peers.

> (Rose Report, 2009, p 11)

Observing and assessing children: what are we looking for?

Table 11.1 shows some of the difficulties and differences that a classteacher can observe, which may contribute to the decision to formally assess a child. These traits will vary between children as each has their own strengths and weaknesses.

As the child moves through school, there is an increased emphasis on the acquisition of literacy skills. If the child fails to acquire these skills or shows difficulty in acquiring them, they will start to fall behind their peers.

Table 11.1 Difficulties, effects and evidence associated with dyslexia

Difficulty	Effect	Evidence
Verbal memory	Working memory and short-term memory are particular issues for a child with dyslexia. This affects the child's ability to manipulate, store and use information. It also affects the organisational skills of the child.	• Has difficulty following and repeating instructions • Forgets words • Forgets what to write
Sequencing	Problems putting things in the right order and remembering sequences.	• Difficulties sequencing the alphabet, days, months etc • Difficulties sequencing stories and events
Directional confusion	Finds it difficult to get directions and orientations correct.	• Confuses left/right and up/down • Confuses letters that look similar: b/d, p/g, m/w • Has difficulty finding their way around school
Time	Finds it difficult to understand the overall concept of time.	• Difficulty remembering their date of birth • Confuses yesterday and tomorrow • Difficulty understanding what happens next • Difficulty with appreciation of time spans
Cross-laterality	Lack of preference to use one hand for all activities.	• Maybe ambidextrous
Poor concentration	Finds it difficult to concentrate for any length of time.	• Poor auditory memory • Restlessness • Short span of attention, will 'zone out' of lessons
Co-ordination	May have difficulty with basic co-ordination.	• Coping with laces and buttons • Poor pencil grip • Struggling with drawing, tracing and writing • Poor letter formation
Self-esteem	Often conscious of their difficulties. They often do not understand why they are failing.	• Tires easily • Is anxious • Becomes frustrated • Can result in negative behaviour • Can become the 'class clown'

Dyslexia is displayed in many ways, as shown in the table, but in the school setting there are other indicators to look for.

Reading:

- makes poor progress;

- reading is slow and laboured;

- strugges to blend letters together;

- unusual pronunciation of words;

- level of comprehension exceeds level of accuracy;

- misses out, or adds, words;

- loses place easily;

- fails to recognise familiar words;

- fails to recognise words from one page to the next;

- difficulties grasping rhyme and alliteration.

Writing:

- standard of written work is poor in comparison to verbal ability;

- poor handwriting, with letters formed incorrectly;

- work is messy: words crossed/rubbed out and attempted several times;

- reversal of letters;

- inconsistent use of capital letters;

- lack of punctuation;

- same word spelled different ways within one piece of writing;

- transposition of letters;

- work not clearly set out;

- erratic spellings;

- words omitted;

- inaccurate copying;

- use of a basic vocabulary;

- struggling to apply any learnt spelling patterns and rules;

- an inability to recognise their own mistakes.

The importance of phonological awareness

Underlying some of these difficulties is the ability to grasp and understand phonology. Phonological awareness is one of the most important predictors of reading in normally developing children (Rack et al, 1994).

Phonological awareness involves understanding that words are made up of smaller units of sound (phonemes) and that by changing these units new words can be created. Children with dyslexia often have difficulties with phonological processing.

A child with poor phonological awareness may not be able to correctly answer the following questions (www.nhs.uk).

1.   What sounds make up the word *hot*? Are these different from the sounds that make up *hat*?

2.   What word would you have if you changed the *p* in *pot* to an *h*?

3.   Can you think of five words to rhyme with *cat*?

Training in phonological awareness can greatly improve dyslexic children's reading skills.

CASE STUDY

The weekly spelling test: how can this task be made less stressful for a child with dyslexia?

Each week the children in Year 2 have a list of words to learn for a test.

The classteacher was aware that Freya struggles with spelling so sought help from the school Special Educational Needs Coordinator (SENCO). The SENCO advised her to give Freya a short list of structure based words (words with the same letter pattern, for example, day, clay, play, away), explaining that this is more helpful for Freya than random words, as the visual repetition of pattern and the rhyme will make the task less challenging. She advised the teacher to write the words onto handwriting paper and use different colours to show the phonemes in the words, then use the same colour throughout to highlight the common pattern.

In addition, and in order for the task to be manageable and achievable, the teacher gave Freya and her parents suggestions for learning the words at home.

- Use magnetic letters to practise word building.

- Use an action, such as tapping the table, to demonstrate the individual sounds.

- Use coloured pens to identify phonemes and spelling patterns, as the teacher did.

- Write on coloured paper or a white board – this takes the focus off handwriting but will encourage the motor memory for the spellings.

- Write the words in air, in sand, with water and a paint brush, with paint – again this takes the focus off handwriting but will encourage the motor memory for the spellings (see Chapter 9).

- Use the computer, for example, Wordshark and Nessy.

- Use the *Look, Say, Cover, Write, Check* method.

The teacher also made sure that she gave Freya enough time and support during the test, to enable her to successfully use the techniques that she had been given to support her spelling.

By approaching the weekly spelling test in this way, the teacher found that Freya was able to complete her spelling test alongside her peers. This built her self-esteem and made Freya feel more positive about the weekly test, and gave her the best opportunity to demonstrate what she knows.

The difficulties experienced by a dyslexic child are often exacerbated by the fact that within the school setting children are judged by their standard of written work. Their ability to communicate clearly and intellectually is not reflected in their writing and this can be a source of frustration, and lead to a sense of failure. Beyond school, dyslexics often come into their own as they have different strengths, such as creativity, thinking outside the box and determination, and have developed coping skills which can lead to success. We only have to look at some famous dyslexics to see the truth in this: Richard Branson, Kiera Knightley, Steven Spielberg, Benjamin Zephaniah, and Tommy Hilfiger.

Supporting dyslexic children with their writing

The Code of Practice states that with the right staff training, strategies and support in place, children with special educational needs (SEN) should be educated in mainstream settings. Dyslexia is now recognised as a special educational need, and so a mainstream school has a responsibility to address the needs of the dyslexic child.

All mainstream schools must appoint a special educational needs co-ordinator (SENCO). Part of their role is to co-ordinate additional support for pupils with SEN. They will also advise and support other members of staff; so, for advice on dyslexic children, the SENCO is an invaluable resource.

This section looks at different ways to support dyslexic children with their writing. Supporting dyslexic children's learning requires a range of approaches, depending on the child's abilities and needs. It involves differentiating and adapting lessons and putting in specific provision for individual children. For example, this could mean that an outcome does not need to be produced in written form as alternatives to writing such as drama, problem solving and art could be used. If the learning objective for a class of Year 2 children is *to organise instructions sequentially*, this could be met by sequencing a set of pictures or acting out the order. Part of the instructions could be given so that the exercise is a cloze activity (a text is provided for readers to complete by inserting the missing words) thereby limiting the writing required. The learning could be assessed verbally, by providing opportunities for the child to talk things through with the teacher, who would then record how successful the pupil has been at meeting the learning outcome. Teachers can also support dyslexic children's learning by creating a dyslexic-friendly classroom.

The case studies below demonstrate different ways to adapt lessons to enable children with dyslexia to engage with the given task, and record it in a way that demonstrates what they know and can do.

CASE STUDY

Recording learning through mind mapping

Conor is a Year 6 pupil who has been identified with dyslexia. In their history lessons the class is studying the Victorian era. The teacher asked the children to assemble ten facts about the life of Queen Victoria to share with their peers and to record the facts in a style that they prefer. The teacher discussed options with Conor and suggested that he should produce a mind map. The teacher explained that it would limit the amount of writing he would have to do, but at the same time would show the key facts, thus demonstrating his understanding. Conor is good at producing mind maps. He likes the idea of organising his work visually, using a mixture of writing and drawing, and feels confident that he can achieve the learning objective using this skill. He is a fluent reader and is able to use his skills to find plenty of interesting facts. He chooses a range of coloured pens to help organise the mind map. The teacher talks to Conor reminding him about copying carefully. Conor, aware that this is one of his weaknesses, has developed a strategy for copying, which he finds to be successful. He places a small object (rubber, Lego brick etc) above the word he is copying. His eyes are then directed to the word and, depending on the length of the word, he copies it out in chunks.

Conor uses different colours for each *branch* of his mind map. He knows to limit the written part of key words and, as a keen artist, chooses to draw some details. The end result is clear, and Conor is happy to share this with his teacher and his peers. As he talks through the mind map, he uses his strong verbal skills to add detail to the information.

CASE STUDY

Using writing frames

Being presented with a blank sheet of paper can be very daunting for children who struggle with the process of writing. It can be difficult for them to know what is required to produce a good piece of writing. Liam was one of those children. He would spend 15 minutes writing the date and the title, and then sit not knowing what to write. Liam's teacher sensed his anxiety and decided to use writing frames to get him started on his writing, providing structure and enabling Liam to focus on the lesson content.

James, Liam's teacher, designed the frames to match Liam's ability. The frame made it clear to Liam the amount of writing he was expected to produce. James knew that Liam was a reluctant writer and so there was little to be gained from asking him to write the title and date. James therefore decided to do this for Liam, allowing him to focus on the objective of the lesson. The blank sheet of paper now looked more attractive, with clear font, space to write that indicated how much he needed to write, and relevant pictures – altogether much more appealing.

James' intervention enabled Liam to be less daunted by a blank page, and therefore to produce some work. This, alongside other strategies, motivated Liam to continue to try hard with his writing.

Once Liam was used to the writing frame, James wanted to move his learning forward. He was aware that Liam should not become too dependent on them, so, he allowed Liam to design his own writing frames, encouraging him to include a variety of styles. In this way Liam had greater control over his writing tasks, and he gained greater satisfaction and enjoyment from these lessons.

CASE STUDY

Using a scribe

Thomas, a Year 3 teacher, wanted his class to re-write in their own words the fable of *The Hare and the Tortoise*. As a way of assessing the children, he wanted them to include the points they had covered in previous lessons. This included the use of adjectives and adverbs, setting the work out in paragraphs and the use of speech marks, as well as basic punctuation. There was no emphasis on the spelling and handwriting; these were not learning objectives. The teacher realised that for Adam, a child in his class who was dyslexic, this would be a challenging task.

Adam is eight years old. Thomas is aware that he has difficulty presenting his work clearly. His handwriting, although joined, varies in size and he struggles with the spacing between words. His spelling is poor and there is little evidence of learnt spelling patterns. When writing, he uses a limited vocabulary which does not do justice to his verbal ability. Adam is reluctant to write and the poor quality gives the impression of low academic ability, although he has a verbal IQ of over 130. However, he is able to re-tell the story orally; he enjoys this and he is also good at it. Thomas decided to use Adam's strength at oral re-telling to adapt his lesson.

To enable Adam to be included in this lesson, and the outcomes reflect Adam's ability, Thomas needed to consider how he could support Adam with his written work. As handwriting and spelling were not included in the learning objectives, Thomas decided to take them out of the equation. He decided that as he was looking for the use of speech marks, adjectives, adverbs etc, then Adam did not need to write the story himself. So, to include Adam in the lesson, and for Adam to remain motivated and to show what he is capable of achieving, Thomas asked the teaching assistant to scribe for him.

Once the lesson was over, Thomas talked with the teaching assistant and looked at Adam's work. They both agreed that without the hindrance of handwriting, Adam was able to organise his ideas clearly. He used imaginative vocabulary, included adjectives and similes, and his work flowed. He was able to tell the teaching assistant where appropriate punctuation was needed, including starting new paragraphs. Importantly, the teaching assistant had noticed that Adam was proud of his achievements.

As this had been so successful, Thomas and the teaching assistant agreed that they would continue to adapt some lessons in this way. Additionally, to encourage Adam to become more independent in his writing, they would begin to teach him to touch type, as this would greatly reduce the need for handwriting, and errors could be easily corrected. They discussed this with the SENCO who agreed that this was a good strategy, as Adam would be able to increase the amount of work he produces, and this would boost his confidence and increase his motivation to write. In addition to supporting his handwriting, it would also help him with learning to spell, as using a keyboard would develop his motor memory for words.

Activity 1

Read through the case studies above.

» *Revisit some of your own lesson plans and reflect on how you could have adapted them to ensure that a child with dyslexia could successfully record their learning.*

» *What have you learnt about adapting and differentiating lessons to enable children with dyslexia to succeed that you can apply to future lesson planning?*

The dyslexia-friendly classroom

Creating a *dyslexia-friendly* classroom will help all children who have dyslexia, and also those who are displaying dyslexic traits (see Table 11.2). In addition, many of the strategies will contribute to providing a supportive learning environment for all children.

Classteachers must be flexible and willing to adapt their environment to allow achievement by all; for example, ensure that the classroom is calm and quiet as some dyslexic children find background noise and visual movement distracting. In addition, an organised classroom with clear routines is important. These aspects of classroom management will clearly be of benefit to all children, including other children with SEN, as they are likely to thrive in a classroom which emphasises clarity and routine and provides visual cues and support. In addition to providing a positive learning environment, it is vital that the confidence and self-esteem of children with dyslexia is considered and supported, as they are important factors in academic success.

Table 11.2 A dyslexia-friendly classroom

Timetable	Provide a visual timetable Have clear routines
Teacher talk	When asking questions, give the child time to respond Limit instructions – keep them clear and precise Do not overload with information
Pens	Use different coloured pens on the white board Allow children to write with different pens, for example gel pens, tripod pencils, as giving a choice of pencil/pen often appeals to children, and makes the task more engaging
Paper	Use larger font with double spacing Print on cream rather than white paper Modify worksheets by reducing the amount of writing that needs to be done – what can you pre-prepare?
Spellings	Have the alphabet on display Provide lists of high-frequency words/topic words Ensure displays contain key vocabulary Learn spellings with a set pattern
Organising ideas	Encourage sub-vocalising when writing as it helps organise thoughts Share writing with the teacher or partner
Handwriting	Encourage cursive handwriting – starting all letters on the line causes less confusion Use a scribe
Copying	Give notes to copy from rather than using the white board Use smaller white boards placed in front of the child
Time	Allow extra time for tasks Add movement breaks into the lessons as regular movement will increase children's focus and retention

Activity 2

Read through the chart above.

» *Reflect on classrooms that you are familiar with.*

» *In what ways could you adapt the environment to ensure that children with dyslexia have the best possible opportunity to access the learning in the classroom?*

Think about:

– *quick changes, that could be implemented within a few days;*

– *medium-term changes;*

– *longer-term or whole school changes.*

CASE STUDY

Creating a supportive learning environment for all children

A group of Year 1 children had been practising letter formation with the intention of joining their letters, and it was clear that Sophie was struggling to form her letters correctly. The classteacher spoke to the SENCO who suggested that Sophie be taught to use lead-in strokes: all letters start on the line with an entry stoke and lead out with an exit stroke – the aim being to minimise confusion. The SENCO explained that once this is established, Sophie will be able to join all letters as they will naturally flow into each other. The teacher decided to use this method with the whole class so as not to single Sophie out.

Before putting pen to paper the teaching assistant took the children outside in small groups and, using water and paint brushes, they *wrote* their letters on the playground, they formed them in the sand pit, and formed them in the air. The teacher's aim was for the children to develop their motor memory for the formation of the letters.

When the children eventually came to using pencil and paper, the teacher marked a green dot on the line where she wanted the letters to begin, and told Sophie that this was her *green for go* dot. Sophie placed her pencil there to start the lead – in stroke.

With practice, the formation of Sophie's letters became more secure. However, the teacher was concerned about the size and unevenness of her handwriting, so she provided Sophie with *ground, grass and sky* handwriting lines, hoping that the colours (brown, green and blue) would help Sophie. She explained that all small letters fit in the grass, tall letters reach for the sky and letters with tails touch the ground. Sophie enjoyed being guided by the colours, and, with practice, her letters became smaller and her writing acquired a greater fluency.

Specialist support

Most children are able to make some progress with support and differentiation in place in the classroom, but for others, with more severe difficulties, specialist support may be required. The Rose Report (2009, p 13) makes clear why this is important:

> *Effective interventions 'personalise learning' by matching provision to meet the children's individual needs and quicken the pace of learning for those with literacy difficulties thus narrowing the attainment gap with their typically developing peers.*

The provision of specialist support will vary from school to school depending on the size, location and type of school. However, regardless of these factors, access to the necessary expertise and appropriate intervention programmes should be available. Two class-based interventions are outlined below.

The Five Minute Box

This is a multisensory system designed to boost literacy skills for children finding it hard to maintain progress with their literacy. The child receives additional teaching on a daily basis, usually with a teaching assistant, with progress being monitored by the SENCO and class-teacher. In this intervention, skills are divided into different areas which allow for them to be taught and reinforced at varying paces.

PAT (Phonological Awareness Training) programme (Frederickson and Wilson, 1996)

This is used to help children in reading, spelling and writing phonically regular words. Children build their knowledge of word sounds and apply them to other words by forming the rimes. This daily ten-minute programme can be led by the classteacher or teaching assistant. The programme contains pre-tests and post-tests in order for progress to be evaluated.

FOCUS ON RESEARCH

What do pre-service teachers know about dyslexia?

Washburn et al (2013) found that pre-service teachers in the UK displayed some accurate knowledge about dyslexia, but they also held some common misunderstandings.

For example, pre-service teachers understood that dyslexia is not caused by home back-ground and that language processing is affected by dyslexia. However, the common misunderstandings were that dyslexia is caused by a deficit in visual perception, that dyslexia is characterised by letter reversals and that children can outgrow dyslexia.

They conclude that teacher misunderstandings about dyslexia may lessen the likelihood of individuals with dyslexia receiving needed and appropriate literacy instruction, and that when popular misconceptions are perpetrated, appropriate instruction may become distorted.

In terms of teacher training, Washburn et al (2013) recognise that the term dyslexia may not always be welcome, because of misuse and the promotion of a negative label (Elliott, 2005), but that pre-service teachers should receive the most recent, accurate and evidence-based information about the nature and characteristics associated with dyslexia.

Conclusion

It is clear that during your teaching career you will encounter children with dyslexia. As a classteacher you may have as many as three children in your class experiencing dyslexic-type difficulties. It is important that you understand what you can do to ensure such children make progress and are able to realise their potential. While the dyslexic child may have poor self-esteem in the classroom, their self-esteem may be much higher on the sports field, in the music lesson or in the art room. It is worth considering whether you are nurturing these talents? Are you giving them opportunities to shine?

Teachers need to be equipped with the skills to identify and support these children. At the moment this does not always happen, and the dyslexic pupil can go unrecognised. In September 2009, it became law that every new SENCO in a mainstream school should gain, within three years of taking up the post, the Master's level National Award for Special Educational Needs.

There is now the call for dyslexia awareness training to be part of the initial teacher training. As Mike Storey from Dyslexia Action states, '*Although I praise the fantastic work of SENCOs in schools, there is an urgent need for all Initial Teacher Training (ITT) programmes to include a mandatory module on dyslexia.*' Currently this is not a government requirement.

Critical points

» *Dyslexia is a neurological disorder, which is present from birth and is a lifelong condition. It affects the skills involved in accurate and fluent word reading and spelling. It should be viewed as a continuum rather than a specific category as children with the label* dyslexic *will have different difficulties, which vary from slight to severe.*

» *There are a range of indicators that a child may be dyslexic. As a teacher you need to be aware of the indicators so that you can intervene as soon as possible to support the child's learning.*

» *There are a range of ways in which you can support a dyslexic child with their writing. This includes adapting and differentiating your lessons, using support staff effectively, focused interventions, seeking additional support from the school SENCO, and creating a dyslexic-friendly learning environment.*

» *A dyslexic-friendly classroom involves adapting the organisation and interaction in your classroom to meet the needs of children with dyslexia. These aspects of practice have the potential to support the learning of all children, as well as children with dyslexia.*

Critical reflections

» *How confident do you feel about identifying and supporting children with dyslexia?*

Make sure that you understand the indicators for dyslexia, and how you can meet children's needs. Reflect on your own practice and identify ways in which you can adapt your classroom, organise your interaction and your lessons plans to enable children with dyslexia to make progress with their writing, and record their work in ways that reflect what they know and can do.

Taking it further

Elliott, J and Grigorenko E (2014) *The Dyslexia Debate*. Cambridge: Cambridge University Press.

This book examines how we use the term *dyslexia* and questions its efficacy. It considers research in cognitive science, genetics and neuroscience, and the limitations of these fields for professional practice.

Smythe, I (2010) *Dyslexia in the Digital Age*. London: Continuum (Bloomsbury).

This book looks at the use of technology in schools to support children with dyslexia. It discusses the merits and limitations of using technology, including how to get the most out of it, and what more needs to be done to make technology truly enabling for children with dyslexia.

References

Barclay, S (2013) I Wonder What It's Like to Be Dyslexic. [online] Available at: https:// www.kickstarter. com/projects/1150582455/i-wonder-what-its-like-to-be-dyslexic. (accessed 12 February 2015)

British Dyslexia Association. [online] Available at: www.bdadyslexia.org.uk (accessed 21 November 2014).

Casserley, A (2012) The Socio-emotional Needs of Children with Dyslexia in Different Educational Settings in Ireland. *Journal of Research in Special Educational Needs*, 13(1): 79–91.

Elliott, J (2012) The Dyslexia Debate Continues. *The Psychologist*, 18: 728–9.

Frederickson, N and Wilson, J (1996) Phonological Awareness Training: A New Approach to Phonics. *Dyslexia*, 2(2): 101–20.

Mellors, C (2000) *Identifying and Supporting the Dyslexic Child*. Scunthorpe: Desktop Publications.

Rack, J, Hulme, C, Snowling, M and Wightman, J (1994) The Role of Phonology in Young Children Learning to Read Words: The Direct-Mapping Hypothesis. *Journal of Experimental Child Psychology*, 57: 42–71.

Reid, G (2011) *100+ Ideas for Supporting Children with Dyslexia*, 2nd Edn. London: Continuum.

Reid, G (2012) *Dyslexia and Inclusion: Classroom Approaches for Assessment, Teaching and Learning*, 2nd Edn. London: David Fulton

Rose, J (2009) Identifying and Teaching Children and Young People with Dyslexia and Literacy Difficulties. [online] Available at: webarchive.nationalarchives.gov.uk/20130401151715/ http://www.education.gov.uk/publications/eOrderingDownload/00659-2009DOM-EN.pdf (accessed 12 February 2015).

Saunders, K and Cochrane, K (2013) Dyslexia-Friendly Schools Good Practice Guide. [online] Available at: www.thedyslexiashop.co.uk/dyslexia-friendly-schools-good-practice-guide.html (accessed 12 February 2015).

Special Educational Needs and Disability Code of Practice: 0 to 25 Years (2014) Department of Education. [online] Available at: https://www.gov.uk/government/publications/send-code-of-practice-0-to-25 (accessed 12 February 2015).

Shaywitz, S (2005) *Overcoming Dyslexia: A New and Complete Science-based Program for Reading Problems at any Level*. New York: Vintage.

Washburn, E K, Binks-Cantrell, E and Joshi, R (2013) What Do Pre-service Teachers from USA and UK Know about Dyslexia? *Dyslexia*, 20: 1–18.

Websites

www.patoss-dyslexia.org – Patoss, the Professional Association for Teachers and Assessors of Students with Specific Learning Difficulties (SpLD)

www.dyslexiaaction.org.uk – information about dyslexia

www.bdadyslexia.org.uk – British Dyslexia Association '*a dyslexia-friendly society enabling all dyslexic people to reach their potential*'

www.dyslexic.org.uk – Dyslexia Research Trust

www.nhs.org – symptoms of dyslexia

www.fiveminuitebox.co.uk – intervention programme

www.nessy.com – website of ideas/approaches

www.wordshark.co.uk – website of ideas/approaches

12 Learning from pupils who have English as an additional language

KIRSTY ANDERSON AND GEETA LUDHRA

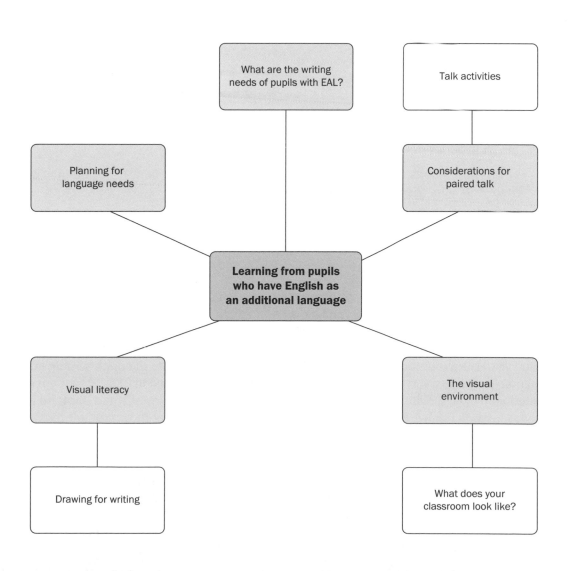

What are the writing needs of pupils with EAL?

Talk activities

Planning for language needs

Considerations for paired talk

Learning from pupils who have English as an additional language

Visual literacy

The visual environment

Drawing for writing

What does your classroom look like?

Teachers' Standards

5 Adapt teaching to respond to the strengths and needs of all pupils

- know when and how to differentiate appropriately, using approaches which enable pupils to be taught effectively

- have a secure understanding of how a range of factors can inhibit pupils' ability to learn, and how best to overcome these

- demonstrate an awareness of the physical, social and intellectual development of children, and know how to adapt teaching to support pupils' education at different stages of development

- have a clear understanding of the needs of all pupils – including those with special educational needs, those of high ability, those with English as an additional language and those with disabilities – and be able to use and evaluate distinctive teaching approaches to engage and support them

Critical questions

» *What are the specific writing needs of pupils with English as an Additional Language (EAL)?*

» *How can we ensure that planning is focused to meet their needs and ensure that bilingual pupils make highly effective progress?*

» *In what ways does talking support writing development, and how do you need to be more critical of the role of talk to support writing?*

» *How can we draw on visual and multimedia literacies to support the progress of bilingual pupils effectively?*

Introduction

This chapter outlines some of the effective strategies which have proved successful in supporting the writing needs of pupils with English as an additional language (EAL). In particular, the chapter will discuss ways in which teachers can move pupils with EAL beyond the early writing stages. This can be done through explicit planning techniques, strategic use of talk, valuing visual representations and evaluating the variety of language in our classroom environments. In addition, it is hoped that the effective strategies outlined in this chapter are recognised as highly relevant to all pupils in some way. The strategies presented are tried and tested ones which have been used by the authors and observed both by student teachers and experienced qualified teachers.

As the Teachers' Standards make clear, it is important to '*respond to the strengths and needs of all pupils*' (TS5). According to research from NALDIC (2013), one in six pupils at UK schools is described as having EAL. This is an estimated one million pupils, where the number of languages represented by these is around 360. This therefore places a significant training need on student teachers to understand how to adapt teaching to include bilingual learners so that they make progress. EAL pupils are not a homogenous group, but they may comprise a wide group from newly arrived beginners of English to advanced bilingual learners who have had all of their education at schools in the UK. They may read, write and speak in more than two languages. It is important to understand that the needs and types of EAL pupils are diverse, so one size does not fit all (see Conteh, 2012).

To develop pupils' writing skills you must ensure that you understand what pupils can already do (particularly in their first language), and recognise that for pupils with EAL, there will be additional aspects to consider at the planning stage. As Ofsted (2014, p 3) explains,

> pupils learning EAL are not a homogeneous group ... be aware of the possible variations between individuals and groups of EAL learners. Pupils come from diverse linguistic, cultural and educational backgrounds.

NALDIC (1999) identifies systematic approaches for teachers when working with bilingual pupils. The principles of these can be summarised as follows:

- *Activate prior knowledge.*

- *Provide a rich contextual background to aid comprehension.*

- *Encourage comprehensible input.*

- *Clarify the relationship between the language form and function.*

- *Develop learner independence.*

(Adapted from NALDIC, 1999)

In diverse classroom settings, you can scaffold language learning by valuing children's prior knowledge and experiences, ensuring that clarity of meaning is achieved through highly relevant contextual supports that include culturally specific resources. It is important to recognise the value of activating and building on prior knowledge, as bilingual pupils are more likely to make progress when they feel that their learning connects to existing experiences.

FOCUS ON RESEARCH

Cognitive demand and context

When planning teaching and learning opportunities to develop the writing skills of bilingual pupils, it is vital to identify two considerations: *What is the academic language proficiency of the pupil?* and *How cognitively challenging is the task?* Bilingual pupils can quickly develop social skills in the *right* conditions, and learn the survival language of the playground through play. However, as Cummins (2000) notes, socialising with peers is likely to be highly contextualised and cognitively undemanding in relation to the academic language requirements of the curriculum. Playground language follows informal grammatical patterns and rules of standard English. For Cummins, playground language would be a context-embedded, cognitively undemanding activity (A in the figure).

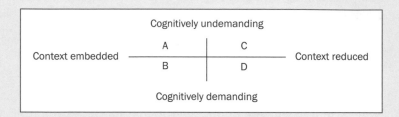

Activities to develop writing skills in a context-embedded form might include writing instructions for a game which they are highly familiar with; writing a recount of a visit that they have experienced through high quality talk and guidance or writing a version of a well-known story that they have rehearsed through drama and role play. Learning will become more cognitively demanding if, for example, wider and more varied vocabulary is gradually introduced. In primary schools, assessment of pupils' independent writing might be an example of an activity that is context reduced. Cummins further highlights the need to ensure that pupils with EAL are supported carefully to move from A type activities towards D activities. Gibbons (1996) supports this further, indicating that in developing writing skills, pupils may need continued teacher support to de-contextualise their learning. Moreover, as the *quadrant* illustrates, tasks located in D are *context reduced* and not necessarily *context removed*. Perhaps for pupils with EAL it is best to ensure the transition process is gradual. Indeed, as Cummins indicates, teaching and learning activities fall into the different aspects at different times. When introducing new learning, it is likely that even cognitively demanding tasks will be context embedded to ensure understanding. All pupils will be undertaking new learning, so they should be moved gradually from what can be understood with contextual support to more context reduced or even abstract independent learning.

Cummins' (2000) aim with this *quadrant* is to support an understanding of the demands different activities might place on academic language proficiency. By understanding the nature of different learning opportunities, teachers can begin to map out appropriately supportive and challenging activities. As teachers, you can plan activities carefully in relation to cognitive demand and context.

What are the writing needs of pupils with EAL?

When teaching pupils with EAL you need to recognise that their needs are diverse, and not simply language focused. Although it has already been recognised that the EAL learner can range from being a beginner to an advanced bilingual learner, there are some considerations you will need to plan for in relation to supporting their writing development.

- Do the pupils need to make rapid progress to catch up with their peers?
- Do they need to learn a new language?
- Does the writing context connect to previous experiences?
- How proficient is the pupil in writing in their first language?

- What are the grammatical structures of their first language and how does this compare with English grammar and writing conventions?

- What support structures will the child need to write, for example word bank, visual images, bilingual dictionary?

You need to recognise that the pupils with EAL will be learning a new language and a new curriculum in that new language. Alongside the new language, you must also remember that pupils might need to learn new or different social skills, values and cultural expectations which will need to be configured within their existing ones. To be a highly effective primary school teacher, it is important to find ways to ensure that these different influences and variables are built on and nurtured. More advanced bilingual pupils will have different writing needs, such as understanding colloquialisms or complex aspects of grammar.

Moving pupils beyond the early stages of writing requires a strong subject knowledge of language development and an awareness of their current positions in their first language. When working with pupils with EAL, it is essential that the language needs of every task are planned for across the curriculum. When children with EAL are learning to write, therefore, you need to explain the language demands of the learning objective by discussing the types of language they will need to successfully complete the activity.

CASE STUDY

A newly arrived beginner to English

Maros had been part of a Year 4 class for four months. Maros was described as a newly arrived beginner to English. His family moved to the UK from Slovakia as migrant workers. Maros had one year of elementary schooling in Slovakia. He knew *survival* and playground vocabulary to talk with his peers in English and was beginning to make attempts to copy his name and the English alphabet. Kath, Maros' teacher, knew that he needed support to develop his spoken English alongside an understanding of the language. She carefully planned group activities which can both develop understanding of different texts and develop knowledge of language.

In one activity, Maros worked in a group to create a *jigsaw story*. The children were each given an image to describe. Maros was supported with a word mat to help him select appropriate vocabulary. Some of the vocabulary was already familiar, as Kath had chosen vocabulary which reflected games she knew Maros played with his friends. After each picture was described, Kath asked the group to order the pictures into a story. She encouraged understanding of the function of the language used by providing a checklist of features which included conjunctions, verbs and adjectives. The group used the ideas to create sentences which tell the story. Using whiteboards, the group tried sentences and then worked together to talk about the features their sentences should include.

Activity 1

» *Which stories might be useful to create a jigsaw story? Consider stories with predictable language and/or events and with universal contexts.*

Planning for language needs

When planning learning activities to develop writing for pupils with EAL, you need to be clear which aspects of written English they will develop during the course of a lesson. For example, when writing recounts, a pupil like Maros may need support with use of articles and determiners, alongside understanding the generic features of writing a recount. He might, for instance, write '*I went shops*'. His teacher would first establish the meaning of any writing (which can be supported with drawing, as will be explored later in this chapter) before addressing specific grammatical needs. By ensuring that writing is context embedded, you can more quickly recognise the meaning and support development of grammatically correct written English. Successful teachers will make sure that they explicitly plan for frequent and early opportunities to share attempts at writing. Teaching children to recognise what might be missing from their own writing can be more successful than simply reminding children of what may seem to be abstract rules of standard English.

Reviewing the plan: how careful planning can make a real difference

When planning for the writing needs of pupils with EAL, it is essential to exploit every opportunity to develop language, and in particular vocabulary. Having a limited vocabulary can result in writing which lacks fluency and range. As a teacher, you need to seek opportunities to expand vocabulary at all times through high quality spoken language experiences. Writing uses deliberate vocabulary choices and specific grammar structures. It is important to teach children to recognise this. When planning, you need to consider what the spoken language demands will be, who and what pupils will listen to, the texts you will use and the technical grammar and vocabulary which need to be taught. The latter should ideally be noted on the lesson plan, as they are more likely to be explicitly taught then. Children need to develop spoken language and pupils with EAL need frequent opportunities to widen their vocabulary. However, it is important to recognise that when they develop their spoken language in collaboration with other pupils, this spoken language may then need further development to make use of the grammatical rules associated with standard English. It is important not only to appreciate and celebrate different dialects and the grammatical forms used but also to take the time to teach children the grammatical rules of standard English and how these might compare across different languages too.

CASE STUDY

An advanced bilingual learner

Maryam is a Year 5 pupil who enjoys writing stories. Maryam might be described as an advanced bilingual learner. Her educational experiences have all been at school in the UK. At school, she speaks English the majority of the time. At home, Maryam speaks Sylhethi with her family who are from the Sylhet region of Bangladesh. Maryam understands rules for spelling and generally follows conventions for grammar, but has some difficulty with the correct use of the past tense.

Maryam's teacher, Sophie, has planned opportunities to enable Maryam to practise using the past tense correctly. With a *talk partner*, Maryam practises transforming sentences from present into past tense. Together they write down what they think, as well as rehearsing it aloud. The next task is to find out if they have used the correct form of the verb. Maryam has written '*I goed*' for the past tense of '*I go*'. With her partner, she investigates whether or not she is correct, using a dictionary. Her teacher also plans for the talk partners to look for examples of people talking using standard English on the internet.

Activity 2

» *Make a list of examples of spoken language characteristics used in the region where you live.*

» *Are there any past tense forms which are commonly used, but which do not follow the grammatical rules of standard English? For example, do you say 'I was …' or 'I were …', 'We was' or 'We were'? When using negatives, do you say 'I ain't …' or 'I haven't …'*

» *If you have an opportunity to work with children with EAL, listen to the syntax of their spoken language. Do these children use phrases such as 'I go shops …'? Which language features can you focus on when pupils use spoken language in this way?*

Considerations for paired talk

Without doubt, high quality talk can and does support the writing process, particularly at the beginning stages. Education theorists including Vygotsky (1978) and Bruner (1996) agree that we learn best through social interaction. As a teacher, you will frequently encourage children to rehearse their sentences out loud before writing them and to discuss and generate ideas with a *talk partner or more knowledgeable other*. At the same time, however, it is important to remember that there are distinct differences between talk and writing (see Chapter 2). When you talk, you tend to use utterances and chains of clauses rather than sentences. Often, when you are involved in speech it is interactive with a person or persons from whom you can take cues. Writing, on the other hand, tends to be more detached, and writing, unlike speech, can be an individual process. Skilled teachers might try out different classroom approaches which include paired and group writing, which can be of particular benefit to pupils with EAL, especially if use is made of bilingual buddies (an advanced bilingual and a less fluent pupil). Bereiter and Scardamalia's (1987) research found that conversation does indeed support composition. Conversational support is extremely effective for pupils with EAL. The aim though for all pupils is, of course, independence and self-reliance, but this must be scaffolded and support provided for pupils with EAL to move beyond conversational support towards producing writing without prompting.

One of the dangers for pupils with EAL is an over-reliance on the talk partner where they struggle to make the transition to working independently. You need to ensure that contributions are made by both parties so there is a balance of cognitive thinking. Ensuring that there are opportunities for all pupils to rehearse their writing out loud can be accommodated easily. You should also ensure that pupils with EAL are enabled to directly discuss the language they have used. By providing pupils with a visual word mat or grammar mat relevant to that particular writing activity, you can remind pupils which are the key components of a sentence in English and provide a reference upon which they can base their knowledge. Rather than simply asking children to read aloud the sentence they are trying to write, ask children to identify the word classes: verb, the connective or the adjective, for example. This can support pupils to develop a metalanguage with which to discuss the features of language.

Talk activities

It is essential to provide adequate *thinking time* for children. While you may want to measure progress and check the pupils' understanding of a lesson through the use of questions, for pupils with EAL this may be quite a daunting task. Even the most skilled teachers, who quickly rephrase questions to include all learners, would benefit from allowing time for silence. Remember that for pupils with EAL the cognitive processes will be different. They will need to formulate an answer and then translate their answer into English – their second language.

It is not only when you question pupils that you need to allow for reflection. When children are writing independently, they need to draw on their memory in order to plan large units of writing. Children also learn to revise their writing by working as both the writer and the reader. You need to support pupils with EAL in this process by facilitating opportunities for silence to allow children time to think of the words they want to use to ensure the sentence carries sense, and to work as readers checking the sense of their own writing. During times when children are interacting with their own writing, it is essential to make use of supporting tools. Word mats, vocabulary lists and checklists of genre features are useful reference points for all children as they develop independent writing skills.

Visual literacy

What are visual texts and how are these used effectively?

A visual text is an image in which a narrative can be found. Television and film are obvious examples, but narrative can also be found in paintings, photographs, games and comics. These are less traditional sources and stimuli; however, you should make use of the diversity of children's experiences. Given the conversations and playground re-enactments of and about favourite programmes, it seems wise to make use of this medium to extend the range of all learners.

Think about how often we hear or ask this question: *'Did you see the latest episode of ...?'* Primary school children are asking this same question. Sometimes teachers silence classroom chatter about the latest film or sensational episode of a reality TV show and redirect it to the playground. But what if we exploit the omnipresence of the media to our advantage in stimulating classroom writing opportunities? Considering how often children re-enact what they have viewed, it could be a potential goldmine! With episodic dramas, we might explore cliff-hangers. Animation aimed at children can be a rich source of comedy. The melodrama and play-acting in wrestling might be useful to develop scriptwriting. The possibilities are potentially endless.

As children grow as writers, you will teach them to refine and edit their ideas so they learn to communicate effectively through the written word. Importantly, children need to have ideas to communicate. Newly arrived pupils will be learning to read in English. It is important to remember that the cultural experiences of pupils from other countries are likely to be different. Some pupils in Maryam's class for example, will be readily accessing demanding and age appropriate texts from which complex language structures for writing can be developed. Texts for early readers might be useful as examples of sentence structure; however, the content would be inappropriate for older pupils like Maryam. Therefore, visual texts can help to support planning to engage *all* pupils, and can draw upon their prior knowledge to help them make connections and move their learning forward. Animated films from different cultures not only provide an additional resource from which writing can be generated, but they also provide opportunities to celebrate and explore the experiences that pupils in your class may have had. For example, *Pat a Mat* (Pat and Mat) are popular animated characters from the Czech Republic. The short animations of the two characters, widely available on YouTube, are ideal for use in classrooms as there is no dialogue. Similarly, *Staflek a Spagetka* (telling the mishaps of two dogs) is a dialogue-free Czech cartoon widely popular across Europe. Using the short films as starting points, learning outcomes can be wide-ranging, depending again on the language proficiency of the different learners. From captions and dialogue, to descriptions and different types of narratives, short films offer a supportive context. (For more details see Chapter 7.)

Vocabulary, in particular, can be developed quickly through the use of images. Moreover, this vocabulary is likely to be remembered as it is contextualised, or *context embedded*. Pictures and labels are often shared with young children as they begin to recognise the graphic version of a word. This practice is continued with pupils with EAL as they develop vocabulary. Starting any topic with children necessitates sharing new vocabulary and this can be more powerful when the vocabulary is generated through a more natural discussion by looking at relevant images.

It is important that a pupil with EAL has access not only to supporting visual aids, such as pictures with corresponding labels, but also to key visuals. The difference between the two is easily explained if you consider a butterfly. A visual aid can be a photograph labelled *butterfly*. A key visual would be the life cycle of the butterfly. When planning for pupils with EAL, it is important that appropriate and effective challenge is available. A key visual like the life cycle of a butterfly is more cognitively demanding by enabling organisational skills to develop, which can in turn be useful as a support for writing.

CASE STUDY

Cross-curricular writing

In Salem's Year 2 class, the pupils were learning in science to observe and describe weather connected to different seasons. Matthew, a trainee teacher on his final placement, decided to fully develop this cross-curricular opportunity for writing. Salem was given a key visual of seasonal changes illustrated by photographs of trees. Initially, Salem was only able to label the different trees using key words: no leaves, new leaves, green leaves, brown leaves. Matthew then mixed up the key visuals and asked Salem to re-order these. Salem did this and was introduced to key vocabulary *first, next, finally*. Salem talked through the seasonal changes with a partner and was then given the opportunity to record his talk using the class iPad. With this talk as a memory aid, and a word mat to help, Salem then wrote descriptions of the key visuals independently. Salem then repeated the activity using other images of weather from different seasons. Matthew noticed that he became increasingly confident with his use of sequential vocabulary and was more willing to write independently.

Activity 3

» Make a list of the different non-fiction genres which can be supported by using key visuals. Note, too, some experiences you might plan for children to support this.

Drawing for writing

Not only can you provide pupils with visuals which can support and prompt independent writing, but you can also facilitate the use of drawing as a memory aid. Encouraging pupils to draw during or after an experience can provide structure for any follow-up writing tasks. For example, when learning to write instructions, effective teachers will aim to make the experience real by baking a cake or playing the game, which they will later write instructions for. To support the writing needs of pupils with EAL, you can encourage them to sketch each step they undertake. By doing this we are providing pupils with their own supporting key visuals as well as providing a reminder of the context so that, as Cummins (2000) suggests, support is not completely removed (a situation which can be difficult for some pupils). Story mapping, as suggested in the Talk for Writing materials from the National Strategy (2008), also makes effective use of drawings which provide a reminder and scaffold for the writing process.

FOCUS ON RESEARCH

Visual stimuli

Using different visual stimuli can be very effective in supporting children to develop their ideas. At the same time, their own drawings can support the development and indeed the recollection of their ideas for writing. In a research study published in 2013, Adoniou found that the writing of English language learners was improved when they were given the opportunity to record their experiences as a drawing first. In the study, pupils were given a context-embedded experience of following a recipe. Those children who were encouraged to draw the process as they worked were able to recall much more and in turn transfer this into their recipe writing. In addition to recalling more, the pupils in the study made greater use of technical vocabulary than those who did not record the stages as they worked.

Picture books are no longer just for the youngest children, and visual media plays a large part in our everyday lives. It is sensible then to recognise and exploit this. Not only can it be stimulating for children, but it also ensures that the practices we use in the classroom are relevant to the everyday lives of all children.

The visual environment

Teaching in a primary school is often busy and demanding. However, if you spend time considering your classroom, then your pupils' writing skills can be developed and supported through the visual environment. Children learning EAL need to have a scaffold for their language development. Making effective use of interactive displays which use examples of grammatically correct English expected in writing can help children to become confident as they write independently. Sharing errors, such as the non-standard past tense forms of frequently used verbs (eg, *to go* or *to be*) on display next to the standard English form of the verb, is a simple but effective aid.

What does your classroom look like?

Considering how displays can be useful for learning is only one aspect of developing writing. The use of visual support, such as art work and films, has already been discussed, but one can go further to develop ideas for writing for children learning English. Children who are effective learners ask questions. Researchers such as Neil Mercer from Cambridge University (2008) have found that exploratory talk is most effective as the learning generated from discussion offers children opportunities to explore other people's points of view and to thus make connections with their own learning. There are many opportunities which we can exploit in the visual environment to generate talk which can then stimulate ideas for writing. Some teachers transform their classrooms wholly into different environments, for example, a polar region or a Greek temple. Other teachers make use of enquiry-based learning such as the Mantle of the Expert (Heathcote and Bolton, 1996). In this, a classroom is transformed into a *real* working environment, such as a museum, and children immerse themselves in role with different jobs. (For more on drama and writing see Chapter 4.)

CASE STUDY

Introducing a story to pupils with diverse backgrounds

Louise, a trainee teacher, wanted to introduce E B White's *Charlotte's Web* to the Year 3 class she was working with. Louise recognised that the pupils had diverse backgrounds and therefore the experiences and understanding which they would bring to the text would be different. In the week before the text was first introduced, Louise began to gather an understanding of pupils' experiences. She placed toy spiders and webs around the classroom without explaining this to the children. She listened to their conversations. To support the English language learners in particular, Louise started to record the questions which were asked and displayed these on her *learning wall*. As the week progressed, Louise introduced labels for different objects. She also copied illustrations from the text and included examples of the description dialogue used in the story on the learning wall. To ensure that the English language learners' needs were met, Louise annotated the description to highlight the use of standard English past tense verb forms as a reminder to pupils like Dominika who made errors in this area. Dominika, from the Czech Republic, was conversationally fluent but made errors when using the past tense forms of some verbs, for example writing wented instead of went. When the text was introduced the following week, Louise had a good understanding of the pupils' experiences of spiders and farm animals.

Activity 4

»   *Look at Roald Dahl's* Danny the Champion of the World. *What items, pictures and key words might you place around your classroom to stimulate language and to understand prior knowledge?*

Conclusion

Pupils with EAL have varied writing needs. Most importantly, you need to remember to ensure that they are given the opportunity to learn appropriate types of language for each activity. Careful planning should include a record of an outcome and a record of the types of language learnt and practised by the pupils. This will support teacher reflections on learning and progress. Using talk is essential for learning and to practise the skills of standard English forms, which impact on the written grammatical structures. Carefully ensuring that partner talk is focused and checking contributions from both pupils, as well as valuing time for reflection, can facilitate more productive talk. Varied visual texts can and should be used to stimulate ideas for writing, to promote inclusive practice through the use of culturally relevant visual texts and also to ensure that the classroom is not a standalone environment which neglects something so prominent in society today. These different aspects should be carefully considered to meet the needs of all learners.

Critical points

»   *Pupils with EAL have specific writing needs, but the strategies which can be used to address these may benefit other children too.*

» *Detailed planning which focuses clearly on targets, clear outcomes and language expectations can enable highly effective progress.*

» *As a teacher, you need to facilitate directed partner talk and allow opportunities for silent reflection to allow all children time to contribute.*

» *Drawing, as a guide and reminder for writing, is demonstrably supportive for pupils with EAL. Pupils with EAL have different cultural backgrounds, but use of multimedia can aid inclusion and support understanding of different cultures.*

Critical reflections

» *This chapter has explored the specific writing needs of pupils with EAL. It is important, however, that as a teacher you think carefully about the writing needs of all pupils. The two essential qualities for teachers to meet the needs of all pupils are flexibility and reflection.*

Taking it further

Short animations *Pat a Mat* (Pat and Mat) from the Czech Republic can be found at: www.youtube. com/watch?v=YS3Mt_5wYLE (accessed 17 April 2015)

Further suggestions can be found at: www.expats.cz/prague/article/prague-entertainment/the-best-czech-cartoons/ (accessed 17 April 2015)

Useful picture books include:

Browne, A (1999) *Voices in the Park*. London: Picture Corgi Books.

Tan, S (2007) *The Arrival*. Sydney: Hodder Children's Books.

Wiesner, D (1991) *Tuesday*. New York: Clarion Books.

Useful guidance on assessing the progress of children with EAL can be found in the QCA publication: A Language in Common (QCA, 2000). Available as a pdf download at: www.naldic.org. uk/Resources/NALDIC/Teaching%20and%20Learning/1847210732.pdf (accessed 17 April 2015).

Gibbons, P (2002) *Scaffolding Language: Scaffolding Learning*. Portsmouth, NH: Heinemann.

Gibbons, P (1996) *Learning to Learn in a Second Language*. Portsmouth, NH: Heinemann.

Both works from Gibbons include useful ideas and exemplified good practice.

References

Adoniou, M (2013) Drawing to Support Writing Development in English Language Learners. *Language and Education*, 27(3): 261–77.

Bereiter, C and Scardamalia, M (1987) *The Psychology of Written Composition*. New Jersey: Lawrence Erlbaum Associates, Inc.

Bruner, J (1996) *The Culture of Education*. Cambridge, MA: Harvard University Press.

Conteh, J (2012) *Teaching Bilingual and EAL Learners in Primary Schools*. London: Sage Learning Matters.

Cummins, J (2000) *Language, Power and Pedagogy: Bilingual Children in the Crossfire*. Clevedon: Multilingual Matters Ltd.

Dahl, R (1977) *Danny the Champion of the World*. London: Puffin Books.

Gibbons, P (1996) *Learning to Learn in a Second Language*. Portsmouth, NH: Heinemann.

Heathcote, D and Bolton, G (1995) *Drama for Learning*. Portsmouth, NH: Heinemann.

NALDIC (1999) *Working Paper 5: The Distinctiveness of EAL – A Cross-Curriculum Discipline*. Watford: NALDIC.

NALDIC (2013). *A Language in Common: Assessing English as an Additional Language* [online] Available at: www.naldic.org.uk/ (accessed 19 February 2015).

Ofsted (2014) English as an Additional Language. Briefing for Section 5 Inspection. [online] Available at: www.naldic.org.uk (accessed 16 February 2015).

Talk for Writing (2008) [online] Available in pdf format at: http://webarchive.nationalarchives.gov.uk/20110809101133/nsonline.org.uk/node/163592 (accessed 12 February 2015).

Vygotsky, L S (1978) *The Mind In Society*. Cambridge, MA: Harvard University Press.

Answers

Activity 1

There will undoubtedly be regional variation in response to this activity. For further information see the British Library Sounds Familiar web pages on the English language at www.bl.uk/learning/langlit/sounds/.

Activity 2

Traditional tales and fairy tales often follow similar patterns. *The Three Little Pigs* and *The Three Billy Goats Gruff* have similar structures for instance. *The Little Red Hen* is an example of a story with universal context.

Activity 3

Genres which can be supported through use of first-hand experiences include (but are not limited to) instruction, recount, persuasion, discussion, explanation. First-hand experiences include following a recipe; a visit; sharing a favourite film; taking part in a debate and undertaking a science experiment.

Activity 4

In preparation for sharing *Danny the Champion of the World*, images might include traditional and modern caravans, cars and service stations. Images of pheasants, stately homes and woods might also be useful. In the classroom, items such as raisins could be scattered around alongside vocabulary including shooting season, pheasants, gamekeeper, land.

13 Beyond pen and paper

JOHN BENNETT

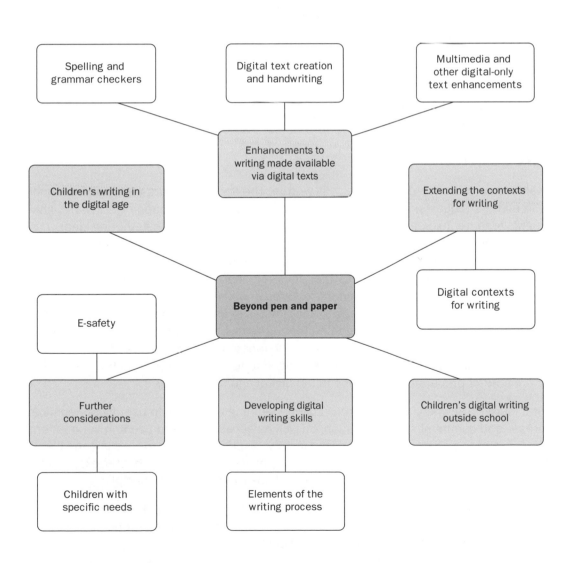

Teachers' Standards

3 Demonstrate good subject and curriculum knowledge

* have a secure knowledge of the relevant subject(s) and curriculum areas, foster and maintain pupils' interest in the subject, and address misunderstandings

* demonstrate a critical understanding of developments in the subject and curriculum areas, and promote the value of scholarship

* demonstrate an understanding of and take responsibility for promoting high standards of literacy, articulacy and the correct use of standard English, whatever the teacher's specialist subject

Critical questions

» *What and how do children write digitally?*

» *How can we ensure that the writing curriculum is relevant to the twenty-first century writers?*

» *How can we ensure that the writing curriculum goes beyond pen and paper?*

» *How can we develop the skills needed to write digital texts as effectively as possible?*

» *How can developing digital writing enhance the development of writing skills?*

Introduction

Consider how this chapter was physically written. The first notes were via email, responding to the editor's requests. In planning the chapter, I used concept-mapping software, linking thoughts together to create clusters of text to organise the content. In gathering ideas, I used two electronic notes programmes (*Evernote* and *OneNote*), on a PC, an iPad and a smartphone. As I wrote, I created and edited, changing words and sentences as I went along and correcting typos. The editing process then involved sharing drafts with the editor, with the use of *track changes* and *add comment* features enabling the process. The only time I put pencil to paper was to add brief notes to sticky notes in physical books. Everything else was written digitally. It is this world of digitally creating writing which children live in now, and the writing of their future is almost guaranteed to be created without the use of pen and paper. We need to take children beyond those analogue tools and give them both the experience and the correct preparation for writing in the digital age.

Digital literacy (Bawden, 2008; Martin, 2006), meaning the ability to use digital technology to create and communicate information, as well as access, find and use it in various forms, is the focus of this chapter, particularly the first two aspects, relating to creating and communicating in textual form, referred to hereafter as digital writing. This chapter explores what digital writing means for classroom practice and has two underlying principles:

1. Digital writing provides varied opportunities to develop writing skills and the technology can be used to enhance the skill development, the experience, the motivation to write and the final written output.

2. Children must learn how to use technology, to enhance their current and future use of digital writing in their personal and vocational lives.

A useful way of considering the use and impact of technology is the SAMR model (Puentedura, 2013), which has four levels at which technology operates: *substitution, augmentation, modification* and *redefinition.* In this chapter you will find out more about:

- making writing more efficient through enhancements;

- extending the possibilities for writing contexts;

- transforming the experience from the relatively limited pen and paper tools, to the broad ranging possibilities of digital approaches.

Children's digital writing outside school

What reasons did children have to write outside school (not including homework) ten years ago? A list for Santa? The odd thank you letter perhaps? Not a lot. But with many children now having their own digital devices, the reasons to write have increased: text messages, emails, even typing a query into a search engine are all forms of writing that are regularly undertaken. Even very young children come to school having experienced keyboards, mice, tablets and smartphones and, as can be seen below, many engage with digital writing technology outside school. Classroom practices should capitalise on the motivation to write that digital media creates (EPPI, 2004).

FOCUS ON RESEARCH

Media literacy

An Ofcom survey of children's media use in 2014 showed that in the UK children's use of a variety of devices to go online is increasing at home (Ofcom, 2014). That use could be for a variety of purposes and while the report does not look specifically at children writing digitally, it does provide an insight into activities which almost certainly include digital writing. Clearly text messaging is a significant part of that and it is probably safe to assume that the 32 per cent of 8–11-year-olds who own a phone will use text messages and the 20 per cent who own smartphones may also use those for email or other text creation.

Some interesting findings about 8–11-years-olds, which can be related to writing digitally, are:

- 75 per cent have access to a tablet computer at home;

- 34 per cent have their own tablet;

- 20 per cent have their own social networking site (certainly requiring writing digitally to set up and maintain);

- they are sending 42 text-based messages a week, on average (email and text messages);

- 84 per cent use the internet for school/homework;

- 8 per cent have created a website.

It seems very likely that the figures above will increase, as access to technology increases. As a primary school teacher, it is very important to have knowledge and understanding of children's writing experiences outside school. It is clear from the survey results that children's writing has extended into the digital world outside school and what happens in school should reflect that.

Activity 1: Exploring children's digital writing

» *Ask a group of children what they write when they are not in school. It is possible that they will start by talking about traditional pen/pencil and paper writing. Point out that writing can be any form of communication where text is created to be read by somebody and can include on-screen writing of any form. Make a list and when it is complete, ask the children the following questions.*

» *Which of those types of writing:*

   – *do you think are the most important and why?*

   – *do you do the most?*

   – *do you never or hardly ever do at school?*

   – *do you think is easier or harder to do electronically and why?*

» *Explore the pros and cons related to writing digitally with your focus group.*

Children's writing in the digital age

Composition using digital texts opens up possibilities for children to be creative, enhancing the text they write and the experience for the reader. Innovative approaches to teaching and learning should engage children with the technology and the possibilities it offers. The view that writing using digital tools is simply an alternative to using analogue, pen and paper methods has certainly been prevalent in the past (Andrews, 2003), but this perspective has been changing rapidly in many schools, due to factors such as OpenSource software, web-based applications and better pupil-to-device ratios in classrooms.

For the development of digital writing skills there are many programs which can be used to create textual content, in the form of word processors, desktop publishers and other text creating software, which are increasingly available as online resources and at low or no cost. Web 2.0 technology, which allows the user not just to view, but also create and share content, provides a wide range of possibilities (Barber and Cooper, 2012; Davies and Merchant, 2009). The range of useful writing apps for mobile devices is also growing. There are some composition programmes specifically designed for children, with a clear focus on developing writing skills, such as the Clicker suite of iPad apps and the main Clicker 6 software (www.cricksoft.com). It is worth exploring these various apps and programs, to identify those which could be used to support writing development in general, as well as provide platforms for digital writing experiences.

Enhancements to writing made available via digital texts

Digital writing technology can enhance the writing experience, making it more efficient than traditional methods and extending the features possible within the created text.

Spelling and grammar checkers

Children should be taught how to use spelling and grammar checkers effectively. A particular point here is that spellcheckers will often *knot pick up sum off the errors children May make*. As you can see from that last sentence, homophones are a particular problem. Therefore, an important lesson for children is that they should not rely on the spellchecker. Spellcheckers should be set to use a UK English dictionary, to avoid US spellings such as *color* and *favorite*.

Many word processors also include further features which can enhance the word level of text creation. For example, using the thesaurus feature children can consider alternative words, which can improve their writing and extend their vocabulary, especially when used with any *look up* feature which gives access to dictionary definitions of the word.

Digital text creation and handwriting

Using a keyboard to create writing has many advantages over traditional methods (as noted elsewhere in this chapter) and is the most common form of writing creation in the developed world. It would therefore be very useful for children to learn typing skills. It is interesting to consider what the impact on productivity, both in education and in industry, would have been if every child in the country had been required to learn how to type at school (see also Chapter 9).

Multimedia and other digital-only text enhancements

Children can create multimedia texts, including hyperlinks, pictures, sounds and animation, relatively easily, using programs, apps or Web 2.0 tools, such as those used to create wikis. Their text can be enlivened with animation and transitions, using presentation software (eg, Keynote and Powerpoint) or online applications such as *GooglePresentations*. Recent developments of web technologies have led to new presentation tools, such as Prezi (www.prezi.com), which adds new dimensions to what can be done with text to provide/create the greatest impact on the audience.

The creation of many digital texts, even using basic word processors, can now include the addition of multimedia and functional elements, such as those listed below:

- hyperlinks;

- mouseover/rollover effects;

- pop ups;

- menus;

- animation;

- sound;

- video;

- contents sections.

Children should be taught how to add these features to their basic text, to create enhanced *documents* and hypertexts, such as web pages and presentations.

CASE STUDY

Creating books

Helen's mixed Year 3 and Year 4 class in a rural primary school had access to tablet computers (iPads), with one iPad for every pair of children. The children used iPads to support work across a range of curriculum areas and it was clear to Helen that not only did the iPads provide a range of different stimuli, but they also enhanced writing, particularly for the lower ability children, who showed more engagement with writing than previously, perhaps due to the fact that they could easily correct errors and the presentation was better than their personal handwriting. Over a year, Helen saw improvements in the quality of the children's writing, which appeared to be due to increased interest and engagement, fostered by the technology.

At the beginning of the year, in pairs, the children created their own interactive class handbook. This was done following a typical writing process. The content was planned and notes were made about what might be seen on each page, which included not only text, but also pictures, movies and sound clips. Part of that development included using an online concept-mapping application (Popplet) to generate ideas. The interactive digital books were created following modelling of the process, using *Creative Book Builder* (iPad app).

The children picked up how to use the program quickly and there were numerous opportunities for Helen to support the creation of the interactive books and for the children to evaluate each other's creations, suggesting improvements and potentially sharing resources which they created, such as photographs and videos (both taken with the iPad). Helen noted that the children appeared much more engaged with this process than the traditional approach. They demonstrated creative thinking in relation to how the text was organised, not just in terms of the content, but also in relation to the placement of text boxes on the page, the use of colour and different text sizes, all of which were taking account of the impact on the reader.

The interactive books were made available through an online depository (Dropbox), so other children could access them. The children therefore had a definite audience for their writing. There was a very clear purpose for the interactive books: providing information for other pupils.

Activity 2: Writing in the digital age

» *Design a lesson based on an aspect of digital writing, for example:*

- *using the thesaurus and dictionary tools to improve a given piece of text;*

- *creating a playscript collaboratively, using copy and paste for the character names;*

- *creating an advert for a school event (using desktop publishing or web page creation software), copying the key text from a word/phrase bank created as a whole class;*

- *creating a branching story, with linking pages.*

» *Think about the* standard *writing skills which will be developed through the lesson, but also think about the distinctive digital writing skills which the lesson could focus on (eg, cut and paste, hyperlinking).*

» *Create learning objectives which relate specifically to digital writing skill development.*

Developing digital writing skills

Modern technology offers ways to enhance all stages of the writing process, potentially enhancing the outcome and certainly helping develop skills in digital writing. What follows are just a few suggestions, in relation to each stage of the process.

Elements of the writing process

Purpose and audience

The audience for children's writing has often been limited to teachers, parents or carers, and peers. Sometimes writing might be done for a national competition, or to be read by younger children, or for other slightly wider *real* or *imagined* audiences, such as a letter to a local MP. Digital facilities, such as email, blogging and Twitter, offer real audiences for children's writing. These can be extended into significant projects, such as multimedia presentations, designing web pages and creating social networking personal spaces. With the right safeguards and careful thought, digital writing with clear purposes and audiences should be seen as a necessity in this digital age.

CASE STUDY

Film club: writing for a purpose and audience

A school runs a weekly film club for the children. After each screening the children are invited to add reviews and comments on the film to a forum set up on the school's learning platform. These submissions are moderated by a member of staff.

It was noted by the school staff that children who would not usually choose to read or write were very happy to add their comments to the forum and in doing so were also reading the comments of other children and adding to the online discussion about the film.

The *real* context of the writing activity provided a meaningful experience within which the children could practise their writing skills.

Planning

Web- and software-based tools are available to help writers gather, shape, sort and organise their ideas and can enhance the process and the quality of the final piece of writing. For example, with concept-mapping software (and other graphic organisers), story maps can easily be created (eg Popplet – www.popplet.com) and 'sticky note' applications, such as Padlet (www.padlet.com), can be used with a whole class to gather and share ideas.

Digital writing offers versatility: ideas, words and whole sections can be moved around in order to create the best flow for the text or the ideas behind it. Possible approaches can be constructed then appraised by the writer to decide if they will work. Once text has been included in one program, it is usually a very simple matter to transfer it to another. So, for example, if a child creates a comic-style version of a discussion between two characters, the words they say can simply be cut and pasted into a prose format. The same goes for extracts of the text or quick write activities, which are designed to feed into the final piece of writing.

Templates created electronically can provide the digital variant of writing frames to help structure children's writing. Hyperlinks could be added to take a child to instructions, or these could even be part of the document as comments or text boxes, which the child can delete once read. The format of the text can be set, so good presentation can be modelled and guaranteed. The writing frame can be pre-populated with text for children to edit, avoiding the loss of creative time to copying text. The frame could include key theme words, which the children can copy and paste, or drag and drop.

Drafting and editing

Digital writing provides the capacity to edit really easily – no rubbing or crossing out, no paper being screwed up in frustration.

Children should be taught and encouraged to use options to delete text, copy and paste (including from one application to another), find and replace, drag and drop, spellcheck, use keyboard shortcuts and also ways of changing the text (font, font size, colour, italic, bold etc). This can all be taken further, over time, to include tabs and tables. Children should also learn file commands, particularly save and print, alongside and the very useful *undo* function.

Presentation

The benefits of good presentation are not just for the reader, but also for the practising writer, who is more assured of presenting text legibly than with handwriting and with enhancements which can make the finished piece look very professional and add motivation to write. However, a child could spend longer choosing a font or a border or a piece of clip art, rather than thinking about the most appropriate word choice or best structure for a sentence. You need to be aware of this and give clear instructions about the writing process using the technology. For example, creating a wanted poster for Goldilocks (after her numerous misdemeanours), requires the key text first, then thoughts about the design. In many activities, elements of the design can be set in a template, or the choices limited.

Extending the contexts for writing

The increase in available technology and software has led to a number of new forms of classroom writing which children can and should engage with, as part of their developing digital writing skills and to prepare them for forms of writing beyond the classroom.

Digital contexts for writing

Context	Notes
Presentations	Using tools such as MS PowerPoint, Apple Keynote and Prezi (www.prezi.com), children can create multimedia presentations on any theme. The ease of use and the versatility of these programs have increased significantly. As a step towards web page creation, developing presentations is an important digital writing experience for children.
Email	Email plays a significant role in modern life and many children will be experienced users outside school. In the same way as letter writing is taught, children should also learn about using email, using actual or 'pretend' emails as a context for writing.
Text messages	This can be seen as a form of dialect and as with other dialect words, textspeak words can appropriately be considered in the curriculum, comparing them with their standard English counterparts and ensuring children learn when it is and is not appropriate to use them in writing contexts.
Online discussions	Forums about just about anything can be found on the web and also feature in many schools' learning platforms. They provide a structured (question/comment – response – comment etc) format for children to practise their non-fiction writing skills.

Blogs	Blogs can be about anything and some schools have started to make use of blogging as a way to provide children with a digital platform to communicate. Personal blogs by children could be in the form of things like learning diaries, reflecting on meeting learning objectives and book reviews. QuadBlogging (quadblogging.net) is also worth considering.
Websites	In creating web pages, writers are free to organise text and media in any way they wish to. The skills required are certainly not too complex for children in primary schools and, as noted earlier, some already create their own web pages.
Wikis	Wikis are effectively online encyclopaedia sites, based around the creation of one or more web pages, and as a context for digital writing and multimedia presentation, these are very useful for classroom activities linked with the themes being studied.
VLEs	Virtual learning environments can include components emulating social networking on the web, providing a more restricted (in terms of audience) facility for children to engage in various types of online interaction (eg MyLearning, Frog Platform www.mylearningltd.co.uk/; www.frogeducation.com/). Components include blogs, forums and even Facebook-style social networking.

FOCUS ON RESEARCH

Text messages

The impact of children's non-standard use of English and errors made during the creation of text messages has been studied by Professor Clare Wood and others, who have found that for older children in primary schools, the use of texting and its abbreviated forms of language and grammar variations had no negative impact on their use of grammar and their spelling (Wood et al, 2014). In fact, one of the studies (Wood et al, 2011) found that for a group of children who were all given mobile phones to use for texting, their literacy skills, particularly their spelling, were enhanced, when compared to a group who were not given mobile phones.

As the use of text messages is a context in which children can write for a real purpose and any incentive to write should have a beneficial developmental effect on literacy, it is important not to dismiss the use of texting. However, a final consideration here is the changes to text message creation, with more sophisticated predictive text and fewer issues with character limits, alongside voice to text facilities, making *textisms* less necessary.

Social networking

As social networking is part of the culture children experience and increasingly become active in, it needs to be part of the curriculum, with appropriate safeguards in place (DCSF, 2008).

Taking account of online safety to ensure anonymity, a class Twitter account can offer a contemporary view of daily writing for millions of people. The character limit of Twitter will set the expectation that tweets are precise, using careful word choices. Twitter can be used to create a collaborative poem, a conversation between two characters in a story, short book reviews, self-assessment commentary and for many other purposes.

Facebook has been described as '*perhaps the most pervasive and commonplace collaborative writing platform in human history*' (Grabill, 2012). Given the prevalence of this form of communication in society, schools must explore this with children, as a way of developing *real-world* (even if virtual) writing skills. There are, of course, issues with children creating an online presence, but secure Facebook-style social networking is available for school use.

Collaborative writing

Using real-time online collaborative writing tools, children can create texts together. These tools can be used in different ways to enhance the writing process and children can become editors, assessors or evaluators of each other's work.

Using the free GoogleDocs environment, or a dedicated collaborative writing online system such as PrimaryPad (http://primarypad.com/), children and teachers can create and edit texts in real time, exploring word choices and sentence construction, thus enhancing the evaluative aspect of the writing process. A simple example of this is the collaborative creation of word banks. Everybody will be able to see the words as they are added and the teacher can edit the spelling or raise questions. The online collaborative writing systems make it easier and faster to work on the texts and each child immediately has a copy of the text to work with.

Sharing of ideas and comments could be done using online *walls*, such as Primary Wall (http://primarywall.com/) or Padlet (http://padlet). These act like online sticky notes, which children view and add to from their own devices. They are ideal for generating and sharing short pieces of writing, for example, alliterative phrases for a whole class poem or evaluative comments on a piece of text.

CASE STUDY

Sharing stories

Alan's Year 5 class used an online story creation resource, Storybird (http://storybird.com/), to create their own online stories. Alan created an assignment for the class by uploading a set of pictures related to the theme the children were working on, *The Egyptians*. The online application works very simply, by enabling the children to drag the pictures onto storybook pages and then add text. The children can then focus on the story or non-fiction text creation.

In this case, the children wrote stories for younger pupils, based on the Ancient Egyptians' gods. The children worked collaboratively on the books over a series of lessons, using a standard template so the format was readily available to them.

While all this could have conceivably been done using traditional methods, the benefits of digital text had a clear impact on the children's motivation and their pleasure in the results. The ability to collaborate on the texts helped in the development of the children's reading skills and their evaluative skills, as they worked at both word and sentence level to improve each other's writing, as well as their own. Having a clear purpose for the text and a clear audience in mind helped the children focus on the particular needs of the reader they envisaged accessing the story online.

Activity 3: Digital writing

» *Consider this following list of activities which demonstrate some of the possibilities in digital approaches to writing. How could each enhance the development of writing skills? What particular aspects of digital writing would be introduced and developed within the activities? What would traditional equivalent writing activities be, if there are any?*

- *Create a web page about an educational visit.*
- *Design a wiki-style information page about an aspect of the current class topic – include hyperlinks to associated web pages.*
- *Create a poster advertising a school event using desktop publishing software.*
- *Design a leaflet to give parents information about the school.*
- *Create a multimedia presentation with a focus on a current class topic.*
- *Create an illustrated set of instructions, using digital photos to illustrate the process.*
- *Write a blog entry for the rest of the class to read.*
- *Create a photo story, which includes digital photographs and captions.*
- *Create a social networking–style page for a story character.*
- *Use a prepared template to plan a story.*
- *Use cut and paste to restructure a story.*
- *Use find and replace to change character names in a story.*
- *Write an email to a local politician.*
- *Create a branching story using hyperlinks (possible with presentation software, such as Powerpoint and Keynote).*
- *Use design software or word processing features (such as WordArt in MS Word) to create a calligram.*
- *Create animated poetry, using text effects, hyperlinks and other special effects.*

- *Write a text message conversation between two story characters.*

- *Write an email to the manager of a local supermarket requesting the chance for the class to visit.*

- *Collaborate with a small group to edit and improve a story using GoogleDocs.*

Further considerations

Children with specific needs

There are often significant advantages to using digital writing with children who have specific learning needs, for example:

- spellcheckers for children with dyslexia;

- speech to text and text to speech for visually impaired children (and others);

- use of pre-prepared texts or word banks to scaffold learning (including using a variety of input devices, such as touch screens, which can have assigned words or enlarged keys for children who have difficulty using a standard keyboard);

- use of coloured text and coloured backgrounds to improve the reading experience for children with scotopic sensitivity.

CASE STUDY

Developing independence and enthusiasm

Simon was a Year 5 boy with behavioural difficulties throughout his school career. Maria, his classteacher, introduced tablet computers for every child to have personal access to. The children had the tablets on their tables and many curriculum activities were based around the use of the tablet. For writing activities, children were often given the choice between using traditional pen and paper methods or the tablet. As the class already had some experience using the tablet computers, Maria was confident that the children knew how to use the basic word processing features and other applications, so felt able to offer the choice and also to introduce a wider range of text enhancement features.

Initial written tasks from Simon proved very difficult to read, due to poor handwriting, and his spelling was weak, possibly due to inadequate knowledge and understanding of phonics, due to his earlier lack of engagement. His motivation to write was minimal and, when he did write, he could not sustain more than a few minutes of focus. His self-image, as a writer, was very negative. In his view he could not write and so frequently would not.

Simon chose to use the tablet for many of his writing activities and while there were still issues to deal with, the amount of writing he produced increased significantly. His motivation to write improved as he saw his writing as *tidy* for the first time and he received more and more praise for the actual content, proving he was capable of sustained and interesting work. He began to see himself, for the first time, as somebody who could write. It was just the tool he used which needed to change, to achieve this transformation.

E-safety

It is critically important that you have a thorough understanding of e-safety when asking children to engage in any kind of online communication. For example, if a class blog is created, which can be accessed by anyone, it should not be possible for children's names to be published. Learning platforms, or virtual learning environments, often provide a secure environment for interactions just within the school community (see earlier). There are also moderated or limited access websites, which provide safer potential contexts for writing (eg, www.storyjumper.com, www.kidzworld.com).

Conclusion

It is important to note that writing and the tools used for writing are evolving. You need to keep abreast of new applications and developments in technology which can be used to support children's digital writing and enhance the writing experience. One area of development which could have a significant impact on children's writing (and already has some impact for some children) is speech to text software. It is possible now for children to dictate their writing and for it to appear on screen. However, digital writing appears here to stay and even if speech recognition becomes the norm, there will still be a need for an understanding of effective text creation processes and ways of structuring a piece of writing.

Given its dominance in writing in the personal and business worlds, writing using digital tools must be a part of every child's classroom experience. You should make informed decisions about when it is best to use digital approaches to writing, as opposed to traditional methods, but in doing so should take full account of the potential benefits of using digital tools as part of the writing process, as well as the importance of digital writing as part of children's development of skills they will almost certainly use outside school and in the future.

Critical points

» *The writing curriculum should be designed to explore digital writing.*

» *The writing curriculum should look towards future writing methods and activities.*

» *Skills in writing digital texts should be developed.*

» *Children should be introduced to a variety of digital-only writing contexts.*

» *You need to resource and develop strategies for writing beyond pen and paper.*

Critical reflections

» *Consider how you write. How much of it is using electronic devices? What digital writing skills do you use as a matter of course? What digital-only contexts do you write in and which of those are new to you in the last five years?*

» *From reading this chapter, what skills and resources do you think a teacher should be equipped with to meet the needs of the modern writing environment? How should a classroom and children be equipped for the most effective development of their modern writing skills?*

Taking it further

Barber, D and Cooper, L (2012) *Using New Web Tools in the Primary Classroom*. London: Routledge. Contains practical ideas about using web-based software.

Savage, M and Barnett, A (2015) *Digital Literacy for Primary Teachers*. Northwich: Critical Publishing. A completely up-to-date text on digital technologies in the primary classroom linked to the new curriculum and computing programmes of study.

Useful online applications to try out:

www.docs.google.com

www.padlet.com

www.popplet.com

www.primarypad.com

www.storybird.com

References

Andrews, R (2003) Where Next in Research on ICT and Literacies. *English in Education*, 7(3): 28–41.

Barbor, D and Cooper, L (2012) *Using New Web Tools in the Primary Classroom*. London: Routledge.

Bawden, D (2008) Origins and Concepts of Digital Literacy, in Lankshear, C and Knobel, M (eds) *Digital Literacies: Concepts, Policies and Practices*. New York: Peter Lang.

Davies, J and Merchant, G (2009) *Web 2.0 for Schools: Learning and Social Participation (New Literacies and Digital Epistemologies)*. Oxford: Peter Lang.

DCSF (2008) *Safer Children in a Digital World: The Report of the Byron Review*. Nottingham: DCSF Publications.

EPPI (2004) *Motivation: A Systematic Review of the Impact of ICT on Literature-Related Literacies in English, 5–16 Review Conducted by the English Review Group 2004*. London: Institute of Education, University of London.

Grabill, J (2012) Why Digital Writing Matters in Education. [online] Available at: www.edutopia.org/blog/why-digital-writing-matters-jeff-grabill (accessed 12 February 2015).

Martin, A (2006) Literacies for the Digital Age, in Martin, A and Madigan, D (eds) *Digital Literacies for Learning*. London: Facet.

Ofcom (2014) Children and Parents: Media Use and Attitudes Report. [online] Available at: http://stakeholders.ofcom.org.uk/binaries/research/media-literacy/media-use-attitudes-14/Childrens_2014_Report.pdf (accessed 12 February 2015).

Puentedura, R R (2013) The SAMR Model Explained by Ruben R. Puentedura. [online] Available at: https://www.youtube.com/watch?v=_QOsz4AaZ2k (accessed 12 February 2015).

Wood, C, Jackson, E, Hart, L, Plester, B and Wilde, L (2011) The Effect of Text Messaging on 9- and 10-Year-Old Children's Reading, Spelling and Phonological Processing Skills. *Journal of Computer Assisted Learning*, 27(1): 28–36.

Wood, C, Kemp, N and Plester, B (2014) *Text Messaging and Literacy – The Evidence*. London: Routledge.

Conclusion

We hope that reading this book has helped you consider the many facets of teaching and learning writing. With a range of abilities and a diverse school population, it is clear that there is no one-size-fits-all recipe for success, so the variety of strategies and stimuli described here should give you a menu to choose from to meet the needs of your class.

We hope, too, that you will make use of the many recommendations for wider reading and links to useful websites to broaden your knowledge and understanding. There is a wealth of material available, most of which can be acquired for little or no cost.

If this book has prompted you to reflect upon your practice as a teacher of writing, and to consider how you can make writing an enjoyable and productive activity for your pupils, then it has been worthwhile.

David Waugh, Adam Bushnell and Sally Neaum

Index

You might also like ...
Beyond Early Reading

BY DAVID WAUGH AND SALLY NEAUM

An essential text for primary trainees and teachers focusing on a range of issues to develop children who can read into children who do read.

Introduction

A current key focus in primary education is the teaching of systematic synthetic phonics to early readers. For some children, this has been done within *a broad and rich language curriculum that takes full account of developing the four interdependent strands of language: speaking, listening, reading and writing and enlarging children's stock of words* (DfES, 2006, 70). However, others may have been less fortunate, enduring a literacy curriculum lacking engagement with texts beyond those which are easily decodable, and featuring limited opportunities to hear their teachers bring texts to life in reading sessions. This book is designed to offer both ideas and a rationale for developing children's reading once they have mastered the early stages, and to show how teachers can engage children with texts, perhaps when they have become disillusioned by an earlier 'thin' diet.

In Chapter 1, Prof Steve Higgins describes the role research can play in helping us to identify problems and issues. He cites a key piece of international research (the PIRLS survey), which shows that children in England perform well compared with their peers in other countries.

However, the study also shows that while the highest attaining pupils in England do as well as the best countries in the world for reading, we are not as good as these countries in supporting the reading achievement of our lower attaining pupils. Children's attitudes to reading are also more negative in England than in many countries. There is clearly much that needs to be done both to address the needs of low achievers and to engage the interest of those who can read well, but often choose not to read at all.

In Chapter 2, David Waugh focuses on the development of vocabulary. English is a rich language with a large lexicon acquired from many other languages. Good readers draw upon wide vocabularies to enable them to read well, but what strategies can teachers use to develop children's understanding of words and their meanings? The chapter looks at how words are created and at ways of applying our lexical knowledge when we meet new words. A strong case is made for vocabulary development to take place in a language-rich environment, set within meaningful contexts

In Chapter 3, Eve English explores a range of meaningful activities to engage children's interest in reading and aid their understanding of texts. She also stresses the importance of teachers' knowledge and understanding of texts and the value of demonstrating that they are readers too. The chapter includes a discussion about parental involvement in reading, a theme developed in Daniel Harrison's later chapter.

Claire Warner's Chapter 4 explores reading comprehension and in particular the role of adults in making the reading process visible by explicitly modelling and teaching a range of strategies for comprehension. Claire looks at key aspects of comprehension and provides practical guidance on developing readers' abilities to use a range of strategies to help them understand texts.

In Chapter 5, John Bennett examines the nature of modern children's reading, looking at children's reading beyond books. John explores ways in which we can develop the skills needed to read digital texts as effectively as possible. He concludes that the reading curriculum must look towards future reading activities, not just those with which the majority of children currently engage.

Chapter 6 looks at the phenomenally successful Harry Potter series to explore how the themes children have become so familiar with, through both the books and films, might lead teachers to capitalise upon children's interest in Potter in order to engage them in a range of literary themes. Martin Richardson, together with teacher Laura Coote, looks at the potential for discussing character, relationships and social and moral issues, using J.K. Rowling's stories as a starting point.

We are fortunate, in north-east England, to have Seven Stories, the National Centre for Children's Books, nearby. This is a superb resource, not only for local children but also for children all over Britain, since much of the staff's work involves schools around the country. Having seen the Seven Stories staff captivating children with imaginative and inspirational activities, we asked them to contribute a chapter to this book. The result is a chapter that provides a rationale for using a range of stimulating activities designed to engage children as creative and cultural readers for pleasure.

In Chapter 8, David Boorman and Jemma Rennocks examine ways in which children can be successfully engaged in reading by exploring texts actively. They focus on a series of classroom projects that increase children's engagement with reading, and find that active reading and plenty of 'talk' about texts can be harnessed to improve writing skills at text, sentence and word level.

In Chapter 9, headteacher, Daniel Harrison, describes a school's project to engage its children and parents in reading and writing. The school identified a need to work innovatively to encourage enthusiasm and enjoyment of reading. To achieve this, teachers made use of local places of interest including Seven Stories, Antony Gormley's iconic and huge *Angel of the North*, and a local Premier League football club, its stadium and educational facilities. The chapter describes the challenges teachers faced and the successes they and their pupils achieved.

In Chapter 10, educational psychologist, Craig Small, describes a project to develop an authentic approach to reading for children in alternative educational provision. This approach echoes a lot of other work on starting from the child's interests in order to engage reluctant readers. There are implications here for teachers in mainstream provision who seek approaches to engage disengaged readers.

Jayne Stead, a secondary English and drama teacher, shows in Chapter 11 ways in which teachers can tune into children's interest in narrative forms and use this to develop their engagement with texts. In particular, she describes how this can be achieved in the transition from primary to secondary school.

Each chapter provides critical questions, points and reflections to encourage you to consider your own practice in light of what you have read. There are also case studies to demonstrate how teachers and trainee teachers have used the ideas in the classroom. Many chapters include recommended further reading, to enable you to develop stronger insights into how teachers can help children move beyond early reading to become fully engaged with the pleasures of reading.

To read more why not order a copy? Visit our website at www.criticalpublishing.com.

Introducing *Critical Focus*

Critical Focus is an exciting new series from Critical Publishing. Each 'Focus' represents key extracts from one of our existing titles, made available exclusively as an e-book, to serve both as a taster for the main book and as a concise summary of one of the key ideas or concepts from the book.

Key Points

»   Available only on Kindle

»   Short and concise

»   Cover key topics

»   Handy for assignments and essays

»   Fully referenced and indexed

»   Excellent value for money

First titles available February 2015

»   An Introduction to Primary Inclusion

»   Primary Inclusion and the National Priorities

»   Teaching Phonics and Early Reading

»   Social Policy and Drugs and Alcohol

»   Voices within Mental Health

For further details and a completely up to date list of all the titles available go to our website www.criticalpublishing.com